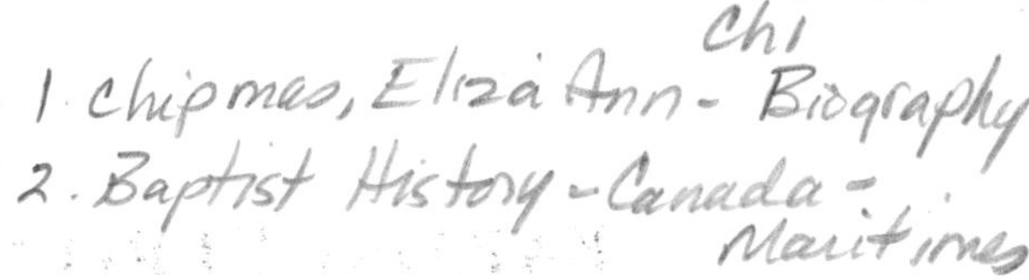

MEMOIR

OF

MRS. ELIZA ANN CHIPMAN,

WIFE OF

THE REV. WILLIAM CHIPMAN,

OF PLEASANT VALLEY,

CORNWALLIS.

EDITED BY

ALLEN B. and CAROLENE E.B. ROBERTSON

Published by
LANCELOT PRESS

for

Acadia Divinity College
and the Baptist Historical Committee of the
United Baptist Convention of the Atlantic Provinces

1989

BAPTIST HERITAGE IN ATLANTIC CANADA

Documents and Studies

A Series sponsored by

Acadia Divinity College

Wolfvillè, Nova Scotia

and

The Baptist Historical Committee

(United Baptist Convention of the Atlantic Provinces

Baptist Heritage in Atlantic Canada: Documents and Studies

A series sponsored by Acadia Divinity College
and The Baptist Historical Committee
(United Baptist Convention of the Atlantic Provinces)

PUBLISHED VOLUMES

1. *The Diary of Joseph Dimock,* ed. George E. Levy, 1979.

2. *Repent and Believe: The Baptist Experience in Maritime Canada,* ed. Barry M. Moody, 1980.

3. *The Journal of John Payzant,* ed. Brian C. Cuthbertson, 1981

4. *The Journal of Henry Alline,* eds. James Beverley and Barry M. Moody, 1982.

5. *New Light Letters and Songs,* ed. George A. Rawlyk, 1983.

6. *Newlight Baptist Journals of James Manning and James Innis,* ed. D.G. Bell, 1984.

7. *The Sermons of Henry Alline,* ed. George A. Rawlyk, 1986.

8. *An Abiding Conviction: Maritime Baptists and Their World,* ed. Robert S. Wilson, 1988.

9. *The Memoir of Mrs. Eliza Ann Chipman,* eds. Allen B. and Carolene E.B. Robertson, 1989.

10. *Baptists in Canada 1760-1990: A Bibliography of Selected Printed Resources in English,* Philip G.A. Griffin-Allwood, George A. Rawlyk and Jarold K. Zeman, 1989.

Additional volumes in preparation.

The series is printed and distributed by Lancelot Press, P.O. Box 425, Hantsport, Nova Scotia B0P 1P0

In Memory Of

MADELINE E. (Harvey) BISHOP

(1894-1973)

and

MARY L. (Welch) ARENBURG

(1891-1975)

Printed and distributed by
Lancelot Press Limited
P.O. Box 425
Hantsport, N.S. B0P 1P0
Canada

ISBN 0-88999-411-0

CONTENTS

ACKNOWLEDGEMENTS

We wish to thank the Baptist Heritage Committee for the opportunity to prepare the first volume in its series devoted to a woman's religious experience. We are especially indebted to Dr. Jarold K. Zeman whose patience, tireless efforts and good humour helped to bring this work to fruition. The comments, criticisms and encouragement of Dr. Barry Moody and Dr. George A. Rawlyk helped our work immeasurably. David G. Bell of the University of New Brunswick kindly brought to our attention the misidentified Porter alias Rev. William Chipman journal. The various aspects of persona in spiritual diaries discussed by Dr. Gwendolyn Davies at the New England Planter Conference (Acadia 1987) proved most helpful. A special note of thanks as well to Patricia Townsend of the Atlantic Baptist Archives; and to Timothy L. Sanford who served as typist for our manuscript.

INTRODUCTION

The *Memoir of Mrs. Eliza Ann Chipman* is a spiritual journal written by a nineteenth-century rural Nova Scotian woman. The product of neither a Baptist saint nor a wanton sinner, nor yet an example of high literary style, the *Memoir* nonetheless can make its claim to be a valuable part of the evangelical Protestant heritage of the Maritimes. Eliza Ann Chipman has left us a record of her inward religious thoughts and reflections from 1823 to 1853. Mirrored in the *Memoir's* pages is the religious faith of eighteenth-century New England and Nova Scotia as bequeathed to Eliza Ann by an indigenous Baptist denomination and a family highly conscious of its past.[1] In spite of the journal's often stereotypical language much is still said about Eliza Ann's expectations as a woman in the early nineteenth-century, the state of family values, and the vital role which the church played in late Georgian-early Victorian Nova Scotia. The *Memoir* also brings us face to face with the darker side of intense, introspective piety and how one individual, an intelligent, socially well-placed woman, encountered and lived with that aspect of evangelical calvinistic faith.

Spiritual journals played an important role in the religious and literary traditions of New England and Nova Scotia. Within her own family Eliza Ann had examples of such diaries, notably among the voluminous writings of her grandfather Handley Chipman, Esquire. An understanding of the use of hymns in Eliza Ann's time and in the time of her parents' youth in the colony adds another dimension to the *Memoir*. Often Eliza Ann's quotations from the verses of Isaac Watts or John

Wesley are the only rays of light in otherwise dark reflections on her soul's state. Altogether there is more depth and richness to this diary of the soul than at first appears evident.

Eliza Ann Chipman was born 3 July 1807 to Holmes and Elizabeth (Andrews) Chipman in Cornwallis Township, Kings County, Nova Scotia. Her father, a farmer and blacksmith, served the community as a quarter-master in the militia, a term as president of the local Agricultural Society, and as a deacon in the First Baptist Church of Cornwallis (of which he was a founding member in 1807).[2] The family itself was highly literate and endorsed basic education, both of which were of great benefit to Eliza Ann. At the age of nineteen years Eliza Ann entered into marriage on 24 May 1827 with another prosperous farming householder, her first cousin (and a widower) William Chipman (1781-1865). 'Captain Billy' Chipman, so-called for his role as a militia officer, combined farming and modest business ventures for a successful livelihood.[3] Like his uncle and father-in-law Holmes Chipman, William was a deacon in the Baptist Church at Cornwallis, and further served as a lay preacher. This last calling led him to enter the ordained ministry within two years of his second marriage. Eliza Ann found her status dramatically altered and society's expectations of her changed as a result. Although she supported her husband's new vocation Eliza Ann would intimate later in her journal how difficult the burden of a minister's wife could be.

William and Eliza Ann had twelve children of their own (eight surviving to adulthood), in addition to the eight surviving children of William's first marriage to Mary McGowan Dickey (1779-1826). Two of the latter were older than their step-mother; it took counselling from the Baptist pastor Edward Manning and others for these two elder children to become reconciled to the idea of their father marrying such a young woman.[4] William's move to Pleasant Valley [Berwick] at the western end of the township to take charge of the Second Cornwallis Baptist Church in 1829 provided all the family with the chance to set up a new household free from past associations.

The salary of a poor minister meant that the Chipmans had to engage in farming to supplement their income. Obligations as surety for a bad debt further increased William's financial worries. Efforts by the household to pay off the debt and run the farm, combined with her family duties and the entertaining of visiting ministers, gave Eliza Ann little time for the furtherance of self-study of Scripture and religious tracts. Nonetheless she maintained, however sporadically, a spiritual diary begun shortly after a religious conversion at age sixteen. Not until a few days prior to her death from an intestinal disorder (23 October 1853) did she reveal to William the existence of this hand-made book of meditations.

Two years after Eliza Ann's passing her husband oversaw the editing and publication of the secret journal. He cited her last wishes as the reason for putting the book in print:

> . . . she did not wish it to be committed to the flames, for she had enjoyed much comfort in reading christian Diaries, and therefore, if there could be a selection of gleanings from her own, which might be useful to others, she was willing that her friends and the public should have the benefit.[5]

Unfortunately interest in diaries of this type was declining by the 1850s. In 1856 the editors of the *Christian Messenger* (the Baptist paper for Nova Scotia) tried to promote the sales of the *Memoir of Mrs. Eliza Ann Chipman:* "The intrinsic value of the *Memoir* of sister Chipman furnishes an adequate reason why all the copies of it should be purchased and read . . . . Her Christian Diary is a devotional book adapted to be highly serviceable."[6] It would nonetheless remain of interest only in a few contemporary Baptist homes.

Except for minor references in Maritime Baptist histories the *Memoir* remained obscure until two brief passages were used by Beth Light and Allison Prentice in *Pioneer and Gentlewomen of British North America* (Toronto, 1980).[7] Here Eliza Ann's journal was placed in the context of contemporary women's writings which served to take her out of a solely parochial setting. Carol Anne Janzen's *Dictionary of Canadian Biography* entry for Chipman tried to emphasize her local prominence in promoting social, religious and intellectual development in Nova Scotian in her capacity as religious study group leader, Sabbath School teacher and spouse of one of the founders of Horton Academy and Acadia College.[8] This was an over-strained presentation yet it helped bring the *Memoir* to the attention of the scholarly community (both religious historians and feminist specialists). The *Memoir* has subsequently been examined briefly in Margaret Conrad's *Recording Angels: The Private Chronicles of Women from the Maritime Provinces of Canada, 1750-1950* (Ottawa, 1982), and been cited in the joint effort by Conrad and fellow co-authors Toni Laidlaw and Donna Smyth in *No Place Like Home: Diaries and Letters of Nova Scotia Women 1771-1938* (Halifax, 1988). *Eliza of Pleasant Valley* (1983) by James D. Davison is an interesting biography of E. A. Chipman based largely on excerpts from the diary and antiquarian delvings into the Reverend William Chipman's account books, related local histories and publications relevant to mid nineteenth-century social and religious life.

With the republication of this scarce *Memoir* scholars and the general public will once more have access to a view of life of 150 years ago when Calvinism was a strong feature of Baptist belief. The *Memoir of Eliza Ann Chipman* is the earliest surviving nearly complete copy of a Baptist woman's diary in Nova Scotia. Compared with the published and manuscript works of the so-called 'Baptist Patriarchs', their Newlight predecessors or younger Baptist colleagues, women's religious literary records for the province are slim.[9] Letters do exist from the late 1700s-early 1800s which have now been published.[10] Extracts or summaries from journals (all too brief) which are now lost to posterity in their full form were printed in the *Christian Messenger.*[11] These give evidence of a widespread practice of keeping spiritual diaries, at least by members, both male and female, of the evangelical denominations.

Eliza Ann Chipman in this context was far from unusual.[12] Moreover she might well have been expected to keep a careful account of her life's relationship with God in her position as wife of a leading Baptist minister. Her descent from a New England-spawned Congregationalist (Puritan) family equally made Eliza Ann heir to a well-established religious practice. To appreciate her *sitz in leben* it is necessary to go back again to her own personal and family history.

In 1761, Handley Chipman (1717-1799) brought his family to Cornwallis Township from Rhode Island. He came from a family which possessed considerable social standing in Rhode Island and Massachusetts and numbered one Congregationalist minister (a grandfather to Handley). Before emigrating Handley Chipman served as a Deputy in the Rhode Island General Assembly.[13] He carried on that level of standing and service in Nova Scotia in the roles of Justice of the Peace and first Judge of Probate in Kings County. His sons and grandsons held public offices and seats in the Nova Scotia House of Assembly.[14] As a group the Chipmans were prosperous, educated and of no mean status.

The family had come to Nova Scotia as part of the 1760-63 migration of New England Planters to take up government offers of land for farming and fishing settlements.[15] These Planters brought not only the requisite skills for carving out a new society; they also came with cherished cultural and religious values. The majority of settlers, including those of the predominantly Connecticut Planter townships of Horton and Cornwallis, were Congregationalists. There was in addition a leavening minority of Baptists, Friends ("Quakers") and

Anglicans. The Congregationalists had been split into "Old Lights" and evangelical "New Lights" during the 1730s-40s Great Awakening in New England.[16] This split was repeated dramatically in Nova Scotia in another awakening or "New Light Stir" during 1776-84. Sparked and carried to all the Planter townships by the forceful preaching of Henry Alline the ensuing religious fervour had by the turn of the century produced several changes. A new sense of Nova Scotian identity was forged among the Planters as they shared in the common revival experience. Indeed, a long-lasting tradition of revivalism was implanted as part of the provincial identity. Finally, there was a resurgence of Calvinism which was incorporated into the Baptist polity. This last grew in part from a reaction against extremist sectarian antinomianism which had spread among the New Lights. The New Light Baptists became both conservative in doctrine and in the conduct of revivals.[17]

The second generation of Baptists was coming to maturity by the second decade of the nineteenth century, following creation of the Baptist Association of Nova Scotia (1800). Eliza Ann Chipman's world was one where although the frontier settlement and evangelizing years were receding although they were not yet over. The fervour of the Allinite legacy as exemplified by Harris Harding, Joseph Dimock, Edward Manning and his brother James, Eliza's own uncle Thomas Handley Chipman (prime founder of the Association) and other preachers continued to inspire congregations to perpetuate the days of pentecostal fire.

Dramatic conversions as evidence of God's election to the visible saints became the standard test for admission to membership in Baptist (and continuing Allinite) churches.[18] Eliza Ann, following the set path of prayer, study of scripture and intensive introspective examination, had her own conversion experience in late 1823. Her relation of that change to her minister Edward Manning and the deacons in 1824 was accepted as genuine; she was then baptized and received into full communion with First Cornwallis Baptist Church.[19] However, she left no detailed account of that "new birth" in her diary, unlike the passages in journals kept by Henry Alline, William Chipman, or in loose manuscript by her own pastor Manning.[20] In subsequent years, when doubts about her election or worthiness assailed her, Eliza Ann's morbid meditations may have stemmed from uncertainty as to the veracity of her own conversion. Fear of not living up to the evangelical stereotype of conversion or of departing from whole-hearted devotion to models set by the patriarchs and matriarchs in earlier generations haunted Eliza Ann and many of her contemporaries.[21] One means of expressing that angst was in the pages of a spiritual diary.

It has been noted already that Eliza Ann looked to her family and New England tradition in journal writings. Further, she wrote in her own diary that it was Edward Manning in a sermon who recommended the reading of spiritual accounts and the keeping of one's own 'journey of the soul' on paper.[22] She obviously was familiar with this partly confessional, partly self-exploration technique. A form of self-psychoanalysis, spiritual diary writing if not always offering a cure for Calvinistic fears at least provided a venting for deep tensions, doubts and bouts with despair.[23]

Eliza Ann left little by way of clues as to what diaries she had read. It seems quite probable, however, that she was familiar with her grandfather Handley Chipman's writings. This family leader had bequeathed to his heirs a high regard for education and a deeply ingrained sense that it was a duty to better oneself. In the course of his own studies and reflections Handley left a large number of jottings, autobiographical notes, a family history, writings on religion and a spiritual diary.[24] This last was in a traditional form which at times bears comparison in style to that of the Massachusetts Congregationalist divine Cotton Mather and it contained observations on the world's events, family matters, and reflections on his spiritual health.[25] An entry from 28 October 1795 is typical of his style: "O may I and all professors of Religion See to it that we are not only Nominal but that we be real Vital Christians in heart and Life. Lord lead me and mine in the ways of truth and Soberness here and when thou Shall take us hence receive us to Glory for Christ Sake Amen & Amen."[26] The Puritan tradition of journal-keeping and spiritual autobiographies (either distinct works or partly merged into one format) was a living heritage to the Chipmans of the 1820s, as it was to other Planter families in Nova Scotia.[27]

The *Memoir* itself is a serial diary. The early years have weekly or at least monthly entries. After marriage with its multitude of responsibilities Eliza Ann often waited several months before taking up the pen again. In certain respects these later passages are maturer reflections and examinations since the author had to summarize or extract the most noteworthy observations of an extended period. However, the *Memoir* is not a true spiritual autobiography or reminiscence written much later in life. Consequently this must be born in mind in comparing it with specific studies on diaries and autobiographies as distinct literary creations. Each form presents its own particular problems of interpretation. Eliza Ann's *Memoir* belongs with the spiritual diary yet awareness of autobiographical accounts is necessary for one to appreciate the wide genre of spiritual (soul-searching) literature.

The true spiritual autobiography seeks to impose a pattern of meaning on life's events. Conversion or an encounter with the Holy Spirit is usually the focal point toward which early life is directed and from which subsequent existence is interpreted by the autobiographer. Henry Alline's journal, as Jamie S. Scott has observed in his exacting examination, is in reality an autobiography using a diary format.[28] His 1776 conversion is the fulcrum of Alline's very being, about which the account of his career revolves and from which it is illuminated. The

Chipman *Memoir* by comparison cannot use conversion as the pivot since Eliza Ann is unable to foresee if it will be superceded by some other event. Her diary is more of the present and recent past with an eye to the future.[29] This difference explains the devotion given to the minutiae of perceived failings, backslidings or neglect of prayerful walk. Each session with the diary forces Eliza Ann to bring her conscience before the bar of judgement. In addition to God and the unseen reader, she herself is confessor and judge.

One result of keeping a diary of faith was that Eliza Ann herself was the central focus of everything. It frequently became a ritual of self-castigation which contributed to a morbidity that detracts from the supposed life of Christian joy toward which she aspired. Eliza Ann confided to the journal her acute sensitivity to perceived slights and criticisms from others. Such a vulnerable conscience was constantly under severe strain in the act of diary writing since the author believed herself to be cognizant of greater faults to which she was privy as guardian of her inmost thoughts. Concentration on self at times produced a form of spiritual pride; Eliza Ann believed that she was unique in her degree of sinfulness to the point of challenging the transforming grace of God. This was a dangerous attitude to take for a Calvinistic Baptist since it threatened to make finite the workings of an omnipotent, omnipresent Deity. A Calvinist would always acknowledge that if God so willed it any person, in spite of the blackest sin, could be re-born.

The spiritual diary can become a trap for excessively doubting souls since in its pages the writer must face in him/herself an unveiled judge and defendant, both of whom are aware of thoughts behind spoken words and actions. Robert O. Fothergill in his perceptive survey study *Private Chronicles: A Study of English Diaries* (1974) has rightly shown that a spiritual diary exaggerates and indeed makes disproportionate the author's sins since the latter came under special examination: "Seek indevotion and dulness of desire, and ye shall assuredly find."[30] The *Memoir of Mrs. Eliza Ann Chipman* amply demonstrates this truism as seen, for example, in her entry for 14 February 1842:

> My own exercises for the few weeks past have been truly painful; distressing doubts about my interest in the Saviour, and such darkness enveloping my mind .... I fear my views of myself and of the awful nature of sin, are too indistinct, too much upon the surface, I beg the trial of thine eyes; come over the mountains of my sins, dear Lord, and let me have unfeigned repentance therefore; and experience thy delivering power from this state of insensibility and stupor of mind, that in thy light I may see light.[31]

Here one must come to an understanding of Eliza Ann's writing: was she indeed as distressed as this passage intimates, or did it come out of unconscious exaggeration and adherence to other model diaries?

Eliza Ann Chipman's journal was both personal and standardized. By choosing to record her spiritual progress in this format she already had prescribed the nature of its content, the use of stock phrases and a great inattention to the external world.[32] It is instructive to note the advice given for journal keeping by the eighteenth-century devotional author the Reverend James Hervey (1714-58) who had come under John Wesley's influence. Whether or not Eliza Ann read his instructions she did adhere closely to the steps provided:

> Compile a secret History of your Heart and Conduct. Take notice of the manner in which your Time is spent, & of the strain that runs in your Discourse, how often the former is lost in trifles, how often the latter evaporates in vanity. Attend to the Principle from which your actions flow. Minute down your sins of Omission. Observe the frame of your spirit in religious

> Duties, with what reluctance they are undertaken, with what indevotion performed; with how many wanderings of thought, & how much dulness of desire. Register those secret Faults, to which none but your own Conscience is privy, & which none but the all-seeing Eye discerns. Often contemplate yourself in this faithful mirror.[33]

Hervey put in writing what Puritan diarists and their successors (including Quakers) had been doing since the early seventeenth century.[34] The strong Protestant tradition of the individual encounter with God, accentuated in the teachings of John Calvin and his English and New England disciples, was conducive to the inward-looking focus of self-examination as expressed in spiritual diaries.

The *Memoir* reflects both the expected format of spiritual diaries of the late 1700s-early 1800s and the conscious efforts of a maturing individual to become comfortable with the medium. The early entries are those of a youthful girl trying to emulate standards of 'Christian diaries' and the current religious-social expectations in Baptist circles at Cornwallis Township. Stilted phrases, exaggerated description and the inherent conflict between penning a private journal while at the same time trying to project the objective observations of a third person created an unevenness of quality and lack of warmth. Feelings were expressed but not truly conveyed. An 1823 entry for 25 August brings these aspects into view:

> What! is it possible that another fortnight has rolled its round, and while new scenes have opened to my view, I have omitted relating them here? The busy cares and affairs of life I am surrounded with affect me to that degree, awful to say, that I often lose the remembrance of serious reflections, and forget that I am born to die, that this is not my home, that soon the place that knows me now, will know me no more. Death and eternity are

> awfully great and mysterious, and important subjects for meditation.[35]

Eliza Ann's tone and content altered with the responsibilities first of marriage, then of child-bearing, house-keeping and the duties of a minister's wife. Experience gained with age helped provide a growing sense of mature reflection in the pages of the *Memoir.*

Each new year gave Eliza Ann cause to consider her state before God. In keeping with the Puritan ledger-book approach to life (sins versus devotion) the *Memoir* depicts its author at times such as these poised between berating herself as a sinner yet praising God for permitting her to see another calendar year, as at the start of 1836:

> My frail life is yet lengthened out to witness the commencement of another year; but alas, alas, how do I enter upon it? the same dull careless creature that I too generally am. O when shall that glad day arrive when captive soul shall be set free, and made like the Chariot of Aminadib?[36]

The nature of the spiritual diary itself meant that each entry was opportunity to confront past conduct with the ideal life for which Eliza Ann aimed; the new year's entries were in that respect only special extensions of journal dialogue.

Although the diary kept by Eliza Ann makes references to her family, local church and other items of news, such were not the main concerns of its author. Obviously Eliza Ann's entries were in part responses to external matters. However the world as viewed through her personal history is a rather circumscribed portrait of Eliza Ann's surroundings. Selective memory had filtered everything. It is not known how Eliza Ann addressed her children, nor if there were any special terms of endearment for William. Even in the illness or deaths of children the *Memoir* does not offer an intimate glimpse of a rural Nova Scotia home. Instead, all events were noted as communications from or thoughts on God and the ways of Providence. The loss of her first-born child Leander in December 1830 though upsetting to her was not preserved in the *Memoir* as a vignette of a mother cradling a dying child. After recounting the accident (by scalding) from which the boy eventually died Eliza Ann turned her pen to describing the stern Puritan God of her faith:

> God has seen fit in his wisdom to hand me the cup of affliction to drink of . . . and although I have found it, and do still find it hard to be reconciled to this my lot, yet I know my dear Redeemer has chastened me for my profit, for he scourgeth every son whom he receiveth, and he hath in faithfulness afflicted me . . . . Oh, I needed it; I have been such a rebel against God . . . .[37]

All events, including Eliza Ann's partial hearing loss later in life, were viewed as judgements or providences.

Sufficient details, nonetheless, were recorded in the *Memoir* to make it possible to comment on Eliza Ann's world. In spite of her clinging to Calvinistic Baptist belief she was subject to the religious and social currents in the English-speaking parts of North America and Britain which presaged the end of the late Georgian and dawn of the Victorian eras. The first such influence was felt in her role as a woman in nineteenth-century Nova Scotia. Political, religious and economic leadership were in the hands of men. The vaunted "Mothers in Israel" were women who adhered devotedly to their particular Christian denomination, maintained and inculcated high moral standards in the home, and performed with diligence their expected part as wives and mothers. William Chipman concluded the *Memoir* with a special passage from Proverbs 31: 10-12, 26, 31 which begins, "Who can find a virtuous woman? for her price is far above rubies," and concludes, "Give her the fruit of her hands, and let her own works praise her in the gates."[38] The pastoral-small village imagery of

Scripture struck a responsive chord among rural Baptists. It also served to reinforce the traditional role of women as homemakers and helpmates bound either to the parental or husband's house.

Eliza Ann did fulfill her expected function. However she permitted herself to voice discontent and aspirations in the pages of the secret journal. Prior to marriage and for a period thereafter she was interested in the foreign mission work of the Rev. and Mrs. Adoniram Judson (the first American Baptist missionaries and models for generations of North American Baptists.) Eliza Ann gave voice to a wish to preach but never carried it into action.[39] Youthful enthusiasm was tempered by submission to what her family and society accepted as women's circumscribed sphere of activity. Moreover, the other known examples of female preachers were hardly seen by Baptists as worthy of emulation. There had been Quaker and Shaker women leaders in the United States and Upper Canada. Quaker enclaves indeed existed in Dartmouth and Bridgetown (formerly Hicks Ferry) in Nova Scotia. However, the Quaker emphasis on the Inner Light over the Bible, ordinances and orthodox Christianity linked it in Calvinistic Baptist minds to the New Dispensation movement and Allinite female "prophets" of the 1790s.[40] Neither of the latter was considered orthodox by Eliza Ann's church, while the prophets had upset the relationship of the family commonwealth.[41]

Alternatives to passive church participation did exist for Baptist women in the nineteenth century. These activities were extensions or variations on women's home duties thereby conforming to current socially acceptable endeavours. Female prayer groups, one of which Eliza Ann led herself, were counterparts to self-study of the Bible by individuals. Should the leader be much older than her fellow group members she in effect served as a mother giving religious instruction to her children. Likewise the Sabbath School movement in the Annapolis Valley by the 1830s often employed women to teach the young. Under the guise of prayer groups, it should be noted, women were, in effect, able to preach to women. Finally, religious tract societies and auxiliary missionary societies permitted women to add their support to larger evangelization undertakings.

The *Memoir* revealed how reluctant Eliza Ann was to take on certain of these social responsibilities. Her own sense of unworthiness led to a feeling of inadequacy which was overcome only with great effort.[42] It seems evident that she would have been happier to engage in private Scriptural and theological studies.[43] More than once she complained of having to serve as a Martha rather than be able to listen to ministerial discussions in her home. Eliza Ann's level of education had left her feeling thwarted in some degree, unable to advance her knowledge openly in a manner similar to her husband William. The support she would give to her children's education, both the sons and daughters, was a means of extending that knowledge in addition to perpetuating the Chipman regard for learning.[44]

As a parent Eliza Ann continued the eighteenth-century evangelical conception of children as sinful beings whose willfulness needed to be broken.[45] Predestination as a doctrine had to entertain the idea of infant damnation. This alone encouraged parents in a vigorous child-rearing in order possibly to facilitate the awakening of a soul to salvation. However, as Peter G. Slater has described in *Children in the New England Mind in death and life,*[46] this inculcation of a submissive will and emphasis on seeking out God was a prelude to the nineteenth-century idea of children as innocents; to be properly taught in the home. The Enlightenment *tabula rasa* approach had infiltrated Protestant evangelical thinking. Consequently in the *Memoir* there are passages which alternately portray the stubborn sinfulness of Eliza Ann's children and others which dare to entertain the hope that her children who died young are among the saved. Again, just as her self-perception as unworthy made Eliza Ann reluctant to lead a women's prayer group so too her bouts of uncertainty as to her state of grace coloured her attitude toward her young. Not sure of her own salvation she could never be assured of theirs.

Eliza Ann did feel an enormous burden was placed on her to oversee the religious instruction of the family. At one point in seeming despair she wrote that, "in my view it is crucifying work to be a mother." [15 Feb. 1849] It did not portray her as an overly warm or emotive mother. Had she leaned toward Arminianism she might have had less difficulty in assuming the increasingly widespread idea of mothers as transmitters of religious and moral values in the rising Victorian cult of the home. The 'save by education' approach would in some denominations amount to a nineteenth-century 'Counter-Reformation'.[47] However, Eliza Ann sought to perpetuate the evangelical Baptist tradition of Nova Scotia by urging her children constantly to seek after things of the spirit. Her anxiety over her role as a parent therefore grew from a belief that if the children did not attain conversion not only would they be lost but she would have failed in her appointed task. Moreover, this view conflicted with Calvinist Baptist teaching on predestination according to which a child's fate was set in spite of a parent's hopes. Eliza Ann lived in a tension of duality between this older doctrine and the changing nineteenth-century beliefs in regard to the young.

In her position as a minister's wife Eliza Ann was under additional pressure to promote the spiritual welfare of her family. Although she did not explicitly state it, any sign of waywardness in the children would have reflected badly on her husband William. He had a high profile due not only to his status as a Chipman, former militia officer, and Baptist minister, but also as an active promoter of denominational education causes and a contributor to the *Christian Messenger*. He served as a governor of Queen's (later Acadia)

College at Wolfville. His son Isaac L. Chipman (by the first marriage) was an early professor at Acadia.[48] Indeed, he promoted the creation of a Baptist historical collection. Later, sons of William and Eliza Ann would attend Acadia.

It would be an exaggeration to say that Eliza Ann was a great participant in the advancement of provincial education. At most she was useful in very local causes, the aforementioned prayer groups, Sabbath Schools and endorsement of her children's schooling. In her capacity as a Christian mother Eliza Ann did exert some influence over Acadia students who boarded at her home while serving with William Chipman in ministerial training.[49] Her own sphere remained limited but within it she with her husband ensured that their sons and daughters had access to and time to read the Bible, devotional literature and other reference works.[50]

A part of family activity undoubtedly included the singing of hymns. The pages of the *Memoir* are filled with excerpts of what had been sung on Sundays (when Eliza Ann usually wrote) and other times of the week. Even when they reflect Calvinistic doctrine, these verses, it should be stressed, were often the only bright passages among gloomy introspective musings. The study of Nova Scotia hymnody in the nineteenth-century, or the use of hymns in worship, has so far been largely neglected. Comparative inference must be drawn from British and American works on hymnody although eighteenth-century hymn-singing in Nova Scotia, especially Henry Alline's compositions, has received growing attention.[51]

Eliza Ann's home church at First Baptist and later Second Baptist in Pleasant Valley seem to have permitted the use of the so-called Winchell's *Watts*. This book was edited by James M. Winchell the pastor of First Baptist Church in Boston; it included the verse of Isaac Watts the great English hymnist and about three hundred other hymns by other composers (in the 1818 and 1832 editions).[52] Consequently one can identify in the *Memoir* hymns by John Wesley, Charles Wesley, John

Newton, William Williams, Toplady, Cowper and Steele, though the majority are by Watts.[53] There are apparently no Allinite hymns in the *Memoir* which in itself is a sign of how completely the writings of that Free Will revivalist had been rejected by the close-communion Calvinistic Baptists of Cornwallis Township.

The singing of hymns and spiritual songs outside the Psalms was not fully accepted in most churches until well into the nineteenth century. Evangelicals within the Church of England and Dissenters led the way in spreading their popularity.[54] The Wesleyan revival added a special impetus to the popularity of hymn singing. Among Nova Scotia's New Light Congregationalists and Baptists of the later eighteenth century the Great Awakening had been a means to carry hymnody among the population while hymns and newly composed songs were themselves vehicles for the revival message. As Louis Benson has rightly observed, hymn singing provided a unique communal experience at worship services; all who were present, either converted or still seeking, could share in the emotions which the songs invoked, imbibe the content conveyed and grow to share a common vocabulary and world view shaped by the hymns.[55] Further, hymns and spiritual songs had a portability which printed Scripture did not; even the illiterate could memorize words and tunes to pass on to others.[56]

When Eliza Ann Chipman wrote down hymn verses she was drawing on a vocabulary and imagery which her fellow congregation members would have been able to comprehend. It would be possible to say that in the *Memoir* just as Eliza Ann's prose breathes the Bible through quotation and allusion the verses are songs of faith equally a part of an ingrained vocabulary. She employed hymnody as well to utilize the poetic depth of expression in them to verbalize interior emotions. Often the hymn attained a higher literary embodiment of how she felt than if she had tried to frame words herself, as in the passage from 25 January 1825 in a musing on death:

> How striking is the language of the poet—
> "Eternity, tremendous sound!
> To guilty souls a dreadful wound:
> But oh, if Christ and Heaven be mine,
> How sweet the accents, how divine!"[57]

For some singers, especially for an intelligent individual such as Eliza Ann, hymns were a means of coming into contact with a higher cultural level through examples of verses which possessed both imaginary and literary superiority. Some songs enabled people to join in a trans-Atlantic English-speaking Christian community. Widely sung songs such as Newton's "Amazing grace, how sweet the sound" and Toplady's "Rock of Ages, cleft for me" (both of which are cited in the *Memoir*) are two examples:

The dichotomous content of many hymns were reflections of Eliza Ann's own interior oscillations between praise of God and denouncement of self. Sandra Sizer, in *Gospel Hymns,* has approached the rhetoric of hymns as metaphors, theme and form. The former could alternately portray God as 'refuge' or 'haven' while life was a 'troubled sea' or pilgrim path. This language went further to create contrasts of turmoil versus rest, darkness versus light, guilt versus atonement and so forth.[58] Eliza Ann was attracted, no doubt, to the hymnic formulation which so vividly conveyed her own situation.

After a reading of the *Memoir*, one must confront the person of Eliza Ann Chipman. There is no portrayal of her physical appearance either in paint or words. She was the wife of a man actively involved in Baptist causes (religious and educational) and knew or met most of the province's leading Baptist ministers. Eliza Ann herself was not a great doer of deeds; instead she performed within her sphere at Pleasant Valley the duties of wife, mother and teacher. References to her parents make it clear that she remained deeply attached to them for life. Family was an important part of her existence, though one is left in doubt as to how warm and caring she was with her own children. That she was concerned for their souls is beyond question, yet Eliza Ann was as concerned for her neighbours' salvation too.

It is through the *Memoir* that any assessment of Eliza Ann Chipman must be made. She has left us with the spiritual diary of a soul seeking a comfort it did not possess nor could it give of the same. She spoke often of many failings and sins yet did not specify them (or rarely so). Eliza Ann was burdened by a sense of spiritual inadequacy which she could pen only in broad terms. Her problems lay in the fact that she strove for spiritual perfection as the ideal but failed continually to live life as a saint. Eliza Ann could not reconcile herself to the fact that even saints had human failings. Comments in the *Memoir* by William Chipman, and observations by other writers, portray a devout Christian woman who dutifully fulfilled her role as minister's wife, moral mother, supporter of local church causes and Baptist endeavours in general. The *Memoir* as penned by Eliza Ann more often than not showed her to have been afraid of not meeting her familial, social or spiritual obligations. She stated in her own terminology that her public persona was a facade meant to ensure that her personal weaknesses did not hinder the appearance of Baptist progress or doctrinal certitude.

Eliza Ann Chipman waged a constant internal warfare to resist sin and seek Christ. This combat engendered a dualism based on the tension between perceived ideals as being attainable, expected and promoted on the one hand, while on the other hand there was the stark fact that this earthly existence does demand attention to the mundane affairs of family, social engagements and financial cares. Eliza Ann sought the prolonging of ecstatic experience rather than using the numinous encounters to allow daily activity to be suffered with a quiet, pietistic strength and peace. She proclaimed God's omnipotence on one hand yet challenged the Divine Love by painting herself as an utterly sinful being. She could not fully trust Christ to overwhelm her corrupted nature and to accept her as she was in human weakness. Never being completely comforted Eliza Ann Chipman was unable to be the sincere comforter of others. Therefore illness in her spouse or children, financial setbacks or the death of near kin were not occasions to write at length about her striving to console or encourage the afflicted. Instead all such occurrences were re-directed solely toward her inward-looking self and interpreted as divine scourging meant only to hurt, humble and correct Eliza Ann the unrepentant.

The educational level to which Eliza Ann Chipman had been exposed had enabled her to tap any available literature—the Bible, religious tracts, theological works, hymnals, diaries, histories and denominational journals—with the result that she was an intellectually-aware individual. As a result she had been accustomed to probing for answers and appealing to recognized authorities. Her references in the *Memoir* to reading narratives or finding in Scripture and hymns situations reflecting her own life's state and quandaries showed that she never ceased in her quest for interpretive guidance. Eliza Ann's acute sensitivity, then, in mental perception albeit a mind not systematically trained added that finer edge to her spiritual diary which served to increase her anxiety in not finding immediate solutions to pressing worries and in being unable to balance intellect, emotion and spiritual faith. Through the repetitive language, borrowed phrases and stereotyped vocabulary we glimpse a woman wrestling with spiritual doubt and a desire to be able to spend time like her husband engaged in theological study and meditation. Confined by the social strictures of her condition, residence and sex, Eliza Ann Chipman had only her letters and especially her secret diary as outlets for her frustrations and ever-active introspective

NOTES

TO THE INTRODUCTION

1. George Edward Levy, *The Baptists of the Maritime Provinces 1753-1946* (Saint John, N.B., 1946); John Hale Chipman, *A Chipman Genealogy* (Norwell, Mass., 1970), pp. 21-22, 37-41; Journal of Handley Chipman [c. 1798: contains a genealogy of his family and that of his wife]: MSS: Atlantic Baptist Archives [A.B.A.], Acadia University.
2. Chipman, *Chipman Genealogy,* p. 40; William Chipman, ed., *Memoir of Mrs. Eliza Ann Chipman, wife of the Rev. William Chipman of Pleasant Valley, Cornwallis* (Halifax, N.S., 1855), p. 5.
3. Chipman, *Chipman Genealogy,* p.79; Ingraham E. Bill, *Fifty Years with the Baptist Ministers and Churches of the Maritime Provinces of Canada* (Saint John, N.B., 1880), pp. 251-61.
4. See reference in James D. Davison, *Eliza of Pleasant Valley* (Hantsport, N.S., 1983), pp. 53-54.
5. Chipman, *Memoir*, p. 3.
6. *Christian Messenger* 9 April 1856.
7. Beth Light and Allison Prentice, ed., *Pioneer and Gentlewomen of British North America* (Toronto, 1980), pp. 60-61.
8. Carol Anne Janzen, "Eliza Ann (Chipman) Chipman" *Dictionary of Canadian Biography* Vol. 8, s.v.
9. Barry M. Moody, "Edward Manning" *D.C.B.* Vol. 8, s.v.; The Baptist Heritage in Atlantic Canada series has made available in print the most recent studies of these denominational founders, including Joseph Dimock, John Payzant, Henry Alline, James Manning, James Innis and Harris Harding.
10. George A. Rawlyk, ed. *The New Light Letters and Spiritual Songs 1778-1793* (Hantsport, N.S., 1983), pp. 89-90, 96-100, 103, 106-110 and ff., and pp. 273-78.

11. *Christian Messenger* 10 July 1855: Obituary of Mrs. Elizabeth Rand ae. 75 years, of Cornwallis: "After the death of Mrs. Rand, a long and interesting paper was found, in which she recorded her early exercises of mind in religious things, and the means by which she was brought to devote her heart to and life to the Saviour."

12. Mary Coy Morris Bradley of New Brunswick (1771-1859) was a convert to Methodism whose part-diary, part-autobiography was published in 1849 as *A Narrative of the Life and Christian Experience of Mrs. Mary Bradley* (Boston, Mass., 1849); see also, Jo-Ann Fellows, "Mary (Morris; Bradley) Coy" *D.C.B.* Vol. 8, s.v. Two different diaries concerned more with every day matters are the "Diary of Mary Ann Norris 1818-38" [of Cornwallis], daughter of the Anglican minister at Church Street: MG 1: Vol. 729A: Public Archives of Nova Scotia [PANS]; the "Diary of Margaret (Dickie) Michener" [Margaret Dickie Michener McCullough] 1847-48, 1849-52, 1867-69 was published in the *Wolfville Acadian* Dec. 1923-Nov. 1929: Margaret nee Dickie was a resident of the ship-building center at Hantsport, a Baptist, teacher and cousin to Dickie families in Cornwallis Township; her's is an engaging journal by a literate, Christian woman.

13. Chipman, *Chipman Genealogy*, p. 21; A.W.H. Eaton, *The History of Kings County, Nova Scotia* (Salem, Mass., 1910), pp. 600-602. A recent biography of Chipman is James D. Davison, *Handley Chipman, King's County Planter 1717-1799* (Wolfville, N.S., 1988).

14. Chipman, *Chipman Genealogy*, pp. 37 ff. Handley Chipman's second cousin's son was a Loyalist and member of the Council of New Brunswick: Phillip Buckner, "Ward Chipman" *D.C.B.*, Vol. 6, s.v.

15. John B. Brebner, *The Neutral Yankees of Nova Scotia: A Marginal Colony During the Revolutionary Years* (Toronto, 1969; 1st pub. 1937); James E. Candow, *The New England Planters in Nova Scotia* (n. p., 1986).

16. Perry Miller, *Jonathan Edwards* (New York, 1959), pp. 133-64; Richard L. Bushman, *From Puritan to Yankee: Character and*

the Social Order in Connecticut, 1690-1765 (Cambridge, Mass., 1980), pp. 183-95; C.C. Goen, *Revivalism and Separatism in New England, 1740-1800: Strict Congregationalists and Separate Baptists in the Great Awakening* (New Haven, Conn., 1962). Cf. Maurice W. Armstong, *The Great Awakening in Nova Scotia 1776-1809* (Hartford, Conn., 1948).

17. Gordon Stewart and George Rawlyk, *A People Highly Favoured of God: The Nova Scotia Yankees and the American Revolution* (Toronto, 1972); G. A. Rawlyk, *Ravished by the Spirit: Religious Revivals, Baptists and Henry Alline* (Montreal, 1984), pp. 73-105; George A. Rawlyk, ed., *Henry Alline: Selected Writings* (New York, 1987), pp. 5-17.

18. A study of the development of the concepts of visible saints and admission requirements can be found in Edmund S. Morgan, *Visible Saints: The History of a Puritan Idea* (Ithaca, N. Y., 1963).

19. Chipman, *Memoir*, pp. 14-15; "Diary of Edward Manning" May 8, 1824: A.B.A.

20. Bill, *Fifty Years*, 251-61; Edward Manning Saunders, *History of the Baptists of the Maritime Provinces* (Halifax, N.S., 1902), pp. 27-29.

21. Cf. Allen B. Robertson, "Methodism among Nova Scotia's Yankee Planters" in Margaret Conrad (ed.), *They Planted Well: New England Planters in Martime Canada* (Fredericton, N.B., 1988), pp. 178-189.

22. Chipman, *Memoir*, p.6. Reverend Edward Manning left journals covering fifty years which are replete with commentary on local affairs, politics, the weather and many more matters; however, above all else the Manning journals are a religious exercise. Manning alternately praised God and berated himself as unworthy of divine graces in protracted passages. This style is in part the result of following models in the genre. It also must be understood that in the throws of spiritual wrestling human vocabulary can be all too limited in expressing the transcendent. The use of familiar phrases reiterates this restriction on transmission of the actual experience to others. Cf. F. C. Happold, *Mysticism: A Study and an Anthology*

(Harmondsworth, England, 1970), pp. 117-19.

23. Rawlyk, *Henry Alline*, p. 55-57; P. W. Martin, *Experiment in Depth: A Study of the Work of Jung, Eliot and Toynbee* (Boston, Mass., 1955), pp. 172-75, 230-31.

24. Davison, *Handley Chipman,* pp. X, 45-48; A. B. A.: Journal of Handley Chipman, c. 1798; Memoir of Handley Chipman 1794-1796; Ledger no. 3, 1771-1799, of Handley Chipman; PANS: mfm: biography: Handley Chipman Notebook [c. 1776: extracts relative to matters scientific, political and religious].

25. Robert Middlekauff, *The Mathers: Three Generations of Puritan Intellectuals 1596-1728* (London, 1971), pp. 321-26.

26. Handley Chipman Memoir 1794-1796: A.B.A.

27. Not all diaries of the 1700s-early 1800s were concerned with solely religious matters. The Connecticut born merchant Simeon Perkins at Livepool, N.S., in his many years of faithful diary entries revealed a man aware of economics and political obligations to a degree which made faith one component (though certainly an underlying element) of a very full career. *The Diary of Simeon Perkins* 5 Vol. (Toronto, 1948-78).

28. Jamie S. Scott, " 'Travels of My Soul': Henry Alline's Autobiography." *Journal of Canadian Studies* 17, no. 2 (1983): 70-90.

29. Daniel B. Shea Jr., *Spiritual Autobiography in Early America* (Princeton, N.J., 1968), p. X.

30. Robert A. Fothergill, *Private Chronicles: A Study of English Diaries* (London, 1974), p. 25.

31. Chipman, *Memoir*, pp. 136-37.

32. Fothergill, *Private Chronicles,* pp. 17-18.

33. Cited in *ibid.,* p. 25.

34. Quaker diaries were open to freer expression being less restricted by doctrinal orthodoxies. Shea, *Spiritual Autobiography,* p. 251.

35. Chipman, *Memoir*, p. 7.

36. *Ibid.,* p. 112.

37. *Ibid.,* p. 93.

38. *Ibid.,* p. 188.

39. *Ibid.,* p. 45. Cf. Mary Bradley's interest in preaching: Conrad, *Recording Angels,* p. 9.

40. Lydia Randall of Cornwallis and Sarah Bancroft in Annapolis County were two notorious 'prophets': Allen B. Robertson, "Legacy of Henry Alline: The Antinomian Challenge to New Lights in Nova Scotia" (B. A. Hon. Thesis, Acadia University, 1982), pp. 37-39, 41-42, 55; D. G. Bell, ed., *The Newlight Baptist Journals of James Manning and James Innis* (Hantsport, N.S., 1984), pp. 258-59. Although Methodists permitted women more scope in expressing themselves the ordained ministry was closed to them, while occassional statements against female preachers were made public as in Robert Cooney's *The Female Preacher Nonpluss'd* (Miramichi, N.B., 1828).

41. For a description of family relationships which continued to have validity in early nineteenth century Nova Scotia see John Demos, *A Little Commonwealth: Family Life in Plymouth Colony* (London, 1970). Ruth H. Bloch, "American Feminine Ideals in Transition: The Rise of the Moral Mother, 1785-1815" *Feminist Studies* 4, no. 2 (June 1978): 101-126. Cf. Rawlyk, *Ravished by the Spirit*, pp. 119-20.

42. Chipman, *Memoir,* p. 124.

43. *Ibid.,* p. 121.

44. Cf. Mary Beth Norton, *Liberty's Daughters: The Revolutionary Experience of American Women, 1750-1800* (Boston, Mass., 1980), p. 256-76.

45. Philip Greven, *The Protestant Temperament: Patterns of Child Rearing, Religious Experience and the Self in Early America* (New York, 1980), pp. 32-43.

46. Peter G. Slater, *Children in the New England Mind in death and life* (Hamden, Conn., 1977), p. 133.

47. Cf. Bloch, "American Feminine Ideals" and Ann Douglas, *The Feminization of American Culture* (New York, 1977).

48. Bill, *Fifty Years,* pp. 736-38.

49. See Appendix I
50. Chipman, *Memoir,* p. 160.
51. Margaret Filschie, " 'Redeeming Love Shall Be Our Song': Hymns of the First Great Awakening in Nova Scotia" (M.A. Thesis, Queen's University, 1983); Thomas B. Vincent, ed., *Selected Hymns and Spiritual Songs of Henry Alline* (Kingston, Ont., 1982); Rawlyk, *Henry Alline,* pp. 274-335.
52. James M. Winchell, ed., *An Arrangement of the Psalms, Hymns, and Spiritual Songs of the Rev. Isaac Watts, D. D. To Which is Added a Supplement of more than Three Hundred Hymns from the Best Authors, including All the Hymns of Dr. Watts, Adapted to Public Worship* (Boston, Mass., 1832); this combination first appeared in 1819, and became almost universally used in New England: Louis F. Benson, *The English Hymn: Its Development and Use in Worship* (Richmond, Va., 1962), p. 204.
53. In the *Memoir,* of identified hymns, 23 are by Watts, 6 by the Wesleys, 2 by Steele and one each for Grigg, Robinson, John Newton, William Williams, Cowper, Toplady and Fawcett.
54. See: Benson, *The English Hymn*; Sandra S. Sizer, *Gospel Hymns and Social Religion: The Rhetoric of Nineteenth-Century Revivalism* (Philadelphia, 1978); Susan S. Tamke, *Make a Joyful Noise Unto the Lord: Hymns as a Reflection of Victorian Social Attitudes* (Athens, Ohio, 1978).
55. Benson, *The English Hymn,* p. ix; cf. Tamke, *Make a Joyful Noise,* p. 3.
56. It is true that long passages of Scripture can be committed to memory. However, verse (and song) have traditionally been the means of preserving legend, ritual, and doctrine over the millenia.
57. Steele, "Eternity is just at hand" in Chipman *Memoir,* p. 27.
58. Sizer, *Gospel Hymns*, p. 25.

EDITORIAL REMARKS

The *Memoir of Mrs. Eliza Ann Chipman* is known only from the published version of 1855 by A. J. Ritchie of Halifax. The original journal consisting of folded paper (presumably stitched together in booklet form) is not known to be extant. Court of Probate Records, in particular the will and estate papers of the Reverend William Chipman, make no reference to the autograph copy being passed on to family members. Contemporary records consulted do not allude to the original either.

In regard to textual integrity one is forced to accept the comments of the first editor, William Chipman. He advised readers that he had omitted only certain repetitious passages. That the text was not further altered seems to be supported by the retention of material not flattering to Eliza Ann as well as inserted critical comments by her husband. William Chipman, who would have been completely familiar with the spiritual diary genre, appears to have been a conscientious editor.

The copy of the *Memoir* used for this publication is held by the Atlantic Baptist Archives at Acadia University. This particular volume had attached inside the front cover a letter from George Armstrong to Mrs. Chipman (26 January 1836) which is included as Appendix I to supplement the letters printed with the original 1855 text.

It was not the intention of the editors to provide identification for all biblical passages or allusions. Eliza Ann breathed the language of the King James version of the Bible, as did contemporaries, to an extent which would have overburdened this present edition if all citations were noted.

Instead, the more significant passages are identified while Appendix II offers further commentary on Old and New Testament usage.

Hymns, quoted extensively in the *Memoir*, have been identified where possible. Two main sources have been used in this task: Richard Fuller and J. B. Peter, eds., *The Psalmist: A New Collection of Hymns for the Use of Baptist Churches . . .* (New York, 1879); John Wesley, *A Collection of Hymns, For the use of the People called Methodists* (London, 1847, and 1874 editions). The *Psalmist* identifications at times refer to collections by editors/authors rather than to the composer of the individual hymn so caution is needed with regard to attribution. (The same hymnal includes the Henry Alline composition, "Amazing sight! the Saviour stands" taken from the earlier collection *Hymns of Zion* though Alline is not cited as the hymn's author.) More work waits to be done on the use of hymns and spiritual songs in nineteenth-century Nova Scotia. For an earlier period one is directed to Thomas B. Vincent's studies ["Alline and Bailey" *Canadian Literature* nos. 68-69 (1976): 124-33; *Selected Hymns and Spiritual Songs of Henry Alline* (Kingston, Ont., 1982)] and Margaret Filschie's, " 'Redeeming Love Shall Be Our Song'; Hymns of the First Great Awakening in Nova Scotia" (MA Thesis, Queen's University, 1983).

MEMOIR

OF

MRS. ELIZA ANN CHIPMAN,

WIFE OF

THE REV. WILLIAM CHIPMAN,

OF PLEASANT VALLEY,

CORNWALLIS.

Sold by John Chase, Wolfville—price 3s.

Aug. 1861

HALIFAX:
A. J. RITCHIE, PRINTER.
1855.

PREFACE.

Three days before her death Mrs. Chipman informed her husband that he would find in a small trunk a sketch of her life and experience, in the form of a Journal. She hoped the perusal of it would be profitable to him. She added, that she did not wish it to be committed to the flames, for she had enjoyed much comfort in reading christian Diaries, and therefore, if there could be a selection of gleanings from her own, which might be useful to others, she was willing that her friends and the public should have the benefit. She was not conscious of pride in writing it, but rather of a desire that God's goodness might be acknowledged.

In compliance with that desire the Journal is now published. It has been slightly abridged, by the omission of a few passages which contained repetitions of thoughts already recorded, or descriptions of feeling so similar to other descriptions, which are retained, that it was judged advisable to leave them out, in order to bring the book within moderate compass.

It is earnestly hoped that this brief Memoir of an excellent woman will prove instructive, edifying, and consolatory to her numerous friends, and useful to all who read it.

CORNWALLIS, January, 1855.

MEMOIR,

&c. &c.

CHAPTER I.

HER EARLY LIFE, TILL HER MARRIAGE.

Eliza Ann Chipman was a daughter of Homes Chipman, Esq.,
of Cornwallis, one of the deacons of the first Baptist Church in
that Township. She was born July 3, 1807. While yet a child 1
she was the subject of serious impressions, chiefly produced by
reading the Scriptures. The Lord blessed that exercise; convictions were deepened, and issued in conversion. Faith in the Saviour was followed by obedience to His commands. She was baptized by the Rev. E. Manning on the 6th of June, 1824, and
joined the Church under his care, to which her parents and other
relatives already belonged. On the 24th of May, 1827, she was 2
married to Mr. William Chipman, now Pastor of the second Baptist Church, Cornwallis. 3

The events of her life, and her religious experience, were recorded by herself, from time to time, in a Journal, which was commenced July 20, 1823.

JOURNAL.

July 20, 1823.—This little book was made yesterday, for the
purpose of penning down a few of the exercises of my mind. But 4
filled as I am with a sense of my own weakness and insufficiency,
I rejoice that the Lord is able to bless the weakest means for the
good of his chosen. Oh! I do feel assured that I am one of his
chosen. If I am, why am I thus? why this dull and lifeless
frame? I cannot relinquish the idea that the God of all grace
and mercy called me by his mighty power and by his outstretched
arm to attend to the things which belong to my eternal peace. O
yes, he has called loud to me by taking my dear brother from me
by death. Two years ago last May it sounded in my ears, "Be
ye also ready, for in such an hour as ye think not the Son of man
cometh." About six weeks before his death the Lord was pleased 5
to afflict me with a slight sickness, at which time I was led to read
the word of God more frequently than before, and never could think
of lying down to rest without begging of God to have mercy upon
me, and to shew me in a real sense the vanity of this transient
world. And, O lamentable! since that I have been very much

allured with sensual delights, but not without checks of conscience. If I have not been guilty of the most flagitious crimes, yet my moral sins would equally condemn me to the same punishment.—But I humbly trust the gracious Lord has called my attention more deeply these four months past, to realize my awful state by nature, and to shew me the emptiness of all sublunary enjoyments, and the fulness and freeness there is in the Gospel to save rebel-
6 lious sinners. I can truly say, from the bottom of my heart, that this world has lost its power to charm, and

> "There's nothing round this spacious earth
> Can suit my large desires."

No, nothing short of having an interest in the once crucified but now exalted Redeemer, and having the fallow ground of this wicked and deceitful heart broken up, and of passing through the strait gate of a sound conversion can make me happy in life, in
7 death, and in that world where celestial glory reigns. O, the happiness there is in religion, which, if I am a stranger to, it is yet a theme upon which I love to converse, write, and reflect.

July 27.—Another week has rolled its round. I have let it pass imperceptibly away without ever dropping a word in this little book; but my thoughts have been often with it, and I have thought what material use will it be to me to pen down here some of the incidents that may occur during the short course of my life. Will it be to my own satisfaction and comfort, much more to the real satisfaction of those whose hands these lines may fall into?—But I have often heard my dear Minister, (Mr. Manning,) speak of the comfort persons might enjoy if they would pen down the first exercises of their minds, and how they then felt the strivings
8 of the Holy Spirit; they might look back with joy thereon.—Perhaps the thoughts I have mentioned are suggestions of that wicked enemy, who "goeth about like a roaring lion, seeking whom he may devour." To-day I was favored with the privilege of hearing the blessed Gospel preached. Those everlasting truths that were delivered, how will they rise up in judgment against me if not improved aright! O dear Jesus, forbid that they ever should prove a savor of death unto death. O solemn consideration! I think I feel more impressed with the vanity of this ensnaring, barren land. O for a greater sense of the deceitfulness of this world, and more entire reconciliation to the Divine will, a more sure reliance on the Fountain of all wisdom. Lord Jesus, enable me to put my whole trust in Thee, for time and for eternity.

Having taken a slight cold in my head it appears now to be resting upon my lungs; a hacking cough succeeds occasionally,
9 which flatters me with the idea that time is short. I almost look forward with joy to the hour that shall free me from this body of

sin and death. Willingly would I take a final farewell of my nearest and dearest relatives, and resign all earthly objects to awake with Jesus, and be forever with him. But stop, my inexperienced pen;—is Jesus mine, and am I his? I have never as yet felt satisfied with my convictions;—they have not been so pungent as I should wish for; but I humbly hope the Lord will reveal himself to me as he does not to the unbelieving world. O Jehovah, enable me to wait patiently for thy salvation.

August 10.—Have been permitted to visit God's holy courts this day, and have heard two sermons delivered; one by Mr. Elder, from those words, "I am debtor both to the Greeks and to the Barbarians, to the wise and to the unwise." In the afternoon a colored man preached, from these words, "For we know that if our earthly house of this tabernacle were dissolved, we have a building of God, a house not made with hands, eternal in the heavens." I think I can say it was good for me to be there; many 10
things were said for my encouragement; but this hard and adamantine heart of mine seemed sometimes almost incapable of feeling the influence of the truth. Oh! dear Jesus, if it was not for the consoling words of life left on record for men to build their hopes of heaven upon, where should we seek for comfort and consolation? Yes, they have great consolation that have fled for refuge to lay hold of eternal life. And am I willing to turn my back on the world, and to shew myself on the Lord's side,—to take up my cross, and follow the meek and lowly Jesus through evil as well as good report? If I know any thing of my own heart, (if I am deceived, O Lord, shew me the deception), it is the wish thereof to be devoted to his cause. I do feel thankful to the God of all mercy that he has in the morning of my life, in the vigour of my youth, (though lamentable that it was not at an earlier period,) opened my eyes in some degree to see the beauty and loveliness there is in religion, and to hate sin and every appearance of evil. But I fear the delusive charms of this fallacious world have too much the governing power over my mind.

August 25.—What! is it possible that another fortnight has rolled its round, and while new scenes have opened to my view, I have omitted relating them here? The busy cares and affairs of life I am surrounded with affect me to that degree, awful to say, that I often lose the remembrance of serious reflections, and forget that I am born to die, that this is not my home, that soon the place that knows me now, will know me no more. Death and eternity are awfully great and mysterious, and important subjects for meditation. O Jehovah, let them be engraven on my memory, 11
and written on my heart, that I may always act in reference to eternity,—that momentous period.

O what a privilege have I been favored with to day! I am permitted to enjoy Sabbath and sanctuary seasons, and do not profess to be partaker of the love of Jesus. Though not a professor, and I fear not a possessor, yet I think I can say that the lines have fallen to me in pleasant places, and that I have a goodly heritage, with the hosts of nations in this land of liberty. It is indeed a land that floweth with milk and honey, but this rocky heart of mine seldom or never realizes those things as it ought. Was the illustrious text, preached from to-day, applied to my own situation? Shall "their people be my people, and their God my God? Eat, O friends, and drink, yea, drink abundantly O my beloved." Glorious Redeemer, enable me to make such a wise and holy resolution, that they alone shall be my people, and their God my God, and may I be stimulated to eat and drink of the good that floweth from thy table. If I know any thing of my own heart, I can say that the world with all its pomp and vanities, sinks in my esteem, and the religion of Jesus appears more delightful. When, O when shall I be favored with the light of God's countenance? When shall the day dawn, and the day-star arise in my soul? There still remains the sinful heart; but can I remove one sin therefrom? O no! it must be an Almighty power to effect the great change; but I will, trusting alone in the Lord, come with all my vileness and filthiness to Jesus's flowing wounds. O that precious blood that atoned for sinners, of whom I am chief! Will Jesus condescend to favor me so highly and apply it to my wounded conscience?

September 3.—Three days ago my beloved Cousin arrived at our mansion, in a very debilitated state; but O what was my great surprise in seeing her so thoughtless and unconcerned about her future destiny, and so much allured with the fantastic visions of this nether world! Divine Redeemer, change the tenor of her thoughts, and let her realize that, although young, yet she must die; and O fit and prepare her for her great and last change, which will surely come.

September 8.—For this week past I have been surrounded with young and gay company, and while joining with them in idle conversation, something seemed to whisper within and say, "All is not right, you cannot serve God and Mammon." How necessary it is to have the good of our souls always in view, knowing that we are under an awful responsibility to God, for the many warnings that are lavished upon us.

September 11.—A sad and mournful catastrophe has happened in the Town of Wilmington, North Carolina (far distant from this), a scene that ought to fill every heart with gloom and surprise. Mr. Mason Cogswell, a connexion of mine, was drowned; what

were his motives when going into the boat, we know not; but perhaps Providence had so ordered it, that he should leave this world
in such a distressing manner. That once animating and promising 12
young man is now reduced to a cold lump of clay, and consigned to the narrow house of the grave. O glorious Redeemer, let this heavy news that has reached his parents' ears, shew them the uncertainty of all sublunary enjoyments, and may they be enabled to cleave unto thee with full purpose of heart, and endeavor after more and new obedience. Let it awaken the surviving brothers and sister to a sense of their alienation from God; and O may they realize what an awful thing it is to die without an interest in the crucified Redeemer; that they may remember their Creator in the days of their youth, for the evil days are drawing nigh, when they shall have no pleasure in them. I leave them, Dear Jesus, in the arms (I would fain hope) of thy mercy. O let them not give sleep to their eyes till they have found comfort under the shadow of thy wings!

September 20.—Sabbath day. This blessed and most holy of days, has again returned, and I am yet spared to see the light thereof; though the Sun in the firmament does not shine with his powerful and benignant rays upon the earth, yet I trust the Son of righteousness does arise with healing beneath his wings in many souls this day. Though deprived of hearing the Gospel delivered by our preacher, may I, poor reptile worm, taste and see from the treasures of thy most holy word, that the Lord is good and gracious, that I may drink of those living streams which are never ceasing to flow. O God, impress upon my mind more sensibly, that I must soon take my final exit and enter an unknown region. Why, O why am I so thoughtless and unconcerned about my eternal welfare? What; for a few moments' pleasure, shall I be willing to sacrifice all real happiness in this life, and in a greater degree augmented through the long annals of eternity? how depraved is this heart of mine,—prone to evil as the sparks that fly upwards,—how lost to every thing that is good; Oh where shall I fly for refuge? Jesus, are thine arms stretched out all day long to a gainsaying and rebellious people? will they not listen to thy charming voice? no, they say by their life and practice, they will not have this man Christ Jesus to reign over them. O ye ignorant and blind mortals, will ye not come and partake of the feast of fat things, of wine on the lees well refined? Solid peace, joy, and comfort, you never will have unless you enlist under the banner of King Jesus, and find his banner over you to be love. Well, perhaps I am in the same lamentable situation.

January 30, 1824.—My pen has long lain inactive, which at times has caused me many heart-rending feelings; to be so im-

mersed with the concerns of life is a great hindrance to private enjoyments; but this is not all my excuse, because when a person's mind is rightly exercised, every thing will bow in subjection to the important concerns of their souls. Well, I must call in question what I have been about for these four months as well as all my life through. I would however observe, that in the omission of writing so long a time, I feel safe in saying that, during that time, I
13 passed through what is generally termed a sound conversion. Such was the distress of my mind, that I knew not what to write clearly, and I feared at the same time that my convictions never had been such as they should be preceding conversion; and in addition to this I felt a heavy load of God's wrath hanging over my head, knowing that I was justly doomed to everlasting punishment. But I will say to the praise and glory of Jehovah's name, my greatest extremity was the time of God's opportunity. He brought my feet up out of the horrible pit, and miry clay, and set them upon the rock of ages; he put a new song into my mouth, even praise to our God. Though I cannot ascertain the identical moment in which the Lord passed by, and said unto me, "live," yet I can say, that whereas I was once blind now I see. Happy seasons were enjoyed by me; I would pray for the evidence of divine grace, while Satan would tempt me by telling me I was in possession of none. I am led however to inquire have I found that sweet confidence in my God which I had anticipated? has Christ become the ultimate end of all my wishes? is He formed in my soul the hope of glory? or have I, like the sow that was washed and returned to her wallowing in the mire, returned again to the beggarly elements of this insidious world? God forbid that I should ever be left to my own fleshly lusts! I again enquire, have I made any advance whatever in a religious course? If my treacherous heart does not deceive me, the foundation laid in Zion for men to build their hopes of heaven upon, appears in my contracted view more firm and permanent; but these lofty imaginations of mine must be brought low; this adamantine heart of mine, that is so inflated with pride, must be humbled. I want to be little, more simple, more mild, more like my blessed Master, and more like a child. My frail life has been protracted to the present moment, by the kind indulgence of a heavenly Father. What shall I render to him for all his benefits bestowed upon me, poor unworthy rebel? May I, by assistance of thine Almighty Spirit, resolutely determine to set out this new year to be more watchful and prayerful, for thou hast said in thy word, "Watch and pray, lest ye enter into temptation:" "In the world ye shall have tribulation, but in me ye shall have peace." May I be enabled to lay aside every weight, and the sin which doth so easily beset me, and run with

patience the race set before me, looking unto Jesus, who is the author and finisher of my faith,—who, for the joy that was set before him, endured the cross, despising the shame, and is now set down at the right hand of God to intercede for perishing sinners.

March 1.—Lord's day. I am again spared to behold a day in which thousands no doubt are favored with the privilege of assembling themselves together for the express purpose of worshipping God, which inestimable favor I am deprived of this day. But ought I to complain? scarce a sermon has been preached by the Baptists in our Township, the past winter, but what I have heard. O! I hope and trust it has proved a savor of life unto my soul, many times. Still I have to lament that I have improved so little by them. God of all mercy and goodness, be pleased to look upon the face of thine anointed, and through him, and for his sake, draw benignly near, and may I, O my Father, have sweet communion with thee, the King of Kings, and Lord of Lords; let me feel a sure reliance on thee; may I have faith to look upon Mount Calvary and behold the Saviour of sinners, bleeding, groaning and dying for me, and that it is alone by his stripes I am healed. Have I received an evidence of adoption into the family of heaven? Yes, I am constrained to say that God has given me a new heart, and that I have reason to hope, by his word and Spirit, that he has redeemed my precious and immortal soul from going down to the pit of endless woe and misery. O what cause have I ever to adore that grace which stopped me in my mad career, and bade me welcome to all the privileges of the sons of God. Never, never, may I be left to wound the cause I have espoused: for surely no where else can such consolations be found, such true joy and comfort; it is a peace that passeth knowledge. To be an heir of glory, an heir of God, and joint heir with Christ,—what more can I desire? and I can truly say nothing more I do desire.

March 26.—Am yet the spared monument of God's saving mercy; what a heart of gratitude ought I to have! But in how small degree do I render the tribute of thankfulness for the innumerable mercies I am made the happy partaker of, while Jesus the Saviour of Sinners has declared, "That in his Father's house are many mansions; if it were not so, I would have told you; I go to prepare a place for you; and if I go and prepare a place for you, I will come again and receive you unto myself, that where I
am ye may be also." How can I, under such a solemn consider- 14
ation, remain unanimated? Am I not lost in wonder, love, and praise? O how should my affections work, when Christ the Son of the most High, has given his life a ransom for many, among whom I trust, through boundless mercy, to sit down in the king-

dom of God. What rapturous songs will then tune our harps—what celestial gems of glory shall we then behold! When will the happy day arrive? when shall I be free from this cumbrous clod of sin and corruption? but I will not be impatient in waiting my Lord's time; O that I could be in actual readiness to meet the summons whenever it shall come, and not be taken unawares; for the Son of man cometh as a thief in the night; therefore may I always watch unto prayer, having my loins girt about with
15 truth.

March 31.—I feel much depressed in spirits on account of my lukewarmness in religion, fearing that I am deceived; but to whom shall I look for comfort and consolation in this trying hour? Dare I look up to the heaven of heavens, I should there find a Saviour ready and willing to help,—a righteous God that will abundantly pardon iniquity. Thou, O Lord, art not willing to look upon sin with the least allowance, but with the most consummate abhorrence.

April 6.—Why am I so willing to admit the very thing that is so offensive to the pure nature of an omnipotent God, into my thoughts, words, and actions? Glory be to thy holy name, there is a fountain opened for all sin and uncleanness. Search my heart, O God, and try my reins, and every thing that is offensive to thy pure mind and will, purge and cleanse me from it, that I may be made holy in all manner of conversation and godliness. I have numberless blessings to be thankful for. Thou, Jehovah, hast never left thyself without a witness. I think I can say from the bottom of my heart, "Bless the Lord, O my soul, and all that is within me bless his holy name." He has given me a desire now to take up my cross and follow the meek and lowly Jesus, through evil as well as good report. Surely there is nothing in the blessed religion of Jesus, that I can be ashamed of. When it convinces immortal souls of their undone condition, leads them to look upon their own righteousness as filthy rags, they are enabled by the sweet workings of the Spirit to view the blood of Christ that has atoned for their sins, and the righteousness which he has wrought out and made over to them, to be procured for them. Why then this diffidence to speak of the most important realities that concern our never dying souls?

April 13.—Have been hearing the sacred truths of the Gospel dispensed from those words, "No Servant can serve two Masters." Will it not be well for me to enquire what master I am serving? It has evidently been declared unto me this afternoon, that I cannot serve two. Therefore I would wish and solemnly desire, before God, Angels, and men, to serve the only and good God, and
16 not to have any communication whatever with Belial. The spirit

is indeed willing, but the flesh is weak, and I have a law in my members warring against the law of my mind.

April 19.—The difference has been fully displayed this day between law and Gospel, by one of the servants of God. I have been made sensible that there is no other name given under Heaven or amongst men, whereby I can be saved, only the name of Jesus; only in and through his death and sufferings, burial, resurrection and glorious ascension, can I ever expect to be accepted of the Father; and since I have been brought to realize my insufficiency and helplessness, I desire no other way. O what reason I have to praise that Majestic Being who hath opened my eyes to view religion as the one thing needful! Dear Saviour, brighten up my evidences for future glory, that I may have a lively assurance of obtaining a part of that rest that remains for the people of God. Let me not be so cold and lifeless; the time is fast hastening, and the period when, (if life and health be spared), I contemplate owning my Lord and Master before a wicked and adulterous generation. Ah Lord! how can I speak in thy name, when I am but a babe in religion; but thou hast said, "If ye love me keep my commandments," and this passage continually harasses me, "He that taketh not up his cross and followeth me is not worthy
of me." 17

> "Ashamed of Jesus, that dear friend,
> On whom my hopes of Heaven depend!
> No! when I blush, be this my shame,
> That I no more revere his name." 18

Yes, I have reason to blush when I approach before the "High and Lofty One, that inhabiteth eternity," but who condescends to dwell with the humble and contrite soul, that I no more reverence his omnipotency. In thy name I put my trust, and how can I go if thou goest not up with me? I will open my mouth, and rely on thy promises to fill it. O what a strong consolation is it that I have an High Priest who was "in all points tempted like as we are," sin excepted, to intercede for me to the Father. Have I received the spirit of adoption whereby I can cry, "Abba Father?" If this deceitful heart does not deceive me, I know I have.

April 25.—How sure is my standing if my feet are placed on the rock of ages,—how secure against all the insinuations of a wicked enemy! I think yesterday was a day to be had in long remembrance. I was truly happy in my mind when sitting under the sound of the blessed Gospel. Heard two excellent Sermons, delivered by Mr. David Harris from those words, "Stand still, and see the salvation of God." "Draw me and I will run after
thee," &c. What a rich salvation is thus provided, to save even 19
the greatest sinners; if it were not such, I never could have been

saved. O Heavenly Father, I desire to have a heart of gratitude for the many privileges I am favored with, more particularly for thy presence being manifested to me, who am so unworthy; but Jesus is worthy.

April 27.—Have been meditating much on that sacred ordinance, the Lord's Supper. Well may every one that partakes of the body and blood of a risen Saviour, cry, "Lord, why was I a guest," and is this feast prepared for hungry souls, them that are hungering and thirsting after that bread which came down from Heaven, which, if a man eat thereof, he never shall die? Dear Jesus, thou did'st tell thy Disciples to "take and eat, for this was thy body broken for them;" and "as oft as ye do it, do it in remembrance of me." Shall I, a defiled creature, be so honored? grant Lord that I may receive it in faith, love, and humility, that I may grow in grace and in the knowledge of my Lord and Saviour Jesus Christ.

May 13.—What a solemn transaction has taken place since I
last wrote! I have entered into covenant with God's people, have
cast my lot in with them, the excellent ones of the earth, and have
20 been received into the bosom of the Baptist Church. What unmerited favours am I privileged with! O thou most adorable
Saviour, ever keep me under the shadow of thy wings from straying and wandering from thee and thy fold; keep me humble; may
I always walk in the light of God's countenance, not adhering in
the smallest degree to the insinuations of a wicked adversary;
never may it be my unhappy case to withdraw from the cheering
beams of the Sun of Righteousness. Ever may I keep my leading
star *Jesus* full in view.

May 17.—I am permitted to behold the light of another morning, am yet held in existence by the Supreme power of an infinite
God. I purpose reading for my instruction a treatise on the Lord's
21 Supper. O may I derive holy and heartfelt satisfaction therefrom,
that it may be profitable to my never dying soul. Enable me,
O Lord, to examine myself, and see whether I am in the faith or
not, to know if I am a proper subject for this ordinance, for awfully
aggravated will be my condemnation, if I eat and drink unworthily
and be guilty of the body and blood of my Lord. The period will
soon arrive when I shall be laid in a watery grave, (if spared) and
follow my dear Redeemer's footsteps. What an exalted station is
a poor fallen creature raised to, when brought out of darkness into
God's marvellous light!

June 20.—Sabbath afternoon. I have been meeting with a
22 large assembly, in an Association. The words delivered have dropt
as marrow and fatness. It was indeed food for the hungry soul.
With how much more real satisfaction do I hear preaching since I

united publicly with the people of God, for ever before was my
mind wavering, and being not established therein; I was continually upbraiding my own conscience until I took up my cross and
made known to the world that I was on the Lord's side. God
grant that I may ever be kept in the pathway of duty, and daily
take up my cross. On the 8th of May, 1824, I was received into
the Church as a candidate for the Ordinance of Baptism, and on
the 6th of June was immersed in Jordan's swelling flood, and
communed at the table of the Lord. O how awfully solemn was 23
the undertaking. But I desire to bless my dear Redeemer for
bringing me thus far; I know the glory will all redound to thy
name for rescuing such a hell-deserving sinner as I from the
ruinous predicament I was in. How lamentable was my situation,
living without God and without hope in the world! but God was
pleased in infinite mercy to pluck me as a brand from the burning,
and to set, I humbly hope, my feet upon the rock of ages, which
the Scripture asserts that the gates of hell shall never prevail
against. Oh! how richly am I sheltered from the stormy blast of
impending wrath that is fast approaching! "The munition of
rocks is my defence;" how ought my heart to glow with love and
gratitude to the Author of all worlds, that he has been so compa-
sionate as to shed abroad his love in my heart!

June 25.—I was indulged the past afternoon with hearing an
excellent Discourse from those words, "By the grace of God I am
what I am." How often has my heart adopted that language, since 24
I have been encircled within the rainbow of the new and everlasting
Covenant. O that the poor deluded votaries of sin would consider
their latter end, that the young in particular would remember their
Creator in the days of their youth, for the evil days are drawing
nigh when they shall say they have no pleasure in them. Could
my arm reach your case, fain would I exert all my effort for your
salvation and eternal welfare. I would clasp you in my arms and
endeavour to unfold to you the beauties of the lovely Saviour:
but alas, it is not in my power to save your immortal souls, neither
could I wish it was, since there is such a glorious ransom provided
to save rebellious, lost man; all I can do is to commend your souls,
that are worth ten thousand worlds, to God, and beseech him to
blot out your innumerable sins and transgressions, and to look with
complacency upon you when washed in that efficacious blood, which
atoned for the chief of sinners.

July 2.—Not long since I visited a young female who has been near the verge of eternity, has felt herself ruined and undone, and was confident in her own mind that if she was removed from time to a world of spirits, she must inevitably sink into misery, where hope could never come. Under those apprehensions, what anguish, what torture, must have seized her whole soul, known only to God and herself. But adored be thy ever blessed name, O Saviour of sinners, that thou ever hadst thoughts of mercy, concerning the fallen race of Adam. Thou hast in thy boundless love (we trust) taken her feet out of the horrible pit and miry clay, put a new song in her mouth, even praise to thy great name. How gladdening this is to my heart. How easy it is with thee to humble the pride of man and bring the lofty looks low, "Thou art indeed glorious in holiness, fearful in praises, doing wonders." O what has Zion and all her advocates to fear, since this God is ours, our forefront and rereward, our shield and buckler, a strong tower where the righteous may run and find safety; the Lord is as a stream of broad rivers to those who obey his commandments and walk in his precepts, and no good thing will be withheld from them that walk uprightly. May such be my happiness!

July 18.—Sabbath afternoon. I have been highly favored to-
day in hearing the everlasting Gospel dispensed, but ah must I say
that it has proved a gloomy season to me? I grieve that I am so
cold and insensible, that my attention is in so small a degree engaged, and that I have such slight views of my own infirmities.
With what solemn weight ought the realities of another world to
rest upon my mind. "Oh wretched one that I am, who shall deliver me from this body of death." I find that in me, that is, in
25 my flesh, dwells no good thing. My mind has of late been continually upon the rack. Blessed Redeemer, draw divinely near,
pity and relieve me, I acknowledge I have forsaken thee, the fountain of living waters and have hewn out to myself broken cisterns
that can hold no water. May I rely upon thy promises and cast
all my burdens upon thee Lord, knowing that thou carest for the
oppressed and afflicted.

The texts preached from to-day in my hearing were these,
"O satisfy us early with thy mercy, that we may rejoice and
be glad all our days." Happy art thou, O Israel, who is like
unto thee, O people saved by the Lord, the shield of thine help,
and who is the sword of thine excellency, and thine enemies shall
be found liars unto thee, and thou shalt tread upon their high places." A week ago to-day, I had the privilege of hearing two ex-
26 cellent discourses delivered from these passages, by Elder Harding:
"And of Benjamin he said, the beloved of the Lord shall dwell in
safety by him, and the Lord shall cover him all the day long, and
he shall dwell between his shoulders." "For as many as are led
by the spirit of God, they are the sons of God." On Thursday
following was again permitted to attend the worship of God, when
this illustrious verse was explained to our further knowledge—
"That he might present unto himself a glorious church, not hav-

ing spot or wrinkle or any such thing, but that it should be holy and without blemish." To what a height of blessings am I raised! "surely goodness and mercy have followed me all my days;" but Oh! how unthankful, how unmindful of the hand that bestows such distinguished mercies upon so vile, so great a sinner! how applicable to my case is the language of the poet—

> "Prone to wander, Lord, I feel it,
> Prone to leave the God I love;
> Here's my heart, O take and seal it,
> Seal it from thy Courts above." 27

Very far am I from being in the Spirit on the Lord's day. Heavenly Parent, forgive me, and remove my manifold transgressions far from me and grant me grace for days to come, for the days are evil; make and keep me humble.

July 21.—Have felt a degree of sensibility these two days past; the burden of sinful self is removed in some measure from my notice. I daily find that I am a dependent creature; if forsaken of God I must perish, O that I had faith to view at all times the sufficiency of the Almighty, for "he is God, and his work is perfect." Thou swayest thy sceptre in righteousness, and leadest thy people by ways which they know not. How justly might I have been passed by and left to hardness of heart and blindness of mind; such precious love is too wonderful, too great for hell-deserving sinners to have bestowed upon them; it excites me to say, "Wonder, O Heavens, and be astonished, O Earth, at the goodness and tender compassion of Immanuel."

July 26.—Had the unspeakable privilege of listening to the cheering sound of life and salvation proclaimed through the merits of a crucified Redeemer, from those passages of Scripture—"Who among us shall dwell with the devouring fire! who among us shall dwell with everlasting burnings?" "He shall dwell on high, his place of defence shall be the munition of rocks, bread shall be given him, his water shall be sure; thine eyes shall see the King in his beauty." How different were my sensations from the last Sabbath! I trust the little spark of grace that is implanted was fanned into a flame, and I was made to rejoice in the hope of the glory of the Lord. Oh this blessed Jehovah is so good to me, while I am so unfaithful to God and my own soul; yet the fountain of living water that flows from his right hand runs clear as crystal.

August 2.—It is now a year since I first drew the resolution to write frequently of my own exercises. The infinite God has spared my unprofitable life to the present moment. I am yet permitted to abide here in this tabernacle of clay, whilst thousands,

without a doubt, since the commencement of this year, have met the King of Terrors, and have been arraigned at the awful tribunal, at the impartial bar of God, there to receive their doom. O
28 may these solemn realities rest with due weight on my mind! How negligent do I appear of them! O for heart-searching grace, that all my powers and faculties might be called up to action, when I am so highly favored as to be privileged with hearing God's word expounded from day to day and from time to time. Mr. Manning, our beloved Pastor, spoke from this noble text, "Then Paul stood up and beckoning with his hand said, Men of Israel and ye that fear God, give audience." Only one sermon was delivered, on account of the sacred ordinance of Baptism being administered in the morning to six candidates. Two blooming youths were of the number. How strikingly did it bring home to my mind the interesting season in which I followed the footsteps of my dear Redeemer down into the liquid grave: then I could say,

> "Happy, beyond expression, they
> Who find the place where Jesus lay."

The state of my mind was rather gloomy to-day, and has been very dark all the week, but I trust I got a little relief at the close of the discourse.

August 6.—How solemn and momentous was the occurrence this afternoon! I had an opportunity of beholding a lifeless corpse committed to the silent tomb; this is to teach me the uncertainty and brevity of life. Oh that I might be enabled so to number my days as to apply my heart unto wisdom. Upon the occasion an interesting discourse was delivered from those striking words, "And while they went to buy, the bridegroom came, and they that were ready went in with him to the marriage, and the door was shut." I hope it led me to enquire whether I had oil in my lamp or not: whatever grace my Heavenly Parent sees fit to bestow on poor unworthy me, I trust he will ever grant a heart to make a right improvement of it.

August 9.—Sabbath afternoon. What a hard and ungrateful heart do I possess towards my Maker, and my fellow creatures, not only for the day and means of grace, but for a preached Gospel established in our land, and the genuine showers of heavenly mercy which have fallen upon many of the inhabitants of this place. Daily additions are made to the church of Christ, of such as shall be eternally saved. Fourteen this day were buried with Christ in Baptism; the season was truly affecting; an enlivening sermon was preached by our Minister from this consoling passage in Isaiah, "And I will bring the blind by a way that they know not. I will lead them in paths that they have not known. I will make darkness light before them, and crooked things straight. These things will I do unto them, and not forsake them."

August 17.—I have retired into my chamber for the night with some good degree of thoughtfulness for the common mercies of my life past, and for the amazing love and condescension of the Father in devising (in the council chamber), before creation was brought forth, or the world was framed, such a glorious plan and way of salvation, which will ever bring a revenue of glory to his great name, and which is so well calculated to bring the aspiring rebel low, and to exalt the worthy name of *Jesus*. On this foundation, and on this alone, do I wish my future hopes of happiness to depend; and the few remaining days that I shall spend here on earth, I think, if I know my own heart, I want to be spent in proclaiming the all-sufficiency of Immanuel to save ruined sinners, by a way which they know not; for surely after such distinguishing love has been manifested towards such a vile sinner as I am, the vilest of the vile need not despair. O if they could but for a moment realize what a few more rising and setting suns will disclose to their view, how soon would they call for help! But so blinded is the human heart by the vain infatuations of Satan, that unless eyes are given them from above, they cannot see, neither can their ears hear.

August 27.—Such a round of worldly affairs engrosses my attention that I neglect private duties very much. How much more gratifying would it be, and far more profitable, to have a variety of sacred duties to attend to, such as visiting the fatherless and widows, the sick and afflicted, the poor and oppressed; but while I have to do with the world I want to have my heart where my treasure is, for I humbly hope my treasure is not in the fading vanities of time, but in durable riches and righteousness, that which is substantial and permanent; but alas how little do I realize that I am entitled to a glorious inheritance, purchased for me by the amazing sufferings of my ascended Redeemer. So stupid and inactive is this hard and wicked heart of mine, that nothing short of the warming sunbeams of heavenly love, and the rich influences of God's holy, quickening, and enlivening spirit, can arouse me to a sight of my lukewarmness. Is it possible that a soul redeemed and ransomed from the power of the grave, can be so dark and unfruitful? But why these gloomy apprehensions? God is not impoverished by bestowing his celestial graces upon his needy creatures; then, oh my soul, apply to the fountain and receive "out of his fulness, and grace for grace;" wrestle with the mighty God of Jacob for favors both for thyself and a dying world; plead the merits of his anointed. O Lord, thou wilt not withhold thy tender mercy if I ask aright, and believing that thou art a rewarder of them that diligently seek thy favor. On the morrow I contemplate meeting my covenanted brethren and sisters in conference; this inestimable privilege I have been deprived of some time. Grant, my gracious God, a word to say, that may be to the honor and glory of thy name; may thy presence be realised by all who shall attend; may the little Zion that has increased with numbers be watered, and righteousness run down our streets like a mighty running stream. Suffer no hypocrites to join with us, but may we all be enabled to run the christian race with joy, and with delight of soul walk and not faint.

September 7.—For this week past my outward privileges have been very great. I was allowed to attend two conference meetings, and on the following Sabbath public worship, on the latter of which I commemorated the death and sufferings of our risen Saviour, and was so assisted by the Holy Spirit as to discover that all my
29 hope was in him, and that it is by his stripes I am healed. As a cart is pressed with sheaves, so was my dear Redeemer laden with innumerable sins and aggravations of mine, as well as of a dying world. When he cried out and said "it was finished," gave up the ghost, and declared the work of man's redemption was complete, there was darkness over the earth for the space of three hours. Well may the Poet exclaim—

> "This was compassion like a God,
> That when the Saviour knew
> The price of pardon was his blood,
> His pity ne'er withdrew."

Here is represented the complete atonement that the Lord of life and glory accomplished, after enduring a life of sufferings (for he was "a man of sorrows, and acquainted with grief.") He gave his soul up to the stroke of death without a murmuring word. O, my Saviour has got the victory over all my spiritual enemies. He has conquered death, hell, and the grave, and what was it for? Is it what he was under obligation to do? No. Then how clearly does it shew forth the amazing wisdom and condescension of the three persons in one Godhead, that he who thought it not robbery to be equal with God the Father, should assume such a contemptible depraved nature as I and all the human family are possessed of, and become "sin for us who knew no sin." A week ago to-day I was permitted to hear a very appropriate discourse preached on that solemn occasion, the death of a beloved cousin, (her ill state of health was spoken of in some part of the first of my writings) from Job i. 21. She quitted this tabernacle of clay in full assurance of obtaining that rest that remains for the people of God. Her views of spiritual things were greatly altered while in her last illness, which consisted only of ten days, during which time she professed to have experienced the love of Jesus. What a daily consolation ought it to be to her afflicted parents, surviving relatives, and to the world at large, that she left such evidence of a good hope through grace, when her expiring language was, "glory, glory to God in the highest," and to her parents and brothers she said (the message was delivered by her tender father as she bade adieu to all terrestrial objects in a land of almost strangers, in Columbia, State of Connecticut, whereas her native place was Annapolis, N. S.), "shed no tears for me, but prepare to meet me in heaven." This was striking, to come from the lips of a dying person. Oh that it might have a salutary effect upon all the living, that each one may lay it to heart. This is a loud warning to me, to be ready to meet the bridegroom at his appearing, to be found with oil in my lamp, and it brightly burning. If this is my happiness, I shall be enabled to meet death as the passport to endless felicity, and greet it as a welcome messenger. It would have been just in God ere this to have cut me off as a cumberer of the ground; but for wise and holy purposes I hope my unprofitable life is lengthened out; may such tender loving kindness excite in this immortal soul of mine fresh expressions of love and gratitude.

October 2.—What shall I here say in any degree connected with the solemn and alarming scene that I have very recently been a spectator to? If I had the tongue of an angel I could not describe it. Another cousin is gone the way of all the earth, in the same melancholy manner his dear brother (in a distant land) met the grim messenger. He was drowned when sailing for pleasure in a canoe, with three other youths. It appears that by his unwearied exertions in rocking the little sail, it upset, and all were in great danger, but by the good providence of God, three out of the four (one of whom, since his deliverance, has professed to know the love of Jesus) were saved, while the other, (namely, Wm. Cogswell, Jr.) was summoned to appear before the judge of quick and dead. Such a general mourning as this severe affliction exci- 31
ted in the breasts of his numerous acquaintance, was never witnessed before, within my knowledge, in Cornwallis, and indeed I have heard those that were far advanced in life, say the same. A deep and tender sympathy for the fond parents and sister of the deceased reigned in every countenance. Alas, they mourn as those that have no hope. How many are the warnings in our land, yet how ineffectual to arouse the carnal, the carnally secure, if not accompanied with the finger of God. O that this affecting occurrence might sink deep in every heart, that each one may consider that there is no work nor device in the grave to which we are all hastening. Gracious God, as the heavens are high above

the earth, so are thy ways above ours. In thy mercy thou didst
snatch the surviving sister (a year since) from the flames of hell,
32 and didst impart thy dying love to her immortal soul. Ah thou
knewest what was in the womb of providence; the decree was
designed to go forth, and this dear youth was prepared by thy
grace to meet this heavy stroke, though she complains of unreconciledness of heart. Yet had she and his dear parents not had
grace to support them, I know not what refuge they could fly to.
O that they may sensibly feel that God has done it, and that it
becomes them to be still, and know it is God who rules in the
armies of heaven above, and does as he will among the inhabitants
of time, and none can stay his hand, or say unto him, "what
doest thou?" May they adopt the language of the psalmist and
say, "It is good for me that I have been afflicted; before I was
33 afflicted I went astray." Sanctified afflictions are the bread of
heaven. The parents have but two children remaining, and the
son at a distance from home. May the power of Jehovah accom-
pany the tidings and bring him into the fold of Christ!

October 11.—Yesterday was a Sabbath of rest. I was privileged with hearing preaching from these words, "Work out your own salvation with fear and trembling." Baptism was administered to seven candidates professing godliness, and the Lord's Supper was administered; the number of communicants that sat round the table of the precious Saviour was one hundred and thirty. I sincerely hope they received with penitence and gratitude the memorials of the Redeemer's sufferings, and the emblem of that spiritual nourishment and strength which is acquired by faith in the Lamb of God. I can safely say it was a season to be remembered by rebellious unworthy me; the more frequently I am permitted to commune with the people of God, the more I think it heightens my attachment to them, and to all the ordinances of God's house.

"My soul, how lovely is the place
To which thy God resorts;
'Tis Heaven to see his smiling face,
34 Though in his earthly courts."

October 17.—I, a highly-favored, though hell-deserving sinner, heard a portion of Scripture expounded by my faithful Pastor; it was this, "Let thy work appear unto thy servants, and thy glory unto their children." I felt to bless God, for the precious opportunity, though I lament that I possess such a wretched, wandering mind; I did not hear with that understanding I would wish to; a solemn reflection of the trying scene I not long since passed through, and a particular sympathy for the mourning family, which have so severely been called to mourn, pressed upon my mind with such weight, that I could not refrain from sorrowing, and it engrossed part of my attention at different times.

> "The fondness of a creature's love,
> How strong it strikes the sense;
> Thither our warm affections move,
> Nor can we call them thence."

Health, invaluable blessing, I am allowed to enjoy in a good degree; but does my immortal part flourish, while the mortal is fat and flourishing? Does it grow as the Cedars of Lebanon? For those that be planted in the house of the Lord shall flourish in the courts of our God. Yes, they shall; am I of the number? Can I say of the Lord, he is my refuge and my fortress, my God, in him will I trust? Can I confide in his never-failing faithfulness and believe there shall no evil befal me,—neither shall any plague come nigh my dwelling? I could more sensibly feel it if I could trust in God. Alas, my levities want to be checked, and a greater importunity at a throne of grace is much needed; I feel my wicked heart to rise so much in opposition to the ways of God.

November 8.—I was privileged yesterday with hearing three
sermons delivered; two by my dear Pastor from 2nd Thess.,
i. 7, 8, 9, 10, and one by a Methodist preacher from the Psalm
84, 2. They were all profitable discourses to the believer; the 35
former was very alarming (or it is hoped will prove so) to the careless sinner. O what vast necessity there is for the proclaiming of the gospel of our Lord and Saviour Jesus Christ in the love and purity of it, keeping nothing back, but delivering the whole matter as it is given unto the heralds of the Most High in the word of inspiration, that blessed book, the Bible, which is profitable for doctrine, for reproof, for correction, and for instruction in righteousness, that the man of God may be thoroughly furnished unto every good word and work.

November 24.—I yet have to lament my engagements to the world and worldly things, but I sometimes think, were I rightly exercised, every thought of earthly objects would be brought into subjection: but the law in my members wars against the law of my mind. Alas, how cold, how inanimate are my affections towards heavenly realities; how easy to seize at a shadow and grasp at a phantom! When such distinguishing, loving kindness, has been manifested to me, who deserve nothing but the lowest hell, and to be banished from the presence of the Lamb, and of Him that sitteth upon the Throne, forever. But while I write bitter things against myself, Oh may I, by an eye of faith, look to Mount Calvary, and there believe that He who was once upon earth, and performed miracles, was rejected of the Jews, defied and shamefully entreated by all mankind (excepting a few, and that very few, who were resolved to follow him whithersoever he went), that my only Saviour who shed the last drop of his heart's blood to ransom me with the elect from endless misery,—may I feel assured that on him hang all my hopes, and that I have no other place of safety; he has become "my hiding place from the wind and my covert from the tempest, and as the shadow of a great rock in a weary land." O matchless grace, that gave my soul a hiding place! how many and how great are the obligations I am under to love and serve my covenant-keeping God, to obey from the heart that form of doctrine delivered by the pen of inspiration. My obligations are daily renewed to be for the Lord and for none other.

December 1.—The last month of the year has commenced. O time, how art thou rapidly passing away!

"Our wasting lives grow shorter still,
As days and months increase;
And every beating pulse we tell
36 Leaves but the number less."

It is now rather more than a year since I professed an acquaintance with the dear Redeemer, but greatly to be lamented is my little progress in the divine life. Lord of the worlds above, grant that in the ensuing year I may be more dead unto sin, and alive unto thee. If it should be consistent with thy holy mind and will to lengthen out the brittle thread of my frail life, may I be enabled to testify to the surrounding world that there is a pure reality in religion, and joys that a stranger intermeddles not with. Oh let me trust in thee for safety against all the assaults of the world, the flesh and the devil. They beset me on every hand, and thou alone canst enable me to withstand them. "The weapons of my warfare are not carnal, but mighty through God, to the pulling down of strongholds." I hope I do feel my insufficiency to fight, but only in my Saviour's strength, in him alone can I ever expect to come off conqueror, yea more than conqueror, through him that hath loved me and hath given his life for me.

December 11.—To-day was our conference meeting; I was again deprived of going. Three months have elapsed since I attended and solemnly dedicated myself both to God and his people. Yet I think it has not been for the want of inclination to meet with them. I could say with the Psalmist, "my heart longeth, yea even fainteth for the courts of the living God—when shall I
37 come and appear before God?" I trust I have had special seasons on the Sabbath and other days, when not permitted to hear the gospel dispensed. I hope to be privileged with worshipping God in his sanctuary on the morrow. O my Saviour, furnish me with every needed grace for that and every other undertaking, for

I know not what I need the most; never was a creature more needy than I.

December 13.—The solemn transaction of yesterday is passed, and what shall I say of myself? Have I been benefited by partaking of the broken body of my crucified Saviour? Have I been encouraged to hold on my way, not turning to the right hand or to the left? Ah, what shall I say? My mind was never more gloomy at such an interesting season; so insensible and lifeless was I, that had it not been for the occasion it would have given the world to censure, and the greater evils it might have produced in my own soul, I should doubtless have kept back; still I do not regret my taking a seat among the dear children of God, for I think it is my heart's desire to follow them as far as they follow Jesus, if I only creep after them; but my divine Lord and Master has left us an example that we should follow his footsteps, and if I was more willing to sit at his feet and learn of him, it would add much to my advancement in the divine life, and my growth in grace. How much humility is displayed in his life, from the manger to the cross! "He was led as a lamb to the slaughter, and as a sheep is dumb before its shearers, so opened he not his mouth." A complete and full redemption is finished on 38
the accursed tree, together with everlasting righteousness brought in. It is enough to ravish the hearts of those who have been made the happy recipients thereof. Tongue cannot express, neither can pen paint, the joy that is prepared for such as love the king of saints. Our sermon was evangelical; a very comfortable passage was the text: "Thou hast a few names, even in Sardis, which have not defiled their garments; and they shall walk with me in white, for they are worthy." Yes, made worthy by free and sovereign grace. I confess I was not a little comforted under the faithful preaching; the admonitions there given, if adhered to, will preserve us from defiling our garments while in our journey here in this wilderness. But in God, who is rich in mercy, must we trust.

Christmas evening.—Another of the days is past and gone, in which it is most generally believed Our Blessed Saviour was born, in Bethlehem. I have been deprived of hearing the gospel preached by our stated Shepherd; yet I was favored with going to a good prayer meeting, and this I ought to be highly thankful for, and not despise the day of small things. Much was said, and to 39
profit, but if I were to say I am thankful for the opportunity I had this day, I fear I should do wrong, for I know not how to be thankful; and I find I have so much to awaken gratitude that I often feel as if I had none at all. This, above all other things, should excite love and gratitude, that God the eternal Father

should send his only begotten Son into the world to die for sinners, of whom I am chief. I think if I ever felt love to the Saviour, and desired to know more of his excellency, it was to-day. O how clearly do all his doctrines of grace meet and harmonize together. The Godhead shines gloriously through the Eternal Three.

January 5, 1825.—With grateful acknowledgements, I trust, have I welcomed the commencement of another year. Great transactions have transpired during the last year that is forever gone; many delightful events connected with my own best interests, and I hope for the glory of God, have taken place. I must truly say it has been a year of years to me; in keeping the commandments of a holy and wise God, there is great reward. While the righteous judgments of Jehovah have spread abroad, I am loaded with mercies, and while large numbers have been hurried out of time into eternity, I am yet in a probationary state, and can approach the mercy seat with a spirit of prayer given from above. Oh that my feet may never stray, for they that trust in the Lord shall be as Mount Zion, which cannot be moved, but abideth forever. I think I sensibly feel my unworthiness and unprofitableness at times, and this makes me long and pant after further degrees of grace, long to be more holy, more like my blessed Jesus, to be entirely divested of self, and to have nothing but the merits of Christ for my plea before the throne.

January 18.—Many delightful scenes have occurred since I last wrote; sabbath and sanctuary seasons have been attended and prized, I trust, by the unworthiest creature that exists on God's footstool. Oh that my heart may be made susceptible of the all-important truths of the gospel. The passage our dear Pastor spoke from last Sabbath was this, "My sheep hear my voice, and I know them, and they follow me; and I give unto them eternal life, and they shall never perish, neither shall any man pluck them out of my hand." The inferences drawn were truly of an edifying nature; comforting and consoling to the true-believing sheep and lambs was the whole discourse. How ought the highly-favored Church of Christ in Cornwallis to prize the gospel Minister (for whom grace has done so much) that is placed over them, and sits as a watchman in Zion. He shuns not to declare the whole truth; he is indeed a workman that needeth not to be ashamed; he has long borne the burden and heat of the day, and is almost worn out in the service of the sanctuary; but he will probably ere long receive a full reward in the realms of pure light
40 and love, for his toilsome labors while on earth. Well, my dear Saviour, prepare me to suffer on my three score years and ten, if it be thy will; if otherwise decreed, that I should receive an early

transition from this vale of tears and woe, Oh help me to redeem the time, to give all diligence to make my calling and election sure, and declare to my fellow creatures yet in chains, the necessity of a speedy preparation for death, of flying to the only ark of safety, the Lord Jesus Christ, while the lamp holds out to burn.

January 21.—This is a most delightful morning; the sun shines with brilliancy in the firmament, while the white fleeces of snow add to the beauty of the scene. And does the sun of righteousness, O my soul, arise with healing in his wings? Am I fully assured that I have an inheritance beyond the glittering toys of this vain and trifling world, when death shall disrobe me of my mortal to put on immortality? Then may I say (if feeling my hope firm and unshaken, and relying on the arm of Omnipotence to support me) "to corruption, thou art my father,—to the worm, thou art my mother and my sister." Then shall I enter that unfathomable abyss, eternity. How striking is the language of the poet—

> "Eternity, tremendous sound!
> To guilty souls a dreadful wound:
> But oh, if Christ and Heaven be mine,
> How sweet the accents, how divine!" 41

January 28.—A week has elapsed since I last wrote, in the course of which a precious Sabbath returned. I say "precious," for it was so to me, the joy and delight of my soul; it was then I partook of the Lord's Supper; I trust, with repentance for my sins, and faith in his blood, to wash them clean. The text that day was, "These are they that follow the Lamb whithersoever he goeth." During the discussion of the subject those words came forcibly to my mind, "Then shall ye know if ye follow on to know the Lord; his going forth is prepared as the morning, and he shall come unto us as the rain, as the latter and former rain upon the earth." But oh, how do I follow the Lamb? Is it with sincerity and singleness of heart, a true dedication of myself at all times, and a firm reliance on his promises, desiring to know nothing among men save Jesus Christ and him crucified? Alas, my soul lies cleaving to the dust. Awake, awake, put on thy strength, O arm of the Lord; put on thy strength, O daughter of Zion; put on thy beautiful garments. Arise, and shake thyself from the dust.

February 8.—"Return unto thy rest, O my soul, for the Lord hath dealt bountifully with thee;" nor is it according to my works that he hath thus been so gracious and merciful. Ah no, for I have committed two evils,—forsaken God, the fountain of living waters, and hewn out to myself broken cisterns that can hold no water. But have I not abundant reason to praise my God while life and breath remains? If I am tempted, he will never suffer me to be tempted above what I am able to bear. And my glorious High Priest was touched with the feelings of my infirmities. Am I tried and bound down? He was acquainted with grief; he bore the sins of his people away in his own most precious blood, and now he ever lives to intercede for poor perishing sinners, and for those whose hearts have been renovated by the grace of God, and are expectants of never-fading bliss in the upper and better world above.

"To thine abode
My heart aspires
With warm desires
42 To see my God."

Then how circumspectly ought I to walk among this crooked and perverse nation! How little does my light shine, and beholders take knowledge that I have been with Jesus! O God, give me a greater discovery of the deceitfulness of my heart, that thereby I may fly to thee, who hast laid help on one that is mighty to save. He alone can guard me against the wicked devices of Satan. Oh for more faith, more love and zeal, to run with alacrity the race set before us.

February 16.—A charming morning has again unfolded its beauties; it is prospective of the millenium day, it in some degree illustrates it; but how incomparably short does it come of the glories of the triumphant world above! O how mean and unsatisfactory do all temporal concerns appear to the heaven-born soul, who views them in their proper light and holds them at loose ends! If poor sinners that are heaping to themselves riches which will take wings and fly away, had but one view of the emptiness of all terrestrial objects, of an eternity of happiness or woe, and would consider that they have souls capable of enjoying the one or partaking of the other, how readily would they lay down the weapons of their rebellion, and accept the free offers of life and salvation! Have not I and all the redeemed of the Lord who have returned and come unto Zion with singing, every reason to bless, adore, and magnify the riches of sovereign grace that has reached so many souls, even in our highly-favored land? I fear, Lord, that those that die without an interest in Christ, where they have had line upon line, precept upon precept, here a little and there a little, will be beaten with heavy stripes, and the vials of thy wrath will be poured out upon them; but this is only for thee, who comprehendest eternity, to decide. Oh may I be sheltered under the balmy wings of the Saviour of sinners in that day! The last Sabbath our dear and much debilitated Minister spoke to us from those words, "But to be spiritually minded is life and peace." Under the preaching of the word, my heart was as cold as perhaps it could possibly be. Why, my soul, such deadness in the divine life?

> "The little ants, for one poor gain,
> Labor and tug and strive;
> But I, who have a heaven to obtain,
> How negligent I live!" 43

February 18.—Last evening a very interesting prayer meeting was attended within our walls. O what privileges am I endowed with! I fear I shall never know how to prize them until I am deprived of them. Life and death were set before us in a very striking manner, as the grim messenger that afternoon had summoned a head of a family within our hearing to appear in the eternal world, giving surviving friends but little or no satisfaction that he was going to rest, he being in a state of derangement. May the widow and the fatherless children, and all in similar circumstances, be remembered by thee, O Father, who hast promised to be a husband to the widow, and a father to the fatherless! May it be the means in thine hand of arresting their attention to the serious concerns of eternal realities!

March 17.—How mysterious is my attention towards writing of my exercises! How backward to tell of the loving kindness of Jehovah, even when I believe he has for Christ's sake forgiven my sins, and can only accept of me in and through the Beloved! What a clog is this mortal body to the soul!

> "My soul would fain outfly the wind,
> And leave all earthly things behind."

Oh that grace would inspire all my powers, so that I may not prove a dwarf in religion. May I be honored with a humble seat at the feet of Jesus, and thereby grow and thrive in the divine life, and praise the Lord unremittingly, for his mercy endures forever.

March 23.—Am yet a spared monument of God's saving mercy and grace, I hope; and how, my soul, is it with thee? More ready to resign the world, for the sake of the blessed Jesus, and to count all things but loss for the excellency of the knowledge of Christ Jesus my Lord? Am I in readiness to meet the last enemy, death? Do I hope to participate in those joys which are prepared for the ransomed of the Lord? Then how should I feel the comfortable evidence of a seat at the right hand of the majesty on high and groan, being burdened with this clayey tenement!

> "These lively hopes we owe
> To Jesus' dying love;
> We would adore his grace below,
> And sing his praise above." 44

March 27.—Lord's day. I have not been indulged with the
privilege of hearing extempore preaching to-day, on account of
stormy winds and sleet; and if I had entered the house of the
Lord, our beloved pastor would not have been seen there, owing to
indisposition of body; his animal life seems almost exhausted, the
faculties of nature much impaired by an indefatigable pursuit of
45 labours. Oh that the arms of his hand may be made strong by
the hands of the mighty God of Jacob,—that he may be strengthened in the inner man, while the outward is decaying. And now,
have I sanctified the Sabbath, oh my soul, in a becoming manner?
Should I assert that I have, I fear I might go too far, but still I
trust reading and praying have in some measure been delightful,
and I have been in the use of those means led to view the immutability of Jehovah's promises.

April 9.—Another week has rolled its rounds, and has brought me so much nearer the eternal world; and, should I this night be called to render my account to my Judge, should I not have much misspent time to complain of, how would shame and blushing of face seize my animal frame! Oh what shall I say unto God, when he has put into my hands so many means whereby I might shew forth his glory? What a poor depraved creature I am! How heavy are my sins—grievous to be borne!

> " Oh for an overcoming faith,
> To credit what the Almighty saith."

Cannot I adopt the language of Hezekiah—" Thou hast in love
to my soul delivered it from the pit of corruption, for thou hast
cast all my sins behind thy back; do I not mourn as a dove? I
46 am oppressed, undertake for me, O Lord."

April 10.—Sabbath morning. I am spared to salute the bright luminary of the world on this, the Lord's day. The keeper of Israel, that neither slumbers nor sleeps, has watched, I verily believe, around my bed, and has guarded me from seen and unseen dangers.

> " Oh for a heart to praise my God,
> 47 A heart from sin set free."

That blessed promise cheers my drooping spirits—"He shall feed his flock like a shepherd; he shall gather the lambs in his arms and carry them in his bosom." Before this God " the nations are as a drop of a bucket, and are counted as the small dust of the balance; behold he taketh up the isles as a very little thing." Here, is there not plenty of provision made in these passages for the righteous to rely on as a promise ratified in the salvation of the weak lambs of Christ's fold? I trust I feel to bless God this sacred morning that I was ever sought out from among the ungodly, and have a name and a place among his people. I desire to resign myself, make a free dedication of soul and body to the living God. Oh that I may now and in future life evince that I am of the household of faith, that I am a pilgrim here below, looking and longing for the coming of the Just One. If permitted to attend Gospel worship to-day, may the truths be sanctified to my heart; may I feast on angels' food, and love holiness for holiness' sake.

Have now returned from the earthly courts of the Most High, where a short but deeply interesting passage of Scripture was discussed—" And he lifted up his hands and blessed them." This is the kind dealing of our common Lord to all his disciples; and I will say to the praise and glory of his name, that he has blessed me; I cannot say how much, nor how many times, for they are not to be enumerated, by a finite worm. I trust I feel the blessing to-day, " Glory to God in the Highest, and on earth peace and good will." A fortaste of the joys of Heaven has been in some good degree unfolded to my weak understanding. May I not say, " this is my rest forever, here will I dwell, for I have desired it": if I have any will of my own it is unperceivable to me; I desire to be swallowed up in the will of God. But here I am in an imperfect state, exposed to the stratagems of the enemy.

April 13.—" Bless the Lord, oh my soul, and all that is within me bless his holy name." Who would not resign this vain and tenacious world, with its profits and pleasures, for a hope that is as an anchor to the soul, both sure and steadfast, and it is this, I trust, bears my soul above the delusive charms thereof. Where can such joy and comfort be found as in religion? Away, away, ye gaudy vanities of this life; approach not to disturb my joys. And who is it that will harm me if I am a follower of that which is good? for the Lord of Hosts hath declared, he that toucheth his chosen people toucheth the apple of his eye. " Sing and rejoice, O daughter of Zion, for lo I come, and I will dwell in the midst of thee, saith the Lord."

April 17.—Lord's day. I was again privileged with attending Gospel worship; a truly consolatory discourse was delivered from these words,—" O love ye the Lord, all ye his Saints, for the Lord preserveth the faithful, and plentifully rewardeth the proud doer." I have to lament my insensibility to those grand doctrines of the truth, and to all religious institutions, much more my ingratitude to a wise benefactor who has taken a providential care of me all my days, and has graciously been pleased to bring me to the knowledge of the truth in and through the merits of a crucified Redeemer. It seems almost impossible that a renewed soul can be so void of sensibility. Lord, let me down into myself that

I may see the hidden abominations of my heart, and mourn before God, that I have thus pierced the Lord of life and glory. Three candidates were to-day buried with Christ in baptism; they have in the judgment of charity given good satisfaction that they were redeemed, not with corruptible things, as silver and gold, but with the precious blood of Christ. May they, and all who profess the religion of Jesus, adorn the doctrine of God our Saviour in all things. I will not include a nominal professor.

April 23.—How solemn and important does the article of death appear in my view! But why should I view it as the King of Terrors, when it will, I trust, prove my friend, to release me from the toils of this sinful world (though frail nature shrinks at the
48 thought)? I think, if my heart does not greatly deceive me, I can join with the poet—

> "I would renounce my all below,
> If my Creator bid,
> And run, if I were called to go,
> And die as Moses did."

O that I may be enabled to speak to my dying fellow men of the necessity of being prepared to stand before their Judge, and leave it as my legacy when I shall be laid in the silent tomb. Poor sinners, how will you stand in the great day of final retribution? God only knows; oh that I were more zealous in the glorious cause I have espoused by the drawings of the Holy Spirit!

April 24.—Again heard portions of Scripture expounded, and searching ones, too, for the word of God is spoken of as "being quick and powerful, and sharper than any two-edged sword, piercing to the dividing asunder of soul and spirit," &c. The passages spoken from to-day were these: in the morning, "Search me, O God, and know my heart, try me, and know my thoughts, and see if there be any wicked way in me, and lead me in the way everlasting;" in the afternoon, "Surely the righteous shall give thanks unto thy name, the upright shall dwell in thy presence." O what a precious privilege is it to be favored with, of hearing the sound of the glorious Gospel of truth! I trust I shall ere long be brought to experience the veracity of that Scripture phrase, "Blessed are they that know the joyful sound; they shall walk, O Lord, in the light of thy countenance." I hope I do in some measure feel the application now of the former part, but am led to scruple the certainty of my living continually under the influence of the third person in the adorable Trinity.

April 27.—It has been my high gratification of late to visit a number on beds of languishing, most of whom profess an acquaintance with the dear Redeemer, while others are destitute of the one thing needful. Oh that God would prepare them by grace for

everything that awaits them in his wise and holy Providence, for life or death, that they may ere long receive the end of their faith, the salvation of their immortal souls. In my excursions I went to a house of mourning, where the family had recently heard of the death of a beloved child in a distant land; one of the sisters had so bemoaned his departure, that in giving away to immoderate grief, she is now confined to a bed of sickness. I trust her case 49
is hopeful, and that these afflictions may be sanctified to her never dying soul. These are important lessons for me. A minister of the sanctuary praying with sick persons, and for mourners, is a very striking memento of the solemn scenes witnessed at our mansion four years ago. Oh how much have I to call up my attention to an active zeal and perseverance in my christian warfare, to fight manfully, being armed with the sword of the spirit, the helmet of salvation, and withal taking to myself the shield of faith. But alas, how great is my poverty of spirit, which makes me so cold and so unmindful of the hand that preserves me through all the difficulties in life. I want to lean upon the breast of my beloved, and in him to be made rich unto all spiritual blessings.

May 1.—Another of the days of the Son of Man has risen upon a worm like me. Oh, does my soul salute it as becomes one of Christ's flock, welcoming its appearance, as a day of rest from secular employments, as a day that is set apart for the special work and worship of the Lord of Hosts? It is a new day to me, and the returning of this has left a succession of days and years that are past and gone. O that I may experience a Sabbath day's journey to my eternal home, that it may be long remembered; and as my mind is now burdened with a sense of my unprofitableness, of my deficiencies and ignorance, and I feel as if I were bereft of all support. I may, in the use of the private means of grace (our dear Pastor is absent), derive much encouragement, and be filled with the good things of Christ's Kingdom, to be enraptured with his glory and excellences, that I may verily believe, "The voice of rejoicing and salvation is in the tabernacle of the righteous, the right hand of the Lord doeth valiantly." 50

May 8.—Yesterday and to-day are memorable days to me, having last year at this time obtained grace to move forward in the path of duty. How many changes have transpired since that! I am spared, while others are dead, and have the blessing of health bestowed upon me. But should I be asked what progress I had made in the divine life, I should be ready to answer, none at all; for the past year, which ought to have been spent to the glory of God, above all others, looks like a blank. But notwithstanding all my darkness, I think I can say, I know whom I have believed.

I have felt increasingly united to God's people since joining with them, and to the cause and interest of Zion. I trust I feel stronger in the faith once delivered unto the saints, and can trace the immutability of God's promise to his obedient children, in this passage, "He shall feed them with the finest of the wheat, with honey out of the rock will he satisfy them." In some small measure I realize this passage to be applied to me, in enabling me to follow on to know his ways, for God's unbounded goodness manifested in the tearing down and building up my soul on the sure foundation. Why art not thou, my soul, shouting the high praises of your ascended Lord? Oh sin, that destructive evil, how it deters me from it; it works in my soul, and binds me down with strong temptations; yet amidst Satan's darts through the last week I have found much comfort in these lines—

> "Though seed lie buried long in dust,
> It sha'nt deceive our hope;
> The precious grain can ne'er be lost,
> For grace ensures the crop."

How little experience have I of the windings and turnings of my great adversary! Oh righteous Father, appear for me, or I shall sink beneath the ponderous load of guilt. Where is the faith I profess to have? It is eclipsed; will not my Jesus love me to the end? has he not died for more than past sins? Yea, he has died to expiate all my guilt.

May 9.—After writing yesterday I perused a part of the sacred volume, particularly the last chapter of Hebrews, where it describes Faith so illustriously, and this portion has pressed upon my mind with great weight this morning, "Now the just shall live by faith; but if any man draw back, my soul shall have no
51 pleasure in him." Oh may I view this to be the only way, and feel desirous to walk in it.

> "Why should the children of a King
> Go mourning all their days?
> Great Comforter, descend and bring
> 52 Some tokens of thy grace."

May 22.—My time for this week past has been occupied with visiting my acquaintance in the adjacent town, where the prince of darkness is permitted to spread his baneful canopy in almost every heart; but there are a few, whose chief aim is, I trust, to glorify God, and to proclaim the riches of free and sovereign grace. I think I was led to view more of the emptiness of this world's vain store, and to realize that without my God all the beauties of scenery would become a darksome prison; some rays of light, I hope, beamed upon my soul with refulgent lustre, and I can and do bless God that "Jesus hath loved me, I cannot tell why." On the following Sabbath a very interesting sermon was delivered from these words, "Man that is born of a woman is of few days and full of trouble; he cometh forth like a flower, and is cut down; he fleeth also as a shadow, and continueth not." The mournful occasion of this discourse was the death of a blooming youth (a connection of mine) in a foreign land; he died among strangers, no fond parents to watch over his emaciated frame. Such is the state of man,—he goeth to his long home, and the mourners go about the streets. May this awakening call, knock loud at my heart and bid me prepare to meet my God. Likewise from this passage an evangelical sermon was delivered, "But whosoever drinketh the water that I shall give him shall never thirst, but the water that I shall give him shall be in him a well of water springing up into everlasting life." The place was truly glorious; I think I realized the presence of the Almighty Saviour to be round about us, and O I hope in many of our hearts, causing them to leap for joy, that "the day-spring from on high hath visited us."

May 29.—Another of the days of the Son of Man has returned, and I am privileged with hearing the everlasting Gospel dispensed from these words, "But Mary kept all those things and pondered them in her heart." "Yea, a sword shall pierce through thine own soul, also, that the thoughts of many hearts may be revealed." I think I can bless God for the precious opportunity of hearing about the divine and human nature of our ascended Lord, and may say to my wicked heart, "Begone unbelief," since such a Saviour is held forth in Scripture being born in a manger and living such a life of spotless obedience, when tempted and ridiculed, despised, and knowing that he must be barbarously crucified on the cross and suffer all these indignities for a wretch like me; he became poor that I might be made rich. What love and condescension is exhibited! Oh my soul, ever adore the triune God, and may he make me a bold soldier of the cross!

June 3.—A deep solemnity pervades my mind on account of a variety of circumstances. A beloved young female was yesterday consigned to the narrow house of the tomb; another in our neighborhood is on a bed of languishing—her case very doubtful as to health (the same one spoken of in one of the foregoing pages last July); the rod is laid heavily upon her. O that she may view him that hath appointed it, and acquiesce in the divine will! How repeated is the admonition—"Be ye also ready." Dying is but going home to a believer; how sweet are the accents,

> "Jesus can make a dying bed
> Feel soft as downy pillows are."

Then why is the immortal mind that is richly stored with all spiritual blessings in Christ Jesus, so unwilling that the body should return to mother dust, while the happy spirit will soar to worlds on high and reap a plentiful harvest in glory for the seed sown in the heart in mortality? Is Christ precious to thee, O my soul? Yea his long suffering exceeds all my scanty expectations, his love is unbounded to me a sinner.

June 6.—A pathetic discourse was yesterday delivered from those words, "Whereby are given unto us exceeding great and precious promises, that by these ye might be partakers of the divine nature, having escaped the corruption that is in the world through lust." O what a mercy that I am permitted to attend Gospel worship,—that I am thus highly favored while others that have counted not their lives dear unto them for the love they bore to the cause of Christ have escaped the dangers of the ocean, and reached Burmah's shores, with a degree of encouragement and looking forward with pleasing anticipations to see good done in the name of the holy child Jesus, are persecuted, many in these latter ages falling victims to the sword, chained with fetters, and suf-
53 fering severe punishment. How little do the civilized know what they shall have to encounter among uncivilized nations! But this reflection cheers my drooping spirits—the heavens do rule, and what has Zion to fear? May this be the language of my heart, "In the multitude of my thoughts within me, thy comforts delight my soul."

June 12.—Blessed be the Lord from this time forth and for evermore. A precious season to my immortal soul has this day been in very deed; my obligations are again renewed to be devoted to the cause of religion, having had another opportunity of commemorating the sufferings and death of our dear Lord and Saviour. We had a delightful conference yesterday. Baptism was administered to a candidate this morning, and an appropriate discourse delivered from this passage of Scripture, "And in that day there shall be a root of Jesse which shall stand for an ensign of the people; to it shall the Gentiles seek, and his rest shall be glorious." What a multitude of privileges! Where is my thankfulness? Lead me, O Lord, in the path of righteousness for thy name's sake; subject me to thine easy yoke and reign, and may I have a single eye to thy glory, for I have hitherto come amazingly short of it; that I may believe God will of a truth dwell among us in our little Zion.

June 19.—Again indulged with hearing the sound of the everlasting Gospel in a warm and pathetic manner; a Missionary discourse was delivered from these words, "But I have all and abound; I am full, having received of Epaphroditus the things which were

sent from you, an odour of a sweet smell, a sacrifice acceptable,
well pleasing to God." A handsome collection was made, for 54
almost the first attempt; but in comparison to what is contributed in other parts of the world, it is indeed very small. However I hope each one will consider, that he that giveth to the poor lendeth to the Lord, and that he that deviseth liberal things, by liberal things shall he stand in future. The gold and the silver is the Lord's—may the gold and silver dust be handed down in abundance here and in every place. What aid should be rendered to missionaries who feel it in their hearts to spend and be spent in the service of our adorable Redeemer in proclaiming the rich gospel of salvation, in heathen climes, for many are perishing for lack of knowledge! O that Zion's borders may be increased, that God may be sanctified in the heathen when he shall gather them out of the countries wherein they have been scattered. God, even the High God of Jacob, who sits upon the circles of the earth and the inhabitants thereof are counted to him less than nothing and vanity, "giveth power to the faint, and to them that have no might he increaseth strength." Let this be comforting, O my soul, that Christ's strength shall be made perfect in my weakness. O my soul, arise and call upon God, and he will give thee light.

June 26.—I behold the light of another Sabbath day with pleasure I trust, in hope that from this time henceforth I may be more conformed to the will of God in all things, more dead to sin and alive to holiness. What thanks, praise, and adoration ought I to render to the giver of all my mercies for his unbounded love manifested to me a sinner. What can I say, but adopt the language of the poet—

> "Here, Lord, I give myself away,
> 'Tis all that I can do."

O fill my soul, heavenly parent, with new and more ardent desires after heaven and holiness; for if my hopes are built upon the rock, Christ, and I cannot but think they are, my mountain is strong, the gates of hell shall not ever prevail against it. Impart the sweet streams of grace and love into my soul, and may I rejoice in this my high calling, and give all the praise to God, be laid in the valley of humiliation and sensibly feel my obligations, knowing what manner of person I should be in my life and conversation.

June 28.—The promise bears up my fainting soul, in which our Saviour and our Redeemer, the Mighty One of Jacob, hath declared that his people are "graven upon the palms of his hands and their walls are continually before him." Such love and goodness demands my life, my all. O for a holy devotedness to my covenant keeping God.

" 'Tis Heaven to rest in thine embrace,
And nowhere else but there."

But is my conscience void of offence towards God and my fellow creatures? Alas a guilty world hangs heavy upon my heart; were it not for my living Head, who intercedes for me before the throne, and has cleared me from all guiltiness by his satisfying though painful death.

July 3.—Sabbath morning. Have this day entered upon my eighteenth year; but how stands my mind affected towards the lovely Jesus? Have I pressed on by the direction of the Holy Spirit to further degrees of grace since my last birth day? Can I witness more boldly for God than at that time? Have I never brought up an evil report against the goodly land—if not by open acts of infidelity—yet have I not reason to fear I have proved a stumbling-block in the way of many poor immortal souls who are looking up to me for an example? O for light, life, joy and peace to be communicated to the darkest recesses of my heart, that it may shew me my unworthiness. I think I desire to be willing to become a fool for Christ's sake, to be nothing, that he might be all in all.

July 20.—O what a debtor to sovereign grace am I, running deeply in debt every day, and nothing from myself to pay; numberless have been my privileges since I last wrote, as well as multitudes of obstructions to impede my devotional exercises, which are few, at the best; but without them, the entertainment of a busy life will in no measure supply their place, nor yield the soul immortal food. I have been hearing preaching to-day by my dear uncle Handley Chipman, from those words, "Thou didst hide thy
55 face and I was troubled." O that I were more distressed for my insensibility and the little progress I have made in my christian course. May the great Shepherd of Israel vouchsafe to make me as a green olive tree in his house, that I might grow and thrive in the divine life.

August 1.—Yesterday I was permitted to enter the courts of the living God, and heard two excellent sermons delivered from these words, "He that walketh with wise men shall be wise"—"A true witness delivereth souls." The first discourse was truly the exercise of a christian; the latter was the duty of a faithful watchman. Such is our beloved pastor, and I believe he will by the grace of God be faithful unto death, and then receive a crown of glory which fadeth not away. I believe I have to-day felt some degree of nearness to my blessed Lord and Master. O the riches of that grace that bade me come to Christ and accept of offered mercy.

August 6.—What fresh desires these words create in my breast—"I am my beloved's, and his desire is towards me!" What renewed love and gratitude should it arouse to be assured in scripture, and by every other argument, that Christ's care and love to the church is so manifested in the strongest terms. Oh how unworthy of the smiles of Him whose countenance is as Lebanon, excellent as the Cedars! Lord, lift thou up the light of thy countenance upon me.

August 14.—Yesterday I attended a conference meeting. I cannot say that it was as precious to my soul as I have formerly found them, and what was the reason? Is it not obvious? Have not my sins separated my God from me? But I think I felt troubled because the Lord hid his face. I could tell a great deal about my wicked and deceitful heart, but I forbear at this time. To-day I was allowed the high privilege of hearing the sound of the gospel by the preaching of Elder David Harris, from this short but truly interesting passage of scripture, "Lift up a standard for the people." The Saviour was indeed lifted up upon the pole of the everlasting Gospel. Our pastor spoke from these words, "He was led as a lamb to the slaughter": it was intended as a preparatory sermon to lead the minds of the communicants to the slaughtered lamb of God while sitting around their Father's board, if it had the same effect upon all that it had upon me, and I hope to a greater degree, I do believe it was beneficial. O the privileges of the Lord's Supper to the believer, to whom the Lord has granted strength to follow him in his appointed institutions! I trust the great institution of it will enable me to watch and pray henceforth more than I have ever done; to cleave unto him with more earnestness and zeal, that I may be guided by his spirit, directed by his counsel, and afterwards received to glory through the all-prevailing name of Jesus, whose name is as precious ointment poured forth.

August 18.—How sweet and reviving are the consolations of the Gospel! How rich the provision of heaven for such rebels (as the children of God are) against the throne and dignity of Jehovah, to be nourished with, on their way to the celestial world. The poet says for our encouragement,

"And if you want more grace
He'll not refuse to lend."

August 21.—Owing to wet weather I could not visit the Lord's house to-day, which is indeed a privation I seldom experience. May I duly appreciate my privileges as I go along, and take heed lest there be in me an evil heart of unbelief in departing from the living God. I think I have shuddered at the thought of living in future disbelieving and in sin; but the depth of the deceitfulness of my heart no mortal can fathom.

"Come, dearest Lord, thy grace impart,
To warm this cold, this stupid heart;
'Till all its powers and passions move
In melting grief and ardent love."

August 26.—I trust I feel to bless and adore God for his matchless love made known to me a sinner, in giving me an inheritance among the saints in light, and delivering me from the slavery of sin and Satan. Why am I not serving God day and night, (for his service is perfect freedom) with thanksgiving and prayer, making melody with my heart? Is it possible that I am the purchase of Christ's blood, and yet spend so much of my time in stupidity and lukewarmness? Alas, my wretched heart is the cause of it all.

"O may this love my soul constrain
To make returns of love again;
That I, while earth is my abode,
May live like one that's born of God."

August 28.—I was privileged with hearing two sermons preached from these words—"Behold, I will publish the name of the Lord; ascribe ye greatness unto God." The name of the Lord was of a truth set on high, and surely all the redeemed must ascribe greatness unto God, whose excellency is over Israel, who prepared them to sit under his shadow with great delight. O God, thou knowest my foolishness in wanderings of heart from thee, and my sins are not hid from thee; but be thou my strong habitation whereunto I may continually resort; thou hast given commandment to save me, for thou art my rock and my fortress.

September 5.—Yesterday I attended public worship at a distance from home in our western district (and the day previous, conference meeting); it was indeed good to be there. The enemy was permitted to assail me, but my blessed Jesus, I verily believe, caused the tempest to subside ere the first sermon was ended. The text was, "All things shall work together for good to them that love God, to them who are called according to his purpose." The latter text was this, "Ye were as sheep going astray, but now have returned unto the Shepherd and Bishop of your souls." They were both delightful sermons, and particularly the second; the word came with power to my heart, and to many others, without a doubt. May it not return void! My mind was not wandering as much as common. The Lord's Supper was commemorated—precious privilege! Oh that men would praise the Lord for his goodness, and for his wonderful works to the children of men. Thou, O God, knowest I desire to be consecrated to thy service, to honor thee in my day and generation; may I loathe myself on account of sin and plead the blood and righteousness of the dying Saviour.

September 10.—I have had but few changes through the past week to what I generally have; and what, my soul, is it owing to? Is it a dead slumber that I am so contented with, or is it a composed reliance on the arm of Jehovah! I would fain faintly hope that the latter was the case (though I have too much reason to fear the former, on account of the intricate designs of my potent adversary and the easy compliance of my depraved nature with his suggestions); this I can say, I have realized more fervency in prayer than I have for some time before, and an increased desire after holiness. To be led by the spirit of God is my chief desire, for I am sensible this glorious person will lead me into all truth. Lord thou knowest

> "That more the treacherous calm I dread,
> Than tempests bursting o'er my head."

September 11.—To-day witnessed Baptism administered to
three candidates, who are in the judgment of charity fit subjects
to be admitted into the visible Church. One is a blooming youth;
he, like myself, felt the scriptures of eternal truth to be the first
and greatest means of his awakening. Various are the means 56
made use of to arrest the carnally secure,—"How unsearchable
are the ways of the living God and his judgments past finding
out; He is a God whose way is perfect, and he has declared that
his word shall be as a fire and as a hammer to break the rock in
pieces." Oh that that happy day may soon come when Ethiopia
shall stretch forth her hands, and all shall know the Lord, from
the least to the greatest! We had an interesting and seasonable
discourse preached to us from this text, "Open ye the gates, that
the righteous nation which keepeth the truth may enter in." Oh
that my life may always, by the grace of God, be unspotted from
the world, that I may not cast stumbling blocks in the gate.

September 14.—This evening attended prayer meeting: the petitions put up at a throne of grace, I trust, were the dictates of the Holy Spirit; but alas the state of my mind is too low to enjoy any comfort. The vain entertainments of this world, how they intrude! I must be nailed to the cross to guard against them.

October 12.—This evening heard preaching by Elder Harding from these words, "And said unto them, thus it behoved Christ to suffer and rise from the dead the third day, and that repentance and remission of sins should be preached in his name among all nations, beginning at Jerusalem." The atonement and resurrection of Christ was clearly brought to view; likewise evangelical repentance was beautifully described, though my hard heart is very unfeeling. Yet I hope my going was not in vain. My privileges, how innumerable! Oh for a heart of gratitude to improve them to the glory of God.

October 13.—How different is this evening's occupation from the last,—employed in serving a throng of company. Alas, this is too much the case a greater part of the time. What an enemy to religion is the society of the world! But my conscience can assert before God that I heartily wish it was otherwise; but I am in the wilderness. Oh that every trial may be sanctified to the good of my immortal soul, and make my retired moments the sweeter.

October 17.—Sabbath evening. Have spent the day at home on account of rain; and have I no new mercies to record, no tokens of favor from my covenant God to recite? Yes, I think I may confidently assert, the Lord has been my helper. May he teach me to count it all joy when I fall into divers temptations, that the trying of my faith may work in me patience. "The Lord knoweth how to deliver the godly out of temptation."

October 30.—Sabbath day. I, with pleasure, and I trust, profit, waited upon God in his sanctuary, and heard preaching by our dear pastor (who has been absent five weeks) from this comforting passage, "And I will make an everlasting covenant with them, that I will not turn away from them to do them good; but I will put my fear in their hearts that they shall not depart from me." The speaker, I have not a doubt, was influenced from above; the energy with which his words were spoken truly evinced the happy state of his mind. Oh how good is God to his people, in this highly favored town! A greater part of the time we have stated preaching, while other societies are almost wholly destitute. Oh that church members might be clothed with humility as with a garment, and beg of God to give them a heart that will rightly appreciate their privileges.

November 6.—I was privileged with hearing preaching from these words, "And to walk humbly with thy God." "Verily, verily, I say unto you, except ye receive the kingdom of heaven as a little child, ye cannot enter therein." It was indeed close preaching, and such as is necessary. Oh that each soul hearing it, may be humbled so as to receive the salvation of Christ, offered upon his own terms, that thereby they may be made holy. I have too long risen (as it were) in opposition to the ways of God, and have been strikingly guilty of the sin of unbelief, and this has brought darkness into my mind. Oh that God would grant me pardoning, renewing, and sanctifying grace, that I may not dishonor his blessed name by this sin. Oh what a God have we poor worms of the dust to do with? Who can stand before him when once he is angry? Who would not be willing, methinks, to sacrifice their lives, to be at last found in him not having on their own righteousness, but that which exceeds the righteousness of the Scribes and Pharisees? But alas the carnal heart is not subject to the law of God, neither indeed can it be, till "sovereign grace strikes the blow."

November 16.—Was this evening unexpectedly privileged with hearing the beloved servant of God spoken of above, preach the doctrines of the cross to the satisfaction of many in the church, from these words, "Whom shall he teach knowledge, and whom shall he make to understand doctrine? them that are weaned from the milk and drawn from the breasts." He showed clearly the necessity of our moving on to know more of the Lord Jesus Christ and his blessed ways; it rejoiceth our hearts that salvation cometh only from thee, the Lord our God. I feel this evening to say, I have peace with God through our Lord Jesus Christ. O, I joy to hear the doctrines of the Gospel which are contrary to our corrupt natures, extolled and spoken of judiciously. Oh for a heart rightly prepared to look beyond the creature to the Creator, and to desire more of his royal presence than any gift beneath himself.

November 19.—Sabbath evening. How highly have I been privileged this day! I have waited upon God, through some difficulty, in his sanctuary, and heard the above-mentioned Minister speak from these words, "Thy word is a light to my feet and lamp to my path." The sermon was instructive and demands our close attention. This evening heard him preach very closely and yet plainly from this passage, "If any man be in Christ he is a new creature; old things are passed away, and all things are become new." It was well calculated to shew people what foundation they were on. O for a heart to praise my God! Lord keep my soul in perfect peace by relying on thy faithfulness and on thy fulness, that I may be in a capacity to say,

"'Tis by the faith of joys to come
We walk through deserts dark as night:
'Till we arrive at heaven our home,
Faith is our guide and faith our light." 57

November 24.—How astonishing that my mind is no more captivated with the excellent glory of the Lord Jesus Christ, and that I do not feel more concerned for the welfare of poor sinners! Oh that the solemn Heavens would bow, that the mountains might quake and saints be actuated to duty, that souls may be given to the gospel trumpeters for their hire; and may the love of an infinitely compassionate God influence every heart to be up and doing while it is day. I want to feel that waiting, that depending spirit upon God that will enable me to join with the poet—

> " Lord at thy threshold I would wait,
> While Jesus is within,
> Rather than fill a throne of State,
> Or dwell in tents of sin."

November 30.—Last evening I was privileged with meeting a
58 few in number at a social prayer meeting. However far my mind was from being rightly exercised, I could say it was with sweet delight I turned aside from the busy haunts of life, to wait upon God. My mind was in some measure employed in reviewing past scenes, when the Lord made such manifestations of his saving power upon the hearts of poor sinners in this place, that we were constrained to cry out " This is the Lord's doing, and it is marvellous in our eyes." And now the courts of the Most High are not crowded as they were then. Oh that God would arise for the help of his afflicted people, and purge away the dross of their corrupt natures.

December 3.—Sabbath evening. The last month of another year has just commenced, and I am spared; what a mercy! Oh that I could improve my golden moments to the glory of God! Three years have elapsed since, I humbly trust, the Lord of life and glory saw me in the open field of ruin, and passed by and said unto me, " live." I have every reason to extol the faithfulness, the long-suffering kindness of Jehovah, while I have to exclaim against the evil propensities of my wretched, deceitful heart, that so often has led me from God; but I would desire to trust in God, for in the Lord Jehovah is everlasting strength; and I hope I can say this day, my soul hath caught new fire; I feel that heaven is drawing nearer. Oh I hope my heart does not deceive me when I affirm that God's decree to save me, or any of the fallen race, has been a feast of fat things, of wines on the lees well refined to my soul this day. While I trust I have been humbled under a sense of my short comings, of my little zeal and energy in the divine life, I feel much the force of these words, " Be sober, be vigilant, for your adversary, the devil, goeth about as a roaring lion, seeking whom he may devour."

December 7.—My mind is much elevated and called up to action with these words, " And I saw as it were a sea of glass mingled with fire, and them that had gotten the victory over the beast, and over his image, and over his mark, and over the number of his name, stand on the sea of glass having the harps of
59 God, and they sing the song of Moses and of the Lamb, &c., &c." What a source for meditation does this passage afford! Oh that my mind was fruitfully led into the sweetness of it, that I might discover Heaven therein, and the employment of holy beings who were selected from the wide mass of corruption, and made the

favorites of God. Oh that the positive injunction that is given to christians to come out from Babylon and be not partakers of her sins and of her plagues, might be obeyed both by professors and by those that have not publicly named the name of Christ, that we might be blessed in watching and keeping our garments, having our end in full view.

December 11.—Yesterday and the day before I had the blessed privilege of entering the sanctuary of the Most High, to meet in conference, and hear the eternal truths of the Gospel proclaimed from this comforting passage, "All that the Father hath given me, shall come unto me, and him that cometh unto me I will in no wise cast out." Our beloved pastor aims at preaching the truth, the whole truth, and nothing but the truth, for the glory of God and the good of his people, and for the alarming of poor sinners. The delightful intelligence has reached our ears, that war is no more heard among the Burmans, where Missionaries have been cruelly tortured and expecting death; but the commencement of peace has caused their efforts and their holy energies in the good cause, by the sovereign power of Almighty God, to shine conspicuously and powerfully to influence the hearts of poor benighted heathens. We are rejoiced to hear that the work of Jehovah is spreading with irresistible force, and we hope such great afflictions as the Missionaries have endured (and may yet have to endure), may tend to purify them as silver, that they may come forth as gold tried in the furnace. My better part would gladly unite with them, in teaching the tawny Hindoos the way of life and salvation, were I qualified; but here I must check my inexperienced pen and the ardent desires of a roving mind, and endeavour in whatever situation I am in therewith to be content.

December 24.—Lord's day, Christmas eve. I was privileged with attending on public worship, but to say that I worshipped the living God in spirit and in truth, it appears to me would be an open falsehood in my present view, though I was favored with the hearing ear, when these words were ingeniously spoken from, "Him that overcometh the same shall be clothed in white raiment, and I will not blot out his name, out of the book of life, but I will confess his name before my Father and his holy angels." Yet the wanderings of my mind are indescribable. Oh, I feel as if I needed omnipotent grace as much now as I did when I was translated out of the kingdom of darkness into God's marvellous light, to subdue pride, self-will and rebellion, in this hard heart.

December 31.—The last day of the year has unfolded its light, and I am spared to see it in health. O my soul, art thou in health? Have the enlivening beams of the Sun of righteousness dawned upon thee this morning? Canst thou call heaven and earth to witness the burning love thou hast to thy Redeemer for his goodness and for his wonderful works to thee, and to the fallen sons and daughters of Adam? Oh that my love was more intense, more constant, and more increased; for how I ought to love God seeing he hath done such great things for my immortal soul? When in prayer to Almighty God this morning, my mind was led much to reflect on past seasons of comfort that I enjoyed in God and from the glory of his presence; and I must say to the praise and glory of his grace, they are to be remembered with joy, and I can safely say they are far greater than can be described. Since I went on pilgrimage, my confidence, my glory, and the only ground of my salvation is that Jesus Christ is mine, and that I am a child of God, an heir of the kingdom of heaven, and called to the hope of everlasting happiness, not through my own worthiness, but merely through the grace and mercy of God. O the incomprehensible depth of the eternal love of God! Oh that the path of life may be made plain before me! Oh for holy direction in duty! But why is it that I feel so little compunction at the close of the year, for my many deficiencies and short comings, for my repeated rebellion against God, through the venomous poison, sin, since I entered upon this year? If it is through the stupefaction of sin, deliver me from it, and grant to work in me all thy good will and pleasure, so that I may redeem the time and give all diligence to make my calling and election sure. What strange events have transpired throughout the world within these twelve months! The Church of Christ in Cornwallis is diminished by many of its members being removed to the Church triumphant, and yesterday two were excluded. When shall the time come for this encouraging passage to be applied, "The punishment of thine iniquities is accomplished. O daughter of Zion, he will no more carry thee away into *captivity?*" Oh that rivers of waters might run down mine eyes for the destruction of Jerusalem "and mine eyes affect my heart." Father in heaven, glorify thyself by thine unworthy child, in her life, whether it be long or short, then when death comes I may hail it as a peaceful messenger to dislodge me from this clog of mortality, that I may awake in thy likeness and be forever satisfied. [Surely this prayer has been fully answered in her death.]—W. C.

January 14, 1826.—Sabbath day. Deprived of attending public worship. I have given full vent to my sorrows, the purport of them being contained in the following verse. I shall cite it:

"How seldom do I rise to God,
Or taste the joys above;
This mountain presses down my faith
And chills my flaming love."

And my soul cries unto God in this—

> "Dear Saviour, steep this rock of mine
> In thine own crimson sea;
> None but a bath of blood divine
> Can melt the flint away."

Fain would my inveterate nature and unhallowed disposition attempt to reign; surely I may say, Satan, with malicious art, studies each unguarded thought. Oh, I want more faith to look unto Jesus in this time of need, to subdue and conquer these inbred lusts and corruptions of mine, to humble the pride of my rebellious heart, and make me as a little child learning of him who is meek and lowly in heart.

January 26.—Sabbath evening. Have spent the day in sweet retirement; enjoyed some nearness to God in prayer this morning, or rather felt a supplicating spirit and some fresh discoveries of the Lord's goodness to me, an unprofitable servant, and felt the application of these lines:

> "God will not always chide,
> And when his strokes are felt,
> His strokes are fewer than our crimes,
> And lighter than our guilt."

Yes I can say, Christ's yoke is easy and his burden is light, and it is good for me that I bear the yoke in my youth, though Satan often tempts me otherwise; but I want to be more and more subjected to Christ's yoke and reign, that I may glory in the cross of Christ, and honor God in my day and generation.

January 29.—How beautiful and encouraging has this passage appeared to me to-day, "Thou shalt no more be termed forsaken, neither shall thy land any more be termed desolate, but thou shalt be called Hephzibah, and thy land, Beulah, for the Lord delighteth in thee." Oh that I had a right understanding of it! methinks if I had, my soul would be all on fire with love and adoration of a compassionate God who hath not forsaken me, by taking his holy word from me, which so often has been fastened upon my mind as a nail in a sure place, and cheered my drooping spirits, and increased my faith to hope afresh in God under many discouragements and obstacles in my way. The following passage has been such a comfort to me when accused by a near and dear relative of not having and shewing sufficient affection for those nearly allied to me by the ties of natural affection, that I cannot forbear quoting it—"Hearken, O daughter, and consider, and incline thine ear; forget also thine own people and thy father's house; so shall the King greatly desire thy beauty, for he is thy Lord, and worship thou him." Since I gave myself up to the Lord and his Church in a solemn covenant, the above passage has been a source of unspeakable joy and consolation to my immortal soul. "Bless the Lord, O my soul, and forget not all his benefits." Oh that I felt a greater hatred to sin and the very appearance of evil, and had more faith to put an unreserved trust in the Friend of sinners! Oh for a spirit of prayer and supplication to call down the seasonable showers of divine grace upon me and all the nations of the earth.

February 4.—Sabbath day. Once more enjoyed the sweet privilege (after an absence of three Sabbaths from the house of God) of hearing the wholesome instructions of the pure Gospel. I could say it was sweeter to me than my natural food, when these impressive words were discussed, "Only let your conversation be as becometh the Gospel of Christ, that whether I come and see you or else be absent I may hear of your affairs, that ye stand fast in one spirit, with one mind, striving together for the faith of the Gospel." Oh how little thankfulness possesses my heart for the distinguished favors I am permitted to enjoy! what reason have I to fear that stupidity is too constant a companion of mine!

February 19.—Yesterday was privileged with hearing an excellent Sermon delivered from this important passage, "To them who by patient continuance in well-doing seek for glory, honour, and immortality, eternal life." My soul can affirm it was good to be there; it was truly a precious season to me, we were indeed (they that could bear it) fed with strong meet. Oh the goodness of God to such undeserving mortals in raising us up from the depths of sin, and making us heirs to an inheritance that fadeth not away, and all this by the sufferings and death of the Son of God.

"The Hill of Zion yields
A thousand sacred sweets,
Before we reach the heavenly fields,
61 Or walk the golden streets."

Lord, make me patient, humble, and docile, more persevering in all things, that I may live to glorify thee, the King of Kings and Lord of Lords, that the time may come when I shall be fully authorised, by the witness of thy spirit, to say, "I live, yet not I, but Christ liveth in me."

March 1.—I have been enabled to arise from the bed of slumber at an early hour. I feel that I have too long indulged in that known sin. I want to deny self and all ungodliness, and I think I have experienced some of the good effects which proceed from it in two particulars,—in being (at intervals) abstemious in my food, and (which I have reason to add, was only at intervals) in leaving
62 the bed of sloth. Oh how little do I and many of my dear fellow travellers to the celestial world, know of the happy consequences of being conformed to the cross of Christ! Our blessed Saviour

arose a great while before it was day, and went into a desert place, and there prayed. Oh that all who desire to imitate his example may go and do likewise! I profess to be his follower, but alas, my conduct does not comport with the high appellation; were I his meek and humble follower, decidedly so, what greater indignities should I meet with, and how sweet would be the consolation within my own breast! I trust I feel an ardent desire to seek for that communion with God in secret, which will cause fruits to abound outwardly in humility. Two days since, I visited one of our beloved sisters, and an highly esteemed member of the Church, who is confined to a bed of languishing, racked with excruciating pain proceeding from a cancer, which has spread through all her system; but she is certainly an example of patience and resignation (she has not entered her nineteenth year, and has not been joined to the Church but two years); she is, blessed be God, happy in her soul, and enjoying foretastes of heaven. Thus, thought I, is the happiness and comfort of the soul experienced in the last struggles of dissolving nature, by being obedient to the commands of the King of heaven, and keeping the garments unspotted from the world; and that God who has promised never to leave nor forsake his people, now supports this dying saint; she would often cry out with the poet—

> "See the kind Angels at the gate
> Inviting me to come;
> There Jesus the forerunner waits
> To welcome travellers home."

May I be led to follow her as she followed Christ, though it may be by glimmering hopes and gloomy fears I tread the sacred road. O Lord make me to dwell under thy shadow, that I may revive as the corn and grow as the vine, that when I come to die I may give up my account with joy and not with grief; and on this first day of the month may I begin to feel more the importance of living unto thee and not to myself. Lord teach me, for I am ignorant. 63

March 19.—Lord's day morning. Every thing in creation speaks forth the beauty and glory of an incomprehensible God. Oh that my soul may be visited by the warming and enlivening beams of the Sun of righteousness! Thou knowest, blessed Saviour, that I stand in great need of it, while I am allowed the privilege of entering thy earthly temple. O bestow upon me a true worshipping spirit, that I may give myself up to thee, knowing that thy blessed spirit can instruct me to hear and understand aright. Last Sabbath I was permitted to hear our dear shepherd speak from these words, "The law of thy mouth is better unto me, than thousands of gold and silver"—"The path of the just shineth brighter and brighter unto the perfect day." I trust I could in some degree adopt the first verse, and felt some assurance of the latter in many of my christian brothers and sisters around me. *Sunday evening.*—Have just returned from the house of God, where I again was highly favored in hearing the delightful truths of the Gospel preached. The text was as follows, "I will praise thee, O Lord my God, with all my heart, and I will glorify thy name for evermore; for great is thy mercy towards me, and thou hast delivered my soul from the lowest hell." But alas, stupidity almost overpowered me, or my heart would have overflowed with gratitude for the wonders of Redeeming love.

March 26.—Lord's day evening. Have spent the day at home in sweet retirement. I cannot but hope that unbelief and distrust of God's mercies are banished for the present time in some good degree from my heart, and I feel an assurance of faith which I would not be a stranger to for all the gold of Ophir. Oh that poor sinners who are drinking down iniquity as the thirsty ox drinketh down water, could see the loveliness there is in religion. But unless God moulds their hearts into his image by his renovating grace, they will continue enemies to God.

April 2.—Lord's day. I attended a prayer meeting this evening, where a few in number were assembled, but our wants were many; the state of our minds was lamentable; I could assent to the truths delivered, as knowing them to be just, true and right, but a feeling sense of the power of them was wanting. I plainly see that without the quickening influences of the Holy Spirit my soul is, as it were, a dry barren waste. I need daily supplies of grace to enable me to urge my way on to the heavenly Canaan. The state of Zion in our land is very different from what it was two years ago. Numbers then were concerned for their souls and flying to Christ as doves to the windows; but now, alas, the most fine gold has become dim. Oh that the Lord would make bare his arm and revive his own work in the hearts of his children, and
64 extend it to poor sinners.

April 3.—Oh what language can express the solemn scene I have been an eye-witness to to-day! Little did I think this morning when these words were rivetted forcibly upon my mind, "God is our refuge and strength, a very present help in trouble," that I was to behold a blooming youth (who has been some time ill) struggling with the monster death. And oh what rends our hearts is, he left no satisfaction of a better state. We hope and trust that he was received at the eleventh hour, but his agony of body was so great, that he could not tell what he might have felt. Fain would my anxious soul enquire, whither has thy spirit fled? But
65 this is not for me to know. And can the Judge of all the earth do wrong? O no, he has a sovereign right to dispose of his

creatures as he sees most fit. Give us all a due submission to thy will, and an earnest desire that this affliction may be sanctified to the good of our immortal souls; may it bring death near to our view. Oh that its terrors may be removed by the all-conquering grace of God.

April 7.—What a lively view does the horizon now present, when but a few hours ago, clouds of darkness veiled the sky. Such is his providence and mercy; often the Lord suffers clouds of trouble to surround his people, while he prepares light to shine out of obscurity. Oh that the overruler of all things would cause this late bereavement to work for his own glory, (which doubtless he will) for the effectual conversion of many immortal souls. I have too much reason to fear it has not left that impression upon my mind which it necessarily should; the only benefit I can discover that I have received from it is, I think I have felt strong desires that it might be the effectual means of opening the eyes of some poor unenlightened sinner, that the axe might be laid to the root of the trees, that many may have reason to bless God for this dispensation of his providence.

April 9.—Having taken a severe cold I could not attend the house of worship, and our dear pastor, from the same indisposition, was disabled from attending. Diseases of all kinds are ready to seize upon us, at the word of Jehovah. Surely it is great mercy shown unto us, that we enjoy such a measure of health as we do. Oh that such favors might tend to lead us to Jesus, who suffered so much that his people should be made partakers of an inheritance, where the inhabitants shall not say they are sick. I feel as if I ought to be no other than a beggar at the footstool of sovereign mercy. I feel needy indeed at this present time; past attainments will not satisfy; I want faith to go to the fountain of life.

April 21.—Death has again sounded a loud and monitory admonition in our ears; within a few days two heads of families were summoned to appear before the impartial bar of God. They have left their widows and numerous offspring to mourn the loss of endeared parents. To-day I went to the house of mourning: distress appeared in every countenance. O Lord, may they be initiated into thy family, and "appoint unto them beauty for ashes, the oil of joy for mourning, and the garments of praise for the spirit of heaviness, that they might be called trees of righteousness, the planting of the Lord, that he might be glorified." How loud should it knock at each of our hearts, for surely we have almost daily warnings to prepare to meet our God. Oh that christians may be more watchful and prayerful, sitting at the feet of their divine Master.

April 23.—Sabbath day. Once more I was permitted, through

mercy, to tread God's holy courts, and heard with some degree of interest a very interesting discourse preached by our beloved pastor from these important words, "And they took knowledge of them that they had been with Jesus." The inferences drawn were truly instructing, and such as, I trust, will be deeply rivetted on the hearts of God's professing Israel. When I look back upon my past life, I fear I have given but little ground for beholders to take knowledge of me. Oh for a heart rightly exercised towards my blessed Jesus!

May 6.—Lord's day. Through the goodness of God, I was permitted to hear the sound of the Gospel delivered by a youth, who has just entered his 20th year, son of Elder David Harris, and not a year since he was brought to the knowledge of the truth; and we cannot doubt but he is savingly converted; it is only about
66 seven months since he began to proclaim the everlasting gospel. What wonders God has wrought for this precious youth! The words he spoke from in the morning were the 37th, 38th, and part of the 39th verse of the 7th Chapter of St. John, and in the afternoon from this striking passage, "Watch therefore, for ye know not the day nor the hour wherein the Son of Man cometh." He expatiated largely upon the parable of the ten Virgins, and much, very much, for edification and profit; his zeal for the salvation of poor sinners appears to be very great; in short his soul seems to be fired with love. Lord, all the praise is due unto thy great and holy name: continue to make him useful, that he may be an honest, upright, God-fearing Minister of the Gospel. I can but hope, I had a hearing ear to-day, and more than this, I trust, a thirsty soul. But past and present ingratitude, and the little praise I offer to the wise Governor of the Universe, seems ready to overwhelm me. The royal Psalmist says, "It is a good thing to give thanks unto the Lord, and to sing praises unto thy name, O Most High." What a deep of sin and iniquity lies concealed in my heart, which deters me from glorifying God as I ought! Lord humble me for thy dear Son's sake.

May 12.—This afternoon a goodly number met in conference, where it was evident the Lord was present of a truth by the influences of his blessed spirit in many hearts. O what cause for gratitude have all the redeemed of the Lord, that he does grant them refreshing showers now and then. I could truly adopt the Psalmist's language, "A day in thy courts is better than a thousand"—

"One day amidst the place
Where my dear God hath been,
Is sweeter than ten thousand days
67 Of pleasurable sin!"

May 20.—Again enjoyed the precious privilege of hearing the comforting truths of the Gospel discussed from the following texts, "Having therefore, brethren, boldness to enter into the holiest by the blood of Jesus, by a new and living way which he hath consecrated for us through the vail, that is to say, his flesh"—"Be not carried about with divers and strange doctrines, for it is a good thing that the heart be established with grace, not with meats." The second clause was, principally, the subject of the discourse, and it was of a truth interesting, as was the first sermon. I felt much the power of these words, "Thy word was found and I did eat, and it was to me the joy and rejoicing of my heart." Blessed be God for sabbath and sanctuary seasons, and all the means of grace. Since the last Sabbath I have felt more sensibility than for some weeks previous. I am led more to view the need pilgrims have of patience, that after they have done the will of God they might receive the promise. O Lord, make me willing in the day of thy power; strip me of spiritual pride and redeem me from all iniquity. O keep me from ever dishonoring that holy profession of religion which I have made.

June 2.—Five years ago to-day I followed a beloved brother down to the house appointed for all living; but oh, what reason have I to bless God for that affliction! And again, to-day, have followed the remains of a sister in the Church, and neighbor, the head of a family (namely, Mrs. Wm. Chipman); eight motherless children to mourn their loss; but joy is to be mingled with sorrow —her hope in the Lord Jesus was firm and unshaken to the last. 68
When beholding the tranquil manner in which the saint of God meets the last enemy, we can see what a solid rock religion is, and the foundation which it is built upon, Jesus Christ the chief corner stone, elect and precious. O Lord, let not this bereavement pass away unsanctified to any, but particularly those who are more immediately concerned. We must soon follow. Oh may we be actually prepared!

June 4.—Sabbath day. The Lord hath spoke once, yea twice, to the members of this Church, to double their diligence. He is removing its pillars from the militant family to join the Church triumphant. To-day a funeral discourse was delivered from these words, "He that dwelleth in the secret place of the Most High shall abide under the shadow of the Almighty"; (previous to this, from this passage, "And as it is appointed unto man once to die, and after that the Judgment,") for another valuable sister who has gone to see Jesus as he is, without a dimming veil between. In the afternoon our endeared pastor illustrated that important saying, "I have esteemed the words of his mouth more than my necessary food," very much for our edification.

June 11.—Yesterday was allowed to enter the courts of the Most High and meet in conference, to hear of our fellow pilgrims travel in the divine life. I know not when I felt such a struggle in my own mind, about going; the cross presented itself in full view. Though I oft-times felt desirous of embracing the cross in every shape, I shrunk then; but it is plainly to be observed, that I am cold and sluggish. And I may safely say, I went from a sense of duty, and not from a warm inclination; but it was gratifying to hear the communications of the Lord's poor and afflicted people. I hope my precious Saviour has given me to realize that tribulation is the lot of his chosen ones here on earth; but it is only of a short duration—their everlasting rest awaits them. O then, let us lift up our heads and rejoice, for now is our salvation nearer than when we first believed. Wilt thou honor us so highly, O God, as to exercise us aright in all our trials? Another candidate for Holy Ordinances was added to our number, and this morning three were immersed in a watery grave. As the Lord has been pleased to lessen our number (and there is now prospect of more breaches by severe sickness), so he has increased it. A missionary discourse was delivered from this appropriate passage, "He shall not fail nor be discouraged till he have set Judgment in the earth, and the Isles shall wait for his law." I verily believe the Minister was assisted in a good degree. Grand and noble were the points of divinity advanced, and notwithstanding all my stupidity I was led to view the foundation which is laid in the Gospel for men to build their hopes of heaven upon, to be more precious, more glorious, and such a one that our affections should be deeply placed on as our atonement, our leader and intercessor, the object of our highest love. Once more was permitted to partake of the symbols of the broken body and flowing blood of the Lord Jesus. Oh what cause have I to love my God and shew forth gratitude. But the warfare is rising high; at intervals, I can look away from this body of sin, but a sight of my innumerable infirmities almost overwhelm me; wilt thou, O Lord, enable me to supplicate thy throne aright?

June 14.—While the country is all in commotion with public business, I trust, I behold the vanity of earthly promotion, the short duration of it, and could congratulate those

> "Who have no share in all that's done
> Beneath the circuit of the Sun"—

Who are gone to be present with the Lord, where they are free from all sin and sorrow. It is the fear of sinning that makes me afraid to live. I think I desire to depart and be with Christ, which is far better; but if the Lord will enable me by patient continuance in well-doing to seek for glory, honor, immortality and eternal life,

I hope I would not be impatient, but wait his time with cheerfulness and alacrity. I want to travail more in the cause of Zion, and feel the weight of immortal souls upon me.

July 1.—How highly exalted have I been among a goodly number, through the past week; and O, what cause have we for love and gratitude for such privileges as meeting together in an association, all which blessings were procured by the sufferings and death of the crucified Lamb. The Association was held at Wilmot, County of Annapolis, where the Gospel was preached in its purity. Thou, O Lord, hast promised that thy word shall not return void. And oh, let the fulfilment of that promise be seen many days hence, that thine arrows may be sharp in the hearts of the King's enemies, that they may fall thereby. The texts preached from were in succession as follows: "Preach the word"—"Let the inhabitants of the rock sing, let them shout from the tops of the mountains"—"And God gave the increase"—"And as he reasoned of righteousness, temperance, and of a judgment to come, Felix trembled." A young Minister of the Gospel who offered himself as a candidate for ordination, spoke from these words, "And a woman having an issue of blood twelve years, which had spent all her living upon physicians, neither could be healed of any, came behind Him and touched the border of his garment, and immediately her issue of blood staunched." The state of mankind by nature was beautifully brought to view; how loth they are to come to Christ, the only physician of souls, till every other refuge fails; the character of the lovely Saviour was also exhibited as every way suited to the wants of poor needy creatures. An ordination sermon was preached from this short passage, "Wherein he hath made us accepted in the beloved." The solemn work of
ordination [of John Hull, now in glory.—W. C.] then took place. 69
And exhortations were given after and through all the meetings, when we parted with singing the Union hymn, "From whence doth this union arise," &c. But oh, the idea of parting rent my heart asunder, till I was brought in some measure to realize that we shall shortly meet in the bright courts of everlasting day, never to be separated. It appears to me I never had such a deep view of the important realities of eternity, and the remembrance of them now is sweet; such were the exercises of my heart that for a time I could hardly tell whether I was in the body or out of the body; I did not feel in an exstacy, but a solemn weight dwelt upon my spirits; long may the remembrance of that season fill me with holy
joy. But oh, I cannot live upon it; I want to have further dis- 70
coveries of the kingdom of God, for our intercessor hath declared that it is within us. What a stoop of divine condescension to mortal men! Lord, enable me to call unto thee, and say to me as

thou didst to thy servant Jeremiah, "I will answer thee, and shew thee great and mighty works which thou knowest not." Oh let Zion travail and bring forth children, that sinners may no longer pursue the downward road.

July 2.—By the preserving care and tender mercy of an Almighty God, I was once more permitted to tread his earthly courts in our township, where the words of life and salvation were dispensed to the comfort of God's people, and we would fain hope to the alarming of careless sinners; the texts were these, "Christ hath redeemed us from the curse of the law, being made a curse for us"—"A true witness delivereth souls." At the close of the meeting the lightning flashed, the thunder rolled, and all was in commotion. Many were crying for fear. This, thought I, is but a very faint resemblance of the terrors of the last great day. Happy for those who can say—

"Should storms of seven-fold thunder roll,
And shake the globe from pole to pole;
No thunderbolt shall daunt my face,
For Jesus is my hiding place."

July 3.—This day I am nineteen years old. Why am I spared, while so many are cut off on the right hand and left? Surely it is of the Lord's mercies that I am not consumed. Oh that my heart was filled with love to God and love to man, that I might have such love to my fellow creatures as not to fail exhorting them to take shelter in the rock, Christ, before the great and terrible day of the Lord comes. And now, have I not reason to record the Lord's unbounded goodness to me a sinful worm of the dust, since
71 the last July? Oh, I could wish that my heart and tongue were more ready to shew forth the praises of Him who, I trust, hath called me out of darkness into his marvellous light. Wilt thou, O Lord, teach me good judgment and knowledge under all thy gracious dealings with me, for I desire to believe thy commandments; if I do not, Lord, humble me.

July 9.—Yesterday I assembled with a few in number at a conference meeting. Our dear pastor was absent, but we had two young Ministers to supply his place. Alas, a time of declension is coming; iniquity is abounding, and the love of many is waxing cold. To-day, heard those passages expounded—"How shall we escape if we neglect so great salvation?"—"Put ye on the Lord Jesus Christ." I had been much cast down for a few days under a sense of the many infirmities of my nature, and my cold and unfeeling heart, my lack of knowledge in divine things, until the suffering Saviour was exhibited as bearing the enormous load of our sin and guilt; then, thought I, how little I feel the weight of my own accursed sin which nailed him to the tree, and as a guilty helpless sinner was enabled to cast myself at his feet, realizing that all fulness dwelt in him. But O how little sensibility have I! Lord, I want more of the illuminations of thy blessed spirit.

July 22.—Since I last wrote I have been confined for a few days to a bed of sickness with the measles, and previous to that endured great distress of mind, arising from a deep sense of my backslidings in heart from God; my ears were often saluted with these words, "The backslider in heart shall be filled with his own ways." The Lord's hand was but light upon me in sickness; it was not according to my deserts that he did not afflict me severely, which I desire to praise him for. But oh, the anguish of my mind was inexpressible; but I have found the comfort of these words, "Who is among you that feareth the Lord, and obeyeth the voice of his servant; that walketh in darkness and hath no light? let him trust in the name of the Lord, and stay upon his God." This, I hope, I am enabled to do by the influence of the Holy Spirit, and sensibly feel it will all work for my good. In this exercise I feel to give myself up to God (which is what I ought to do at all times), and if he is only my guide I know he will bring my captive soul into liberty in his own good time, and I trust will purge away much dross and tin of my old corrupt inveterate nature. Lord, I see much unfaithfulness and every other sin in my past life. O make me more faithful to thee and my fellow creatures, and shew me duty, and give me strength to perform it, "for I have seen an end of all perfection, but thy commandments are exceeding broad." Oh that my ways were directed to keep thy statutes! When indisposed one morning, I had a near view of death, and although my mind was beclouded, I felt that my hope in the Lord Jesus would stand by me when time was no more.

> "How can we sink, with such a prop
> As the eternal God?"

I had much time for meditation and prayer, but a deceitful heart often leads me astray. Oh that I may from time to time henceforth be more assimilated to the likeness of my divine Redeemer!

July 23.—Sabbath day. My ears were again saluted with the cheering sound of the Gospel, delivered by Mr. Ansley from the following words—"If ye continue in the faith, grounded and settled, and be not moved away from the hope of the gospel." I can 72
truly say I was much gratified with the discourse, wherein the Minister described the true and spurious faith, and I hope it will have a lasting effect upon every heart. Our beloved Pastor is safely returned to us from Halifax, where he has been administering the word of righteousness, we hope, for the glory of the triune God. His text was, "Who is this that cometh from Edom with dyed garments from Bozrah? This that is glorious in his apparel,

travelling in the greatness of his strength? I that speak in righteousness, mighty to save." I had flattered myself that I should have heard with uncommon solicitude to-day, but alas, my attention was as usual not as much engaged as it should be. Oh for that spiritual life to be communicated which will animate my drowsy
73 powers and quicken me to run the heavenly road.

"Come, Holy Spirit, heavenly dove,
With all thy quickening powers;
Come shed abroad a Saviour's love,
74 And that shall kindle ours."

July 30.—Sabbath evening. Have this day been prevented going to the house of God, by the too tender care (I think) which my parents have of my health. I however enjoyed, I trust, the privilege of retirement, and was led to reflect much on a speedy preparation for death, from a dream that I had last night. I dreamed of being at a meeting where there was a vast concourse of people; it appeared a very solemn time, as there had been many deaths around. One of God's Ministers came to me, namely, Mr. Harding, and said, "such a day thou must die." Not feeling much alarmed, on account of not hearing the sound distinctly, I yet felt anxious to know when. After a few moments I thought I asked Mr. Harding how long it would be before the summons would be sent to call me hence? He answered, "in three or nine days;" this filled me with sensations not to be described. I thought every one who saw me was gazing at me with astonishment, wondering why I was not more alarmed. I awoke, and it seemed to have a great impression upon my mind; how it is, the Lord only knows. He is as able to prepare me for the solemn exit in this short time, as in years. I want to have, whether living or dying, my faith brightened up and increased, and to be so led by the unerring spirit of truth that I may honor my Lord and Master, wheu I am called to pass the swellings of Jordan, which stare me in the face, and make me to tremble in view of it. I trust the Lord will comfort me with his rod and staff, that I may fear no evil, and receive me
75 to his arms, a poor miserable sinner, saved by his unmerited grace.

August 7.—My spirits are much depressed this evening, on account of my enjoying so little of the manifested presence of my dear Redeemer. The busy occupations of life take up my time and thoughts to that degree that the pleasures of sweet retirement are at present but seldom known by me, (oh that while my hands are busily engaged, my heart may be ascending upwards to God, who requires heart-service,) which privilege enjoyed is a great help to the heaven-born soul, that is ardently desiring and seeking for communion with the blessed Jesus.

August 13.—Sabbath day. Three of the days of the Son of Man have forever fled, and I have not visited the house of God on either of them. To-day was employed (in a way of duty) in watching over the emaciated frame of a dear young sister in our neighbourhood, whose case I have formerly hinted at. She has been languishing for a fortnight, and is almost past hope of recovery, but her soul is in a good degree reconciled to the will of God, and she feels willing to go whenever the summons may come. Her beloved father is also confined, but rapidly recovering from a scorching fever; the Lord has done great things for him on that bed of sickness whereof we are glad. He has for the greater part of the time enjoyed a little heaven upon earth, and often says, "if this be a foretaste of future happiness what must the full expanse of the blissful Canaan be," (or in similar language)—he has been made willing to resign his darling child into the hands of the Lord, to do with her as seemed good in his sight. I wonder how I can be so stupid, so cold, when the mercies and judgments of God are abroad in the land,—when others are deprived of health and I enjoy a good degree of it; my proud heart wants humbling. O Lord let my prayer come before thee; incline thine ear unto my cry, for my soul is full of trouble, and I am ready to say, thy wrath lieth hard upon me. Shall thy wonders be known in the dark? Shall the dead arise and praise thee? Whom have I in heaven, but thee? and there is none upon earth that I desire beside thee. Oh may I be enabled to hope in thee, my God, and be of good courage.

August 16.—This has been a day of trial and sorrow: my spirits have sunk within me, and I can scarcely so much as lift my voice to heaven and cry, "God be merciful to me, a sinner." Instead of going from strength to strength till I appear before God, I have every reason to fear I am going from step to step in offending an infinitely wise and good God. Surely the graces of the Holy Spirit do not dwell in me, or I should not be off my guard so much in indulging wrong passions. Lord, hast thou not an ear for my complaint? O grant me true and unfeigned repentance, and may I experience thy pardoning and forgiving grace, for never did I need it more than I do now; and I shall expect to do so more and more while I tabernacle here in clay, for I shall be always sinning against the Lord Jesus, while so much of the old man is cleaving to me, which I desire to have crucified with his deeds. O Lord, be not far from me to help me.

September 17.—Sabbath evening. After an omission of writing for some time, I am gratified to have an opportunity of stating the privilege I have been favored with to-day, of hearing the true Gospel preached from these words—"But to this man will I look,

even to him that is poor and of a contrite spirit, and trembleth at my word." The inferences drawn therefrom were experimentally clear; but I was so far from being one of that character, owing to the darkness that has pervaded my mind of late, (also hardness of heart and impenitency,) that truly I may say my spirit was burdened. Oh that God would in infinite mercy humble me in the dust at his feet, and restore unto me the joys of his great salvation. Since I last wrote I have journeyed by sea and land to see christian friends and relations in a distant place, in which excursion I felt
76 the necessity of endeavoring to maintain the christian character. I trust I sometimes felt the presence of Jehovah in giving me to realize that religion was no subordinate matter. Mercies were lavished upon me; but how do I forsake my own mercies and wander from the fountain of all good! Lord, reclaim a poor backsliding sinner, and cause me to return unto thee with weeping, with fasting, and with mourning, rending my heart and not my garments. O control me to practise self-denial and take up my daily cross, that in doing so by the grace of God I may be enabled to enjoy communion with God for Christ's sake.

September 26.—I have just returned from Horton, where I attended a yearly meeting. Preaching, praying, and other religious duties were performed, solely for the good of Zion's cause. The texts preached from in my hearing (with the exception of one) were as follows—"That as sin hath reigned unto death even so might grace reign through righteousness unto eternal life"—"But if I tarry long, that thou mayest know how thou oughtest to behave thyself in the house of God, which is the church of the living God, the pillar and ground of the truth." "And he said, go ye into all the world, and preach the Gospel to every creature; he that believeth and is baptized shall be saved; he that believeth not shall be damned." Thanks be unto God I was favored with the hearing ear, and I can but hope, an understanding heart, though wandering thoughts and cold affections often interrupted me; but I am so deficient in applying the truth as I hear it, and in putting it in practice, that I often think my accountability is very great; but what am I that my ears should be unstopped, my eyes opened, and my heart broken? O it is all rich, free and sovereign mercy, that saves a worm like me.

October 1.—Sabbath evening. After a long absence of nine Sabbaths from our stated place of worship in Canard, I, with some degree of heartfelt pleasure, heard the comforting truth of the Gospel advanced therein by our pastor from these words—"But this shall be the covenant that I will make with the house of Israel after these days, saith the Lord, I will put my law in their inward parts, and write it in their hearts, and will be their God, and they shall be my people." My soul was joyful in the house of my God, feeling a conviction in my own mind, that although my sins had gone up to heaven and cried for judgment against me, yet the blessed God had borne them all away and cast them into the depths of the sea by his own offering for sin. Oh how great is the goodness of God to me, a rebellious child, in giving me to feel renewed desires to live to him and not to myself! Blessed Jesus, wilt thou enable me with all the whole Israel of God to live as children of a King; and as we are virtually in heaven, make us to have our conversation there also, to be looking for that blessed hope and the glorious appearing of God our Saviour.

October 8.—Sabbath evening. Again enjoyed the delightful privilege of waiting upon God in his sanctuary, where a practical discourse was preached from these words—"Whether therefore ye eat or drink, or whatsoever ye do, do all to the glory of God." The Sacrament of the Lord's Supper was administered. Solemn transaction! here, I thought, I am a spectacle to men and angels; and if my life does not evince my gratitude to God for the gracious displays of his distinguishing mercy towards me, what a monster of iniquity am I! Oh I would lament that I love God so little and follow him at such a distance. But our beloved pastor encouraged me by saying, this was a proof that a principle of love was set up in the heart, that it was perfect in its nature, however defective in its degree. I want my heart drenched with the love of God, that it may stimulate me to a life of obedience and a life of faith on the Son of God, that this light, trifling spirit may be subdued and humbled, seeing I have to do with eternal realities.

October 19.—Many have been the changes in my mind since I last wrote; I have indeed been down to the bottom of the mountains, but think I sensibly realized how necessary it was to be chastised. Oh how desirable to join in the language of the poet—

"Since all that we meet
Shall work for our good,
The bitter is sweet,
The medicine is food."

I want to be panting after God, as the hunted hart panteth after the cooling water brooks, to be hungering and thirsting for righteousness and to have more engagedness in prayer.

October 22.—To-day entered the tabernacle of the Most High, where Christ and him crucified was preached from these important words—"But without controversy great is the mystery of godliness, God was manifest in the flesh, justified in the Spirit, seen of angels, preached unto the Gentiles, believed on in the world, received up into glory." A lecture was also given from the 84th Psalm, much for the edification of God's people. I trust it was a day to be had in long remembrance by poor unworthy me. I do not want to be content with the form of godliness without the power. Oh I want this heart of mine to be more alive to the interest of Zion's cause.

October 29.—Sabbath evening. My mind is much solemnized after returning from the house of the living God, who dwelleth not in temples made with hands, but who condescends to dwell in every place with the humble and contrite soul. Our meeting was highly interesting to-day; the banks of Jordan were once more repaired to, where the solemn rite of Baptism was administered to a young female who was once entangled in the snares of Babylon and followed the traditions of men; now that heavenly prediction of the prophet is verified in her case, "They shall be all taught of the Lord." She most devoutly believes that God has taught her duty by his word and spirit, and now feels that she must obey God in his appointed ways. May the Lord make her a lasting blessing to his church, that she may have grace here and be crowned with glory hereafter.

November 5.—Lord's day. Was again favored with hearing the sound of the Gospel in a very applicable address to this church from Ephs. 5, 14, and Isaiah 40, 10. But the melancholy tidings this morning of the death of a beloved cousin (a blooming youth) interrupted my close attention to the word preached. Oh how often do we hear of the departure of some of our relations in distant places! The fond parents have ere this committed to the dust one of their tender offspring—a young man who had come to years of maturity, had grown up into their love and now twined round their hearts with all the strength of natural affection. Unless thou, O Heavenly Father, hast made them to submit to thy righteous will, and bow in humble obedience to thy sovereign ways, we know that nothing short of thine Almighty power can enable them to be still and realize that the judge of all the earth can but do right. Therefore, Lord, grant to them reconciliation of soul, and make this affliction abundantly to work for their good, that they may say, "The Lord gave, and the Lord hath taken away; and blessed be the name of the Lord." May it be the means in thine hands of crucifying them to the world, and of setting their affections more effectually on things above, where they hope their treasure is. Oh that they may henceforth live as strangers and pilgrims here on earth, live to honor and glorify God by devoting their bodies with all their possessions a living sacrifice to God; let their remaining child, who has arrived almost to manhood, be a child of thine, blessed Father, and oh make it a salutary warning to the rising generation, that many may have reason to bless thy name for this dispensation of thy providence.

November 11.—Have had the unspeakable privilege of hearing
one of the servants of the Most High God (Elder Richardson)
speak of the things of Jesus under our roof; his conversation with
me in days and months that are past has been edifying and instructing; he has under God cherished and nourished my soul, having
entered deeply into my feelings. Oh that I felt a grateful heart to 77
my dear Redeemer for his loving kindness in permitting me to be
thus favored with frequent interviews with the heralds of the Gospel, and for every other sacred blessing. O I feel as if I wanted
to love my Jesus more, and not serve him by halves as I have
done, through insensibility and ingratitude. Am so little acquainted with his preciousness—open thou mine eyes, blessed Jesus, to
behold wondrous things out of thy law. O deliver not the soul of
thy turtle dove unto the wicked; forget not the congregation of
thy poor forever.

November 12.—Sabbath evening. Have spent the day in sweet retirement at home, and have been employed in writing letters to my cousins concerning the late breach that has been made upon us and the afflicted mother of the deceased. Lord, grant it to be for thy glory! Upon the whole I may say it has been a good day to my soul, though I want to feel a more lively sense of my acceptance with God, and to give myself up to him, for I feel as if his robe of righteousness was very near me, to clothe my naked soul, and his arms opened to receive me. Oh for true humiliation! The goodness of God to me, a speck in creation, is beyond all account. I trust (for these few days past) I have, by faith, in some small degree fed upon the immense fulness there is in Christ, finding in him a cordial for every fear, and can read my title clear to mansions in the sky, when my eye is fixed upon the merits of Christ. Lord, by thy favor thou hast made my mountain strong; thou didst hide thy face, and I was troubled. Thanks be unto God, he has revealed himself unto my waiting soul in a way of mercy. Oh that he would instruct me to glorify his great and holy name, that I may be the clay in the potter's hands.

November 14.—Yesterday attended conference meeting; it was indeed a precious, good season to many souls; not so refreshing to my own soul as I have found such opportunities heretofore—but the cause is obvious; I stood in need of humiliation, and an unreserved trust in the God of all my joys. To-day heard a pathetic sermon from Rev. 2, 8 and 9. Oh what seasonable preaching was it to each member of the Church! May good be seen many days hence! Our faithful pastor is greatly assisted of late in dispensing the unadulterated truths of the gospel. I am often led to fear his days will soon be numbered, but I should be submissive to the will of my Heavenly Father. This day's exercise, I trust, has been profitable; O when shall I drink deeper into the mysteries of the cross of Christ, and be alive to the interests of religion? Lord, continue the leadings of thy Holy Spirit with me, that I may be a cross-bearer in every point, be poor in spirit and rich in faith.

November 16.—To-day have realized something of the vanity of human life, and although I may appear to take some part in its fleeting enjoyments, yet my conscience can solemnly assert, nothing of that kind attracts my attention in competition with a more intimate acquaintance with the dear Redeemer. I hope and trust my desires will never be satisfied with any thing short of Christ, that I may never open the wounds of my blessed Saviour, and cause them to bleed afresh, by being captivated with earthly and sensual things. O God, forbid my ever wandering from thee, and getting out of that straight and narrow path which is cast up for the ransomed of the Lord. Alas, one would suppose by my general deportment I wandered far from the path of rectitude; how much do I lack of real devotedness to God!

November 22.—A large ball is attended this evening in this township. I hope I feel some desire to implore the mercy of hea-
78 ven in the behalf of those who go. Oh that an arrow dipped in blood may reach the heart of some one (or more) to shew them the slippery precipice on which they are standing, that all beneath them is eternal ruin, and may they find refuge in the extended arms of the Lord Jesus Christ.

"Why was I made to hear his voice,
And enter while there's room,
While thousands make a wretched choice,
And rather starve than come?
'Twas the same love that spread the feast
That sweetly forced us in;
Else we had still refused to taste,
And perished in our sin."

December 2.—Last evening I was permitted to attend a social prayer meeting. The communications and prayers were such as reached my heart, as I had for some days been conversant with the same observations, but still have to lament the beclouded state of my mind, owing to the inbeing and indwelling of sin. I have prayed to be let down into myself, which prayer is answered in some measure (though I wish to have a greater discovery, that thereby I may learn wisdom and righteousness by relying alone on the meritorious death of the Lamb of God), and the sight overwhelms me; the evening before I was favored with a solemn view of death. Oh how great is the transition from time to a world of spirits! Lord, prepare me for the solemn change.

December 3.—The light of the glorious Gospel is yet obscured to my view and to human view.

> "Every grace lies buried deep
> Beneath this heart of stone."

But I am in some degree comforted with these words—"Now no chastening for the present seems to be joyous, but grievous; yet afterwards it yieldeth the peaceable fruit of righteousness to them who are exercised thereby."

December 4.—Sabbath day. I have been highly favored in hearing the Gospel preached in its purity to-day by Elder Harris, from these words of Scripture—"For thou wast slain, and hast redeemed us to God by thy blood, out of every kindred, and tongue, and people, and nation"; "Then shall ye return and discern between the righteous and the wicked, between him that serveth God and him that serveth him not." Oh what a highly favored people are we, to have the privilege of a Gospel Ministry! Oh that error in principle and practice may subside in every character that names the name of Christ.

December 18.—Sabbath day. I am deprived of meeting with the assembly of God's people to-day, but I think it was laid before me in prayer this morning that I should enjoy as much, and perhaps more, satisfaction to remain at home. The comfort I have felt is inexpressible in praising God for what is past, and trusting him for what is to come, believing he will guide me all the desert through. I think I have felt something of the mind of the poet,

> "Lord, we believe, O chase away
> The gloomy clouds of unbelief;
> Lord, we repent, O let thy ray
> Dissolve our hearts in sacred grief."

December 25.—Christmas day. Almost another year has rolled away. What a solemn consideration should it be that we improve time aright, which is so fast hastening us mortals to the impartial bar of God. When I look back to the last Christmas and see what the Lord has brought me through (notwithstanding my rebellion in revolting from him), I have reason to say, blessed be the Lord who daily loadeth me with benefits, even the God of my salvation, he is my keeper. Oh that he would preserve my going out and my coming in from this time forth and for evermore.

December 30.—How should the closing scene of this year affect my hard and obdurate heart, under a variety of circumstances; but I have to regret that my mind is so insensible of the many favors I daily receive from the hand of a kind benefactor. Oh that at the commencement of the new year I may have some penetrating and abiding sense of the Lord's goodness and my ingratitude, and feel more fervency in prayer. And, oh Lord, permit me never to leave a throne of grace at the peril of my life.

January 1, 1827.—Lord's day. How much praise and adoration is due to the high and lofty One, for allowing such an unworthy worm to enter his earthly courts on this New Year's day, and favoring me with the hearing ear in some good degree. I have felt, O precious Saviour, the sweetness of the Gospel to-day, when it was expatiated upon from this text, "If ye be Christ's, then are ye Abraham's seed, and heirs according to the promise." May this year, if my life is spared, be spent more spiritually, more humbly and more to the glory of God, and by all the ransomed children of God, than ever before. Lord, enable us to plough more in secret that we may reap in public. Oh that while we live, we might live to thee and none other. Eternity, with all its solemn realities, will soon open to our view; then the sinner's doom is fixed, and the saint's joy completed; then in heaven will they enjoy it in its fulness.

"What sinners value, I resign;
Lord 'tis enough that thou art mine;
I shall behold thy blissful face,
79 And stand complete in righteousness."

January 9.—I am spared to see the second sabbath of the New Year, and have much cause for lamentation that the first week has been spent so little to the honor of God, (it appears to me none at all)—how much sin is lurking in my heart, which I do not perceive! "I know that the Lord hath set apart him that is godly for himself; the Lord will hear when I call unto him;" but the Psalmist further observes, "Stand in awe and sin not, commune with your own heart upon your bed and be still,—put your trust in the Lord." In all which I am very deficient. Oh how much I want that living faith that will enable me to endure as seeing him who is invisible, and to preserve me from ever indulging in a dead faith. My soul joins with holy David, "Lead me, O Lord, in thy righteousness, because of mine enemies; make thy way straight before my face." And may thy blessing rest upon me for my sanctification and perseverance!

January 11.—The weather for the time of year is remarkable; no covering of snow on the earth. This morning I was favored with some faint views of the excellent wisdom of the Creator of all things in forming the high hills with the low valleys for the happy convenience of the human family. O Lord God of Hosts, who is a strong Lord like unto thee? Thou rulest the raging of the sea; all nature is at thy control. Oh that I had more implicit faith in thy mighty arm, feeling in my soul, that thou wilt direct my steps. Lord, help me to acknowledge thee in all my ways, that all my deportment may be consistent, for I often feel that I reel to and fro like a drunken man.

February 12.—Sabbath day. It is indeed strange that I should allow myself to be so neglectful in noticing the state of my mind, which I trust has not altogether been unprofitable. A week ago to-day our dearly beloved pastor preached the pure Gospel from these words—"My flesh and my heart faileth, but God is the strength of my heart, and my portion forever." Many were the instructive admonitions drawn from it, and it was one of the most precious sermons I have of late enjoyed, if my heart does not greatly deceive me.

February 16.—This evening was favored with hearing our dear pastor speak from these words, "We are ambassadors for Christ, as though God did beseech you by us, we pray you in Christ's stead, be ye reconciled to God." It was truly an excellent sermon; much was said to believers to exhort them to be reconciled to God in all things, whether prosperity or adversity. I felt that I come far short. I know if I were submissive to the will of God it would be much better with my soul, which requires to be humbled, to take the yoke of Christ upon me, and learn of him, who is meek and lowly in heart, that I may get rest unto my soul. I do desire to be like the wise scribe, well instructed unto the things of the Kingdom.

February 27.—What a sad account have I to give of the exercises of my mind of late! How does my time run to waste, while death is spreading his wide domains among our friends and relatives. Two funerals yesterday, two to-day, and one on the morrow, within twenty miles. Husbands bereft of their bosom friends, and children mourning the irreparable loss of a kind mother, and yet, alas, how little is my mind solemnized and deeply impressed with eternal realities, through the great interruption of company, and the proneness of my wretched heart to evil! How forcibly does it rest upon my mind, this life is a chequered scene of vanity and confusion; my temptations rise to a great pitch; such wanderings of heart in prayer I hope no other creature ever felt; but the worst of all is, I do not sensibly feel my poverty and true state. Father in heaven, suffer me not to murder my precious moments in this lukewarm frame.

"My love so faint, so cold to thee,
And thine to me so great."

O put to thine helping hand, Saviour of sinners, and raise my affections to sublime objects, and transform me into thy blessed image.

February 28.—Have this evening been highly favored in attending prayer meeting; it was good to be there. I think I realized it was spending time well. What a sweet resort is a throne of grace, when difficulties and dangers break in upon our souls? Well, if in this life only we have hope in God, we are of all men most miserable. Though I often feel to say, I would prefer a hope in Christ if there was no reward hereafter, rather than enjoy the pleasures of sin for a season. Oh for holy zeal and energy in the cause of Christ, that I might be a good soldier of the cross, kept in my proper place, by being sufficiently humble.

March 11.—Sabbath day. Have been hearing a sermon preached by a Presbyterian Minister on the solemn occasion of the death of a beloved aunt, from these words—"All things shall work together for good to those who love God and are called according to his purpose." The subject was appropriate to my present
80 situation, having many things to perplex my mind. A new scene of trouble is now opening to my understanding. Oh thou who art the counsellor and director of thy tried ones, condescend to make thy strength perfect in my weakness, that I may be enabled to say, from a full conviction that thou art my helper, "I can do all things through Christ which strengtheneth me." O suffer me not to take a leap in the dark, and go contrary to thy mind and will concerning me. Grant me, dearest parent, true light, wisdom, and meekness, and a double measure of the influences of thy Holy Spirit, that I may act in thy fear, and have a single eye aiming at thy glory. May I feel that I am not my own, but give myself to thee for time and all eternity.

March 18.—Sabbath evening, deprived of waiting upon God in his earthly temple. I seclude myself in my little room to wait upon God in private.

"This little room for me designed,
Will suit as well my willing mind,
As palaces of Kings;
A heart to read and understand,
And faith to trust the Lord,
I'd urge no company to stay,
But sit alone from day to day,
Nor wish to rove abroad."

How do the precious promises of God, with his eternal purpose buoy my mind up under trials of a complicated and distressing nature! I can truly say I feel much consolation in committing all my care and concerns into the hands of God, believing that not a sparrow falls to the ground without his notice. I feel much the force of these words, "Who is he that saith, and it cometh to pass, when the Lord commandeth it not." I know God will do that which is most for his own glory and my best good; I can bless my dear Redeemer for his special kindness manifested to me, in not withdrawing the sweet beamings of his countenance when overwhelmed with inward anguish; but instead of dealing with me according to my just deserts, he gives me to feel patient and submissive under trouble. Oh that it might work out for me a far more and exceeding weight of glory! O how much cause for gratitude, "where'er I rove, where'er I rest."

March 23.—Another Sabbath evening has returned. The dark clouds that pervaded the atmosphere through the day have vanished at the appearance of the bright luminary of our lower world, and a dazzling splendour is again witnessed by the attentive eye. Oh how much need I stand in of having the weighty clouds of sin and unbelief removed by the Sun of Righteousness, Him that is fairer than ten thousand stars. Oh for that life to be communicated to my immortal soul which arouses dead sinners to see their danger. Spring, thou lovely season, art returning and hastening me onwards towards the paradise of eternal bliss, when I shall be judged by the Lord Jesus. Solemn realities! Strange stupidity of mine, to be so regardless of them! Father in heaven, direct my steps in the right way, and enable me to ponder the path of my feet.

March 25.—Once more enjoyed the sweet privilege of hearing the Gospel of the Son of God from these words—"And he shall sit as a refiner and purifier of silver, and he shall purify the sons of Levi, and purge them as gold and silver, &c. &c."—Malachi 3, 3. The sound of the Gospel, I find, is yet solemn and impressive to my mind, though perplexed and captivated with earthly objects, the path of difficulties which now presents itself to my view, if God calls me to walk therein. Oh may I be refined by the powerful operations of the Holy Spirit; thou seest that I stand in need of that wisdom which is profitable to direct. Heavenly Parent, grant it unto thy unworthy child.

March 31.—How shall I record the events of the past evening,
which are so important and weighty a nature! Oh that the God 81
of heaven would direct me. I am now called upon to decide my situation for life, if it is the will of him who cannot err, and who is too good to be unkind. How much hesitancy do I feel on the account, if it should not be for the glory of God. Many things combined make me to shrink and almost recoil at the thought. The person paying his addresses is a widower and father of eight children, some older than myself, and one of them, especially, very much opposed. He is a beloved member of Christ and his Church, which is one particular inducement, as I always was opposed to believers and unbelievers being united. He is situated only half a mile from my father's mansion; every religious privilege granted unto me as at home (though I shall feel vastly different, having the charge of a large family). I was ever averse to leaving Cornwallis

unless God in a very special manner called me. I have often thought (when reflecting upon heathen lands) that my nearest and dearest relatives would be no more than a thread to me, if God would only qualify and call me to go and tell the good news of a Saviour. What is opening for me in my own land heaven only knows. O guide me by thy counsel, dearest Parent, and afterwards receive me to glory.

April 1.—Sabbath afternoon. To my regret I have not entered the sanctuary of God this day, and in vain would I give my attendance unless a worshipping spirit was bestowed. Oh Lord God, suffer me not by this late transaction to get a sink in my mind which I may never recover; how much cause have I to bless thy holy name, that thou hast given me to feel placid and serene this day from a passage of Scripture impressed upon my mind out of the thirty-second Psalm (the whole Psalm with many others has comforted me much)—"I will instruct thee and teach thee in the way which thou shalt go; I will guide thee with mine eye." Oh that I may have understanding! Since I last wrote I have been oppressed with sorrow's weight; the difficulties appear like mountains. I am ready to say, "Send, Lord, by whom thou wilt, but not by me;" at other times, "here I am, Lord, do with me as seemeth good in thy sight." But how can I walk in that path, who am but a child? Why those severe trials, if I am not called to walk therein, but to purge my dross away? Shew me a plain path, oh thou who art the true wisdom, and enable me to trust in thee and not be afraid.

"I trust thy faithfulness and power,
To save me in the trying hour."

May my strength be equal to my day!

"Though dark be my way, since he is my guide,
'Tis mine to obey, 'tis his to provide;
Since all that I meet, shall work for my good,
The bitter is sweet, the medicine is food."

April 5.—I still am the subject of anxious inquiry to know the mind of God concerning me; many promises encourage me to hope that the present anticipated union is the decree of heaven; the following words have sweetly flowed into my mind, when perplexities of various kinds pressed upon me—"The steps of a good man are ordered by the Lord," &c. Though I have no goodness to claim, but only in and through the Lord Jesus Christ. Oh that I could hear that voice that speaks, "This is the way, walk ye in it." Methinks I could "forward then with courage go"—(knowing that) "Long I should not dwell below." I am now upon the point (if the Lord will) of committing myself into the hands of an earthly friend: his solicitations for the same have now risen to their height, and I am left to decide the important question. Will the Lord of heaven grant me wisdom to act in his fear and for his glory? And if the answer should be in the affirmative, oh qualify me for the arduous undertaking, that I may possess the inward adorning of the mind, "a meek and quiet spirit, which is in the sight of God of great price;" that all my conduct in subsequent life may evince my love to God and love to my fellow creatures. Lord, give me more faith to trust in thee, an all-sufficient God, and a spirit of prayer and supplication.

April 10.—This last desire in the above writing I trust has been granted in some degree; my trials are more and more severe, but blessed be my God and King, he is my sure defence: yes, my Jesus is all in all to me; "O how great is thy goodness which thou hast laid up for them that fear thee, which thou hast wrought for them that trust in thee before the sons of men. Thou shalt hide them in the secret of thy presence from the pride of man. Thou shalt keep them secretly in a pavilion from the strife of tongues. Blessed be the Lord for he hath shewed me his marvellous kindness in a strong city." Oh for more humility and gratitude that I may ever continue to wait upon God, knowing that he is my light and my salvation, that as the heavens are higher than the earth so are his thoughts and ways higher than ours; he can bring order out of confusion. I hope I feel like clay in the potter's hand, for into thine hands, O God, I commit my spirit, and trust thee to be my guide and direction.

April 12.—Solemn and important have been the transactions of this evening. I have now, amidst opposition and conflict, given my hand to my nearest earthly friend. I trust it has been in the fear of Almighty God; and in the whole affair the glory of God and the good of a fellow creature have been the governing motives. Oh how arduous is the undertaking! May God sanctify me throughout, soul and body, and qualify for me to serve him acceptably. 82

April 15.—Sabbath afternoon. Once more have been highly favored in hearing preaching by two Ministers of the Gospel, who have come to visit us, to see how we do, if we are pressing on trusting in God, or slackening in the good way; their communications are refreshing. The texts spoken from to-day were as follows—"Bless the Lord, O my soul, and forget not all his benefits." "Behold he cometh with clouds, and every eye shall see him, and they also which pierced him, and all kindreds of the earth shall wail because of him." Methinks my heart is very hard, or else it would melt with supreme love to God. My spirits are depressed and I feel to go mourning, without the warming influence of the Holy Spirit, and am ready to shrink at the cross in anticipation. Oh that God would undeceive me, if I am deceived.

April 22.—Sabbath evening. By reason of stormy weather I was obliged to remain at home. In the morning I felt the disappointment much, for "I love the habitation of God's house and the place where his honor dwelleth." I have, I trust, enjoyed some nearness to God this day, though I fear if it was put in the balance it would be found wanting; if not in nature, in degree. Oh that I possessed more of a spirit of self-loathing, that my soul might make her escape (if only for a time) from these clogs and fetters which bind me down to earth. I have for some days past felt the force of this passage—"Put ye on, as the elect of God, holy and beloved, bowels of mercies, kindness, humbleness of mind, meekness, long suffering." I trust the Lord is giving me to see that I am very much unqualified for the important undertaking in view. Oh that it might lead me to the inexhaustible source, the Lord Jesus Christ, where all my wants can be supplied, that he may be made unto me and all his dear followers, wisdom, righteousness, sanctification and eternal redemption. May the high way of holiness ever be my element, for fools shall not err therein.

April 30.—Sabbath evening. I am glad that I went to hear the sound of the Gospel when it was dispensed from these words, "For thou art my rock and my fortress, therefore for thy name's sake lead me and guide me." There were many things brought to view applicable to my own situation; in particular, respecting the providences of God, whether smiling or frowning, that we should as professors of godliness take the word of God for our rule and strive to be well acquainted with it. I have a faint hope the Lord has led me in this way, first to go to him and his word for direction. My mind is much composed to-day, and have felt that whatever was the will of God concerning my recent trouble, I could say, let it be done. The words of the poet are sweet—

"A frowning world I will defy,
And all its flattering charms deny,
If Jesus stands my friend."

But I shall no doubt soon be tossing to and fro with the waves of anxiety that beat high, and call in question my present exercise.

"Father, what'er of earthly bliss
Thy sovereign will denies;
Accepted at thy throne of grace
Let this petition rise:

Give me a calm, a thankful heart,
From every murmur free;
The blessings of thy grace impart,
And make me live to thee:

Let the sweet hope that thou art mine
My life and death attend;
Thy presence thro' my journey shine,
And crown my journey's end." 83

May 6.—Another Sabbath day has rolled its round, and has left me deeper in debt for the privileges of the Gospel. Our faithful pastor has preached three sermons in succession from the 31st Psalm; he spoke to-day from the 8th and 21st verses. A great variety of wholesome instructions were given us, I hope for our edification and comfort; but alas, I have reason to fear my soul was destitute of divine influence while hearing with some degree of satisfaction the preached word, for a feeling sense of the power of it was wanting. Oh for real panting after God, the living God!

May 13.—Lord's day. Not being favored with attending public worship, I have given full scope to reflection of a serious nature—sometimes on heavenly things, at other times on earthly things. The situation which I shall before long (if spared) be called to fill, occupies my thoughts not a little. I am sensible that I can never discharge the several duties that will devolve upon me in my own strength. Oh that a sense of it might lead me constantly to look to the strong for strength, to the rock that is higher than I. I have for these few days past (when difficulties came in like a flood) felt the sweetness of the following words, "Offer unto God thanksgiving, and pay thy vows unto the Most High; call upon me in the day of trouble, and I will deliver thee, and thou shalt glorify me." How precious is the revealed word of God to the deserted soul, when Christ by his influence comes with it! Lord, give me more spirituality of mind, that I may arise and shake myself from the dust of the earth, and repose such confidence in thee, that I may believe all things shall work together for my good, and that thou canst make crooked things straight. May I feel perfect safety under the shadow of thy wings, knowing that soon the storm of life will be o'er.

CHAPTER II.

HER SUBSEQUENT HISTORY.

The Journal is thus continued:

May 24.—The solemn day has arrived for my union with one of the household of faith and of the same name with myself; and in all probability the sun will never set again upon me (or at
least for a time) in a single life. Oh how weighty and important 84
does the subject appear! I hope I am not deceived, when I say, I feel that I am in the presence of Almighty God, and can make

a free surrender of soul and body, all into his blessed hands, to lead, to guide, and to defend me through this thorny maze. Enable me, righteous Parent, to watch therefore (that I may not be overcome with the cares of this life and so that day come upon me unawares) and pray always, that I may be counted worthy to escape all these things that shall come to pass, and stand before the Son of Man. Solemn is a view of the transaction (my case being extraordinary, how can I ever perform the part of a mother to these orphan children on account of my youth and inexperience? But I can only say, if God has called me thereto, he is able to qualify me for the task; here I find safe trusting); but when I realize that heaven and earth are called to witness my engagements to an earthly friend, and that God and his holy angels are viewing me with minute inspection, I indeed feel weighty impressions. Oh that I may ever hold my precious Jesus up to view by my life and conversation, and be a fountain of praise to my covenant-keeping God. Lord, I implore thy grace to help me in this time of need, for soon must I go to engage in the important undertaking. Oh that the fear of God may be before my eyes.

June 10.—Sabbath evening. After an absenee of five months I was again favored, yesterday, with the precious privilege of meeting in conference, and to-day of hearing the Gospel proclaimed from the three first verses of the 73rd Psalm, and once more communed at the table of the Lord, which has not been celebrated for nine months within my reach. Although I have to lament the wretched stupidity of my deceitful heart, yet I can but hope I was led to a discovery of its hidden evils. Oh the treachery of the enemy of souls, who is ever ready to trip up our heels and lead us astray! Suffer not the enemy to get any advantage over me, O Father, but may I at all times feel to say, "In the Lord have I righteousness and strength."

June 28.—Have been preserved through dangers seen and unseen while journeying to Chester to attend an Association, and am with my companion, through the kindness of our dear Redeemer,
85 safely returned. What gratitude is due to the King of heaven for his unremitted favor lavished upon us. My Jesus did not permit me to come away without a blessing, but was pleased to shew me (though at the last in a more especial manner) that all my confidence was in him, which brought with it a train of reflections, edifying I trust, feeling deep repentance for past transgressions. Lord keep me and guide me.

July 19.—Am still the spared monument of God's saving mercy; have been quite indisposed the day past, but did not feel to murmur, or complain, knowing that God is my refuge and a never failing prop. The words of the poet are very sweet to me this morning:

"Amazing grace, how sweet the sound
That saved a wretch like me;
I once was lost, but now am found,
Was blind, but now I see." 86

Twenty years of my life are gone, never to be recalled; and what have I done for God? Nothing, nothing. I am on a journey towards my eternal home; how it becomes me, to study, to honor and glorify my king and captain. How much I need journey bread! Lord, impart it to me, for there is enough in thine house and to spare.

July 23.—Yesterday I spent a comfortable Sabbath day; my reflections were consoling, while travelling a distance from home with my companion, who joined in the exercises of the day and expounded the third chapter of James, particularly the 13th verse (he has his mind exercised about preaching, but God only knows what is designed for him; I pray God to direct him in the path of duty and to make us all submission); how good is my Redeemer to poor unworthy me, who am continually straying and wandering from the right ways of the Lord! He gives me to lean upon his blessed arm, and believe that he is able to make all grace abound towards me, that I having all sufficiency through Christ in all things, may abound in every good work. I feel as if I could say with the poet,

"Each of his words demands my faith;
My soul can rest on all he saith:
His truth inviolably keeps
The largest promise of his lips."

July 29.—Sabbath day. Blessed with Sabbath and sanctuary seasons, but alas, alas, how little improved by wretched me! had but little or no ears for the preached word to-day; my supineness, how great, when I profess to stand for the defence of the Gospel and to mourn for the afflictions of Joseph! in short, I profess to be a follower of Jesus; but what am I about, grovelling here in the dust, while I ought to be seeking for far superior joys which do in Jesus dwell, and the thoughts of such amazing bliss as I hope to solace in, should "constant joys create?" In the world I find I shall have tribulation, but the blessed Son of God has said, "be of good cheer, I have overcome the world, and in me ye shall have peace." Oh for that nearness to God that I so much stand in need of to qualify me for every known duty. Lord Jesus, be pleased to pour out of thy spirit upon us, that we may know what thou wouldst have us to do.

August 5.—Sabbath evening. Blessed with hearing the sound of the Gospel in a very special manner by our beloved pastor from

Isa. 2, 2. The subject was truly glorious. I seldom heard better than to-day, and I can but think the Minister was greatly assisted. My exercises the preceding evening were of that nature that I think I scarce ever felt more my entire dependance on God, and realized that without his divine aid, direction and support, I never could fill the situation I am placed in to the honor of God, nor to the satisfaction of my own soul. Oh that I could feel my daily dependance on God for life, breath, and being: I know if I did, I should realize God to be near at hand and not afar off. Lord, draw me unto thee.

August 24.—Three months to-day have elapsed since I entered the marriage relation. What cause have I to bless God for his comforting support many times during that period amidst trials and perplexities, though my mind is not so much awake to righteousness as I should wish; but the words of the poet came very forcibly to me this morning,

"Should cares like a wild deluge come,
And storms of sorrow fall,—
May I but safely reach my home,
My God, my heaven, my all, &c. &c."

Oh for a taste of the sweetness and import of them!

August 27.—Yesterday travelled with my partner 14 miles to wait upon the living God; his mind was much enlarged and comforted while speaking from these words, "I the Lord do keep it, I will water it every moment; lest any hurt it, I will keep it night and day." It was indeed a comforting season; but I think if such opportunities had a right effect upon me, they would rest upon my mind with such force that I could not get rid of them through the week; but I am in a wilderness world:

"Lord what a wretched land is this,
That yields us no supply."

Guide me, O Saviour divine, through all the ills and troubles of life.

September 15.—Sabbath day. Am obliged to remain at home, and feel oppressed with sorrow's weight, under a consideration of my distance from God and of my many and great deficiencies, in every point of view. Oh, I feel to lay my hand upon my mouth, and my mouth in the dust and cry, unclean, unclean, before the living God. Oh for the cheering light of the glorious Gospel to be disseminated through my whole soul, that I might once more enjoy the peaceable fruits of righteousness and be capacitated to sing praises unto God, and not live at this poor dying rate, surrounded as I am with mercies temporal and spiritual; but I richly deserve the frowns of Jehovah, and do think I feel a disposition to bear them, because I am conscious I fully merit them; but Lord, how long ere thou wilt cause my light to rise up out of obscurity?

October 13.—Sabbath evening. Seldom do I let such a length of time pass without penning some of the exercises of my mind, but such is my situation in life, that I have but little time to devote to the pen; and another thing is I have not that fulness of matter to notice that I could wish, though I have been highly favored with Gospel privileges; but if the soul is not capacitated to improve them, how lost is our time and usefulness! I have attended 87
a yearly meeting since I last wrote; the Lord was present with many, glory be to his holy name. Yesterday attended conference meeting, and to-day public worship. Heard our beloved pastor preach two excellent sermons from these words, "I am he that liveth and was dead, and behold I am alive for evermore, Amen, and have the keys of hell and death." "Looking for and hastening unto the coming of the day of God," &c. I had to lament that my mind was not in a right frame for hearing; trials befal me and await me, and I can but feel the weight of them. The partner of my joys and sorrows is much exercised about public speaking, and is now called upon by the Church to exercise his gifts. Oh! the pride and corruptions of my wicked heart, to feel so much unreconciledness to his embarking in so good a cause, provided it should be the will of God; but I desire to bless God that I feel more submission than last night, and sometimes think I should glory in the cross. Oh for right tempers and dispositions.

"I charge my thoughts, be humble still,
And all my carriage mild;
Content, my Father, with thy will,
And quiet as a child."
"Guide me, O thou great Jehovah,
Pilgrim through this barren land:
I am weak, but thou art mighty,
Hold me by thy powerful hand." 88

And when my heart is overwhelmed within me lead me to the rock that is higher than I.

November 4.—Sabbath evening. Went a distance from home (to West Cornwallis) to attend the solemnities of divine worship. I cannot say but it appears more solemn and important to me than ever before; not that my mind is more stirred up than usual, but it ought to come close home, when my beloved companion takes the lead thereof. To-day he expounded to us the last verse of the 16th Chapter of John. I feel much need of being made submissive to the will of God in all things, and of having grace to mortify the deeds of the body, and live a life that will comport with the Gospel; but at present am very far distant from such blessed

conformity. Though I do not feel to lift a finger against Mr. C.'s preaching (and sometimes hope it may be the case, if it is the will of God, and long to be a help to him); but I want very much a
89 spirit of prayer and supplication. Oh I want to hold sweet communion with the King of saints! Want of time for reflection has shut me out from the privilege, having been much cumbered of late, owing to a wedding in the house, but I trust not captivated with it, though it might seem to appearance to be so. Lord, grant to shed abroad the influences of thy Holy Spirit in my heart.

November 15.—Have just returned from a prayer meeting; but my mind is so sunk, nothing but the cheering presence of my dear Redeemer can raise me to the enjoyment of real happiness. I am sometimes led to say, "wearisome days and nights are appointed unto me," and to realise the force of that passage, "Because I have said these things unto you, sorrow hath filled your heart." Why so much disquietude and quarrelling within? Why no more reconciled to the allotments of Providence? O Saviour, Lamb divine, hast thou borne my griefs and carried my sorrows? If thou hast, grant to arm me with the armour of salvation and shew it unto me. O give me the "spirit of love and of a sound mind," that I may with christian fortitude bear up under all the trials of this disordered life.

November 30.—Last evening accompanied Mr. Chipman to the house where prayer is wont to be made, where he endeavored to cast light upon the 20th verse of the 26th Chapter of Isaiah; but alas, his mind was not as fruitful as we could wish, necessarily owing in a great measure to the peculiar situation he is in as respects worldly things, so numerous are his offices and avocations; but we have cause to bless God he does not wholly forsake us, though very deserving of everlasting banishment. My partner wishes to be the instrument of comforting the waste places of Zion. I think I have of late realized that none but Christ can do helpless sinners good, and such I feel myself to be.

"Oh how sweet to feel the same,
Passing tribulation's flame."

December 16.—For want of comfortable travelling I am still debarred from going to the house of worship, but I want to feel more sensibly my soul panting and longing for the courts of the
90 living God, and not only that, but nearness to him. I do hope sometimes that my troubles lead me to God, and recently have felt a good degree of confidence in his faithfulness and wisdom. My partner is laboring to-day in the destitute part of the Township; may his labors be abundantly blessed and God glorified by him.

New Year's Evening, 1828.—The lines following are so

expressive, and touch my case so clearly, that I feel extremely anxious to notice them:

> "Look back, my soul, the Lord has been thy friend,
> He's brought the last year's troubles to an end;
> Then, what's to come, Lord, give me strength to bear,
> And at thy feet to cast my every care."

The state of my mind since I last wrote has been calm and unruffled in some measure, or rather I feel to be still and know that God reigns. This passage has enabled me to look up—"The Lord knoweth the way I take, and when he hath tried me I shall come forth as gold:" but when I consider how different the way is I take from what it ought to be, I am ashamed and confounded. I do not seek the glory of God as I should, and humbling myself before him on account of sin, I oftener am found fighting against God, than quietly submitting to his easy yoke and reign. Strange presumption in an expectant of infinite glory! Oh that God would give me grace and strength to set out afresh in the cause and interest of Zion, to be continually waiting for the bridegroom at his appearing, and to be useful to my fellow creatures while in this mortal state. May humility and gratitude be prominent features in my christian character.

January 19.—Sabbath evening. Both my body and mind are in a state of languor; the latter is too much so the greater part of the time; and how astonishing is it that it can be so, when death is making so many ravages amongst us! Two funerals to-day; one a head of a family, leaving a wife and seven children to mourn their irreparable loss; but their loss is his unspeakable gain. Since writing last, my mind has been, I hope, more than ordinarily exercised. I have had a sore combat with the enemy of souls, but it has taught me my own insufficiency, and the necessity of having constant strength and support from Him that is stronger than the strong man armed, though I require to be more deeply hunted and rooted out from my lurking places. Yet I can but wish such seasons to abide. I have also felt in some respects more resigned to the dealings of Providence with me; but oh how little I know and feel to what I ought to feel!

January 27.—Lord's day. This is in some measure a quiet day after a week of confusion, arising from an election within two miles of our house, and my father-in-law being one of the representatives. Alas, how much wickedness has been manifested— 91
enough to sink a world! Oh, if all were as anxious to make their calling and election sure as many have been in these political affairs, how much more safe would their standing be! At the close of the week, my husband being about to attend a meeting in the Western Settlement, and I feeling a burden of care, thought I

could truly adopt the verse before referred to (made for the New Year). I hope and trust I felt my Saviour near, and could repair to him for succour and support, knowing that his watchful eye was over me.

February 17.—Sabbath day. Here I am, confined to the
house (owing to peculiar circumstances), and suffering some pri-
92 vations; but they are small to what many have to endure. We
have family worship statedly, bibles and good books to peruse, and
the same God here as in the sanctuary; the most that is wanting
is a thankful heart for the comforts and mercies, spiritual and temporal, I am favored with beyond many others. My companion
always gives me an account of the meetings, so that I know almost
as much as if I were present. I trust that I am in some measure
made to be still and know that God reigns, who humbleth himself
to behold the things that are in heaven and in the earth. Well
might the Psalmist say, "Praise ye the Lord, the works of the
Lord are great, sought out of all them that have pleasure in
them."

March 2.—I am yet preserved in health and strength, enjoying
many comforts and blessings; but alas, how does that monster
ingratitude swell my breast! My mind is too little exercised
about eternal realities; my whole soul is not swallowed up with
the religion of Jesus as I wish it was, but yet I ought to be thankful for the crumbs which sometimes fall from my Redeemer's table.
I cannot but hope my confidence in God is upon the increase, and
know that he will order our cause for us. All I desire is to be
made quiet and resigned under every allotment of Providence, and
to be taught with equal firmness to sustain when tempted with
alluring pleasure, or assaulting pain. I was thinking yesterday,
I knew not what I should do if I had no God to look to for aid
and support, when difficulty and danger, and perhaps death, are
93 near at hand. I trust I do feel to look to the rock of Israel for
strength and direction in every trying exigency.

March 7.—A slight indisposition deters me from attending to the numerous avocations of life that devolve upon me, which leaves me more than usual time for serious reflection; but alas, if the spirit of God is not granted to quicken and enliven my mind, no outward means are sufficient of themselves. But ought I not to bless God for the smallest intimation of his loving kindness towards me? I see more beauty in the sacred volume of divine truth, and feel some of its sweetness more than for some time past; have felt the force of that passage, "In the Lord have I righteousness and strength." Oh how much I shall need the strength of the Almighty to be made perfect in my weakness in all future vicissitudes. I feel to rejoice in the prosperity of Zion, which is about, we hope and trust, to lift up its head again in the eastern part of our Township. A number have been brought to profess faith in Christ; we hope it is saving faith in every one, but we rejoice with trembling, knowing that it is an easier matter to put on the livery of Christ than to wear it. I feel it in my heart to address the young professors in the following pathetic lines:

"Ye little lambs of my Redeemer,
Ye who feed in pastures green,
Follow, follow Christ your leader,
Ever let your light be seen;
Ever mind and love each other,
And travel on the way together;
Shew the path that leads to woe—
So farewell, brethren, I must go."

But oh, when I think I am only a lamb myself, I ought to shut my mouth.

April 27.—Almost two months have elapsed since I have been able to notice my exercises; but O what thankfulness and praise is due to my covenant-keeping God and compassionate Redeemer for the displays of his unmerited mercy in my late confinement! I am now the mother of a living child, and am raised to a measure of health after a number of repeated indispositions; but the Lord has been kind, he has not suffered me to fall a prey to disease and death; my obligations are greater than ever to live a holy and spotless life (but this is what I never have done, and doubt much whether I shall ever be able to; surely I cannot, only in the strength of the Lord God of Hosts). I feel the weight of an immortal soul committed to my charge. God grant me wisdom and grace to conduct myself aright with it, and before it, for thou hast given us a blessed promise that "wisdom and knowledge shall be the stability of our times, and strength of salvation." Oh if my son is only one of the heaven-born race, all my toil and care will be nothing, and I trust it will be unceasing for his spiritual interest. I already feel him to be a strong cord to bind me to earth, but long to feel, that he is only a lent favor, and to hold him and every other earthly enjoyment at loose ends. I have in my affliction to lament that I enjoyed so little of the manifested presence of Jesus; but I have also cause to bless God, that he has given me to feel quiet and submissive under it, though very crossing to my wishes. 94

May 12.—After an absence of six months from the courts of the Most High, I was again made partaker of the happy privilege. Oh that I could more earnestly rejoice in God my Saviour for such distinguished blessings falling upon our little Zion! What a host do we witness assembling themselves together at conference meetings, at the water side, and at the house of God! May they all have spiritual eyes to discern the Lord's body until he comes! Five were received, in addition to a large number heretofore, for Baptism, among whom was a little girl eight years old, who gave striking proof of the reality of religion; and to-day twenty-six followed the footsteps of their divine Redeemer down the banks of Jordan, and for the first time sat down at the table of the Lord,—a solemn transaction indeed! May they never disgrace the holy religion which they have professed, but on the contrary be patterns of piety, of faith, hope and zeal.

June 8.—Sabbath morning. Duty seemed to call upon me to stay at home to-day, but I was unexpectedly privileged with going to conference meeting yesterday, and desire to bless God for it, for it was a comforting season; the minds of most of the Church seemed to be somewhat awake, to see the necessity of living to God. For my own part I know I am too dull and slothful, but I cannot but rejoice, that God has a people that shall shew forth his praise.

June 29.—Sabbath evening. What reason have I to bless God that I am favored with health and strength to worship him in his courts. We were pleasingly entertained to-day with two discourses from these words, "Unto this man will I look, that is poor and of a contrite spirit, and that trembleth at my word." "Nay, in all these things we are more than conquerors through him that loved us." They were calculated to benefit the Church of God, both the strong and the weak. I think I can say, I love the place where his honor delights to dwell; how beautiful have those lines appeared to me:

"I love her gates, I love the road;
The Church, adorned with grace,
Stands like a palace built for God,
To shew his milder face."

July 6.—I have now passed the twenty-first year of my age; and what shall I render to my God for all his mercies bestowed upon me from the cradle to the present moment—nearly five years of which I have professed to have fellowship with the Father and with his Son Jesus Christ, and have enjoyed the happy privilege of being in fellowship with a Gospel Church?

"Oh to grace how great a debtor,
Daily I am constrained to be;"—

But "prone to wander, Lord, I feel it,
Prone to leave the God I love."

Oh for a constant abiding sense of the obligations I am under to an infinitely wise God, though I too often am murmuring against the dealings of Providence with me, when I meet with anything trying to my feelings; but "whom the Lord loveth he chasteneth, and scourgeth every son whom he receiveth." I hope my trials will all be sanctified, that the true gold may sustain no loss, and I be enabled to glorify God in the fires.

July 16.—I have been blessed with some rather precious seasons of late; have attended conference meetings quite frequently, and go with my companion to hear him proclaim the joyful news of salvation to perishing sinners. I trust he is the means of comforting the weary heritage of Zion amidst a thousand embarrassments and hindrances; but our God is strong and mighty. Oh, to be more consecrated and more given up to God is what I most earnestly desire, and to have a weighty sense of eternal realities rolling into and upon my mind; but I am at present like Martha, "cumbered about much serving."

July 27.—This is a happy day (in some measure) to my immortal soul, having sat with great delight under the preached word by a Minister of the Gospel, Missionary from England (Mr. Tinson) to the Island of Jamaica, who has come hither by the good Providence of God for the purpose of improving his health; he appears to be a man of extensive information, good abilities and education, connected with ardent piety, as we must undoubtedly believe; what could have induced him to make such sacrifices as to leave his native land and many comforts for the thatched cottage in the burning Indies, but love to God and poor perishing sinners? He has been blessed, and so will every one who comes into the service of the great Head and King of Zion. Such soldiers have a large place in my affections, and I earnestly, in the name of God, wish them good success and God speed (sometimes for a moment feel a secret desire to be one of their number, but I have work to do in my situation if I will only do it). The texts to-day were as follows:—"All things shall work together for good," &c. &c. "Will ye also be his disciples?" It was very instructing to hear the same Gospel that we are in the habit of hearing.

August 16.—Lord's day. These three Sabbaths I have been necessarily detained from the continued indisposition of my partner; he seems in a very weak state, I hope not dangerous, but I must leave this for the Lord to decide. I begin to feel the want of the public means of grace. Oh for more ardent desires to meet the living God in his courts! Though deprived of that blessed privilege, the Lord does not altogether forsake me, but I deservedly merit it. Owing to the overwhelming bustle of the season, while the harvest, which is plenteous, is gathered in, I have been deeply immersed in the busy cares of life; but I trust crumbs have fallen from my master's table, and made me to realize that those who love Zion shall prosper. It appears to me, I am by no means in a prosperous state, but I think I have of late ascertained my love to the children of God (dare I say?) very clearly, and if I love the branches why not the vine?

September 15.—Yesterday I was blessed with the unspeakable privilege of attending Gospel worship; and the day before, conference meeting. I know not when my soul has been more refreshed at a conference; in short the spirit of the Most High seemed to be of a truth present. The texts on the Sabbath were as follows:—"Who hath believed our report, and to whom is the arm of the Lord revealed?" "For the great day of his wrath is come, and who shall be able to stand?" The discourses were delivered by two young Ministers raised up among us, and in a very remark-
95 able manner the Lord assists and prospers them. I seemed to get above my trials, and felt my heart light in the Lord, having for a length of time felt the combat between nature and grace very sore; but I hope and trust my proud heart, that seemed to gain the ascendancy so much, is humbled in some measure, while I feel the force of these words, "Mortify the deeds of the body, for if ye live after the flesh ye shall die." The Lord grant it for his name's sake!

October 29.—I have of late been indulged with many privileges, and I think I have enjoyed them in some measure, but not as I ought; what reason have I and all christians to praise the Lord for what he is doing among the sons of men, and even within the limits of our Township? "God who commanded the light to shine out of darkness hath shined into many hearts to give the light of the knowledge of the glory of God in the face of Jesus Christ." Oh, wonderful display of his mercy and goodness! I can but wish I was more given up to God, that I might behold the beauty of the Lord and inquire in his temple. I attended four days not long since, and they were precious seasons.

November 23.—Sabbath evening. I have been blessed with the precious privilege of hearing a very solemn and deeply interesting address delivered by a young servant of God raised up among us, (in the Zion of our God) who is about to take his leave of us, from the following words—"Wherefore I take you to record that I am pure from the blood of all men, for I have not shunned to declare the whole counsel of God." The speaker saw such a world of matter couched under the words, that he said he could only glance at them, but in glancing at them (as he thought) he included almost every point of the christian religion, and was very full and clear, manifesting ardent desire that they might be impressed upon every heart. This discourse was delivered in the neighborhood where he was born and brought up, and when he called his friends and neighbors to witness his life and conversation since his putting on Christ publicly, he said he must put his hand upon his mouth and his mouth in the dust; but after he felt a necessity laid upon him, and the love of Christ constraining him, and a death-blow was struck to his ambition for the world, he never has shrunk from declaring the distinguishing doctrines of grace as far as God gave him ability, though in much weakness; and then he made a solemn application and bade saint and sinner farewell;—the scene was very affecting. It is only a year since he commenced preaching, since which he has wonderfully improved, and we cannot doubt but the Lord is with him. His place of destination at present is about forty miles from this, to be an assistant with an aged Minister: the Lord prosper him and make him abundantly useful, as he has hitherto, and keep him humble, and bless his dear companion; reconcile her to thy will in all things. 96

January 16, 1829.—Sabbath day. I have not been privileged with attending on the public means of grace these four Sabbaths. I feel the want, but wish I could more earnestly say, "my soul longeth, yea even panteth for the courts of the living God." Various have been my conflicts and trials since I last wrote; but what troubles me most is my unreconciliation to the divine will, and that I dishonor my divine Lord so much. I oft-times think some heavy judgment will befal me; but can I hope that thou wilt yet deal mercifully with me and fulfil that gracious promise, "Though I walk in trouble thou wilt revive me!" O dear Jesus, bring me to thy feet, where I ought to be, and make me to learn of thee. O that I could realize more than I do, my noble birth, and my eternal inheritance, and what price the redemption of the elect cost; I think it would help me to smile at the frowns of an ungodly world. How true do I find that passage, "A man's foes are they of his own household." My situation is peculiarly trying, my companion is a great deal of the time from home, (but if I could only feel the Lord's support to enable me to bear those privations) proclaiming the glad tidings of salvation to perishing sinners, and some through his instrumentality are brought to accept of it, which ought to gladden my heart; but without the Spirit's influence what are we? O God, shew me the letting down of thy power, and let my soul arise and live to praise thee.

March 8.—Sabbath evening. The events of the present time are so important, in regard to my companion, myself, and others, that I cannot omit mentioning some of them; but (as a wise author says) "how can I sufficiently adore the patience of my Lord, my gracious husbandman who still bears with me, the weakest of all his branches? He has not cut me off yet, but still dresses me to bring forth more fruit, though like a degenerate plant, I have yielded little else but wild grapes. Why, then, shouldest thou

grumble, O my heart, at the application of his pruning knife? it
is really for thy good. He is angry only with the degenerate,
unfruitful branches; the more these are purged, the more fruit
thou shalt bring forth." This I can say has been my case all
through my life long, but particularly since I united with the
church of the living God; and I view it more sensibly at this
present time, having yesterday received a dismission from the First
Baptist Church in Cornwallis, in order to be received into the
Second Baptist Church in this place, over which my partner in
life is soon to be ordained (two ordinations have recently taken
97 place with members of this Church; what hath God wrought?)
Lord who is sufficient for these things? I trust I in some measure
feel my weakness to perform the duties of a Minister's wife, and
also my responsibility to God, how I conduct myself; but oh my
heart is very bad, a fountain of iniquity lies within, which has for
a time back led me to hew out broken cisterns that can hold no
water. I have experienced a long night of darkness. May the
Lord sanctify it and all my trials. We have in expectation soon
to remove from our present habitation to one more retired, twelve
miles distant from this, where the little Church is principally situated, that if the Lord will we shall dwell among (at least for a
time): we trust it is thy doing, for if thou build not the house, in
vain do they labor that build it; it surely has been a subject of
98 much prayer and deliberation (but alas, too little by me). How
shall we go in and out before this people? Lord, counsel and
direct us.

"Let me but hear my Saviour say,
Strength shall be equal to my day,
Then I rejoice in deep distress,
99 Leaning on all-sufficient grace."

March 30.—I am now comfortably situate in my new habitation, and want much to be thankful for the mercies I enjoy; but
alas, my mind is so secularized with worldly things, that I do not
realize the importance of my situation as much as I ought. O for
a right discovery of it that I may seek only for that happiness that
flows from the right hand of God. O may the Lord of heaven
dwell in me and I in him! Then I shall be richly supplied with
every needed good. A new house is erected for the worship of
God, near our dwelling; the sight of it from the window often
100 creates in my breast a sensation not to be expressed. I hope I
shall never get into such a state of mind that that house will not
look pleasant.

"Peace be within this sacred place,
And joy a constant guest;
With holy gifts and heavenly grace
Be her attendants blest."

April 12.—I still am a probationer of this lower world, and blessed with health, while many others are visited with affliction; and do I feel thankful? alas, I am too insensible to the mercies I am daily made the partaker of; but what shall I say of my spiritual welfare? I am yet too careless and unconcerned about Mount Zion, the city of the living God; but I think I feel increasing comfort in pouring out my soul for myself and others. O that Satan's strongholds may be weakened, and the Lord God who reigns from sea to sea, and whose right it is, may have the uppermost seat in every heart. Lord make me more heavenly minded, that I may forget the things that are behind, and press forward towards (further degrees of grace) the mark for the prize of my high calling of God in Christ Jesus, and be ready to say—

"Could I command the spacious land,
And the more boundless sea—
For one blest hour at thy right hand
I'd give them all away."

May 7.—Since writing last, three Sabbaths of the Lord have passed, and on only one of them was I privileged with hearing the preached word; but I have been favored with going to a good conference meeting,

Where I heard the babes in Zion sing
"Hosannas to their King."

Eight came forward and owned themselves on the Lord's side. May their conduct ever evince that they are true soldiers!—and on the last Sabbath (as rain prevented the Sabbath preceding) seven were baptized according to our blessed Saviour's example. It being the first time my companion administered the ordinance, both he and I felt much trembling, fearing something improper might occur; but God supported him, I firmly believed, and all things were done in a good degree in decency and order; his text following the baptism was, "Go ye into all the world and preach the Gospel to every creature; he that believeth," &c. &c.; the fields are looking white in this corner. Lord warm our hearts, and engage us more and more in thy service, that God may be glorified in, and through, and by us!

June 2.—I am spared while others are sick and dying, enjoying many mercies and privileges. God grant to make me thankful for them, that thereby I may be benefited. Five more have witnessed a good confession before men and angels. O may the unity of the Spirit abundantly increase in this little Church as numbers increase. I sometimes feel to bless and adore God for what he has done and is now doing, and will do till the last top stone be brought forth with shouting, crying grace, grace unto it. There can be no doubt that the latter day glory is fast approaching. O solemn, weighty and happy realities for them that are vitally united to Christ! O that christians were more alive (and I among the number), admiring the riches of free and sovereign grace! Lord, grant us a spirit of prayer and supplication, that we may pray much for the peace of Jerusalem.

June 14.—Sabbath afternoon. Yesterday we had a delightful season at conference: much quickening and animation was felt by the Church in general. O that God would rend the heavens and come down, that the mountains might flow down at thy presence, that saints may arise and put on their beautiful garments, that sinners may tremble and fear. To-day and the last Sabbath, baptism was administered to one, and the solemnities of the day were interesting. To-morrow, if all is well, we take our departure for Yarmouth, to attend an Association; may the great Head and Shepherd of Israel go with us, and satiate our souls with the marrow and
101 fatness of the Gospel. Lord crown the meeting with thy divine presence!

June 29.—The blessed Lord has, in his good providence, returned us in safety to our charge and family. I desire to be thankful for his goodness manifested in our absence to the little flock here (though some division has arisen which pains our hearts), and to the associated body. Much harmony prevailed; the sound evangelical truths of the Gospel were clearly brought to view in preaching; texts as follows—"When he ascended on high, he led captivity captive, &c." "Examine yourselves, whether you be in the faith, &c." "I know that my Redeemer liveth, &c." "And you who were once afar off are, &c." "Upon this rock will I build my Church, &c." "We love him, &c." "We then are ambassadors for Christ, as though God did beseech you by us, &c." I trust all their deliberations met the divine approbation, and that much good may result from it. O that that mind which was in Christ Jesus may be in us.

July 14.—I wonder my soul is not on the wing, praising God for the mercy drops that are falling, which we hope is only a prelude to a plentiful shower. Oh that I was more engaged in the good cause, and had more travailing pangs for poor sinners and for the righting up of God's people. It is a day of great events from what we hear and observations we are enabled to make; the Lord is raising up and thrusting many of his young servants into the Gospel Ministry. Yet the harvest is great and the laborers are few. O that the Lord of the harvest would send forth more laborers.

August 18.—Strange stupidity of mine—where am I? or what am I about? I sometimes feel as if Jesus was saying to me, why are you not more active? Lovely Jesus, I desire to "throw mine arms around, and hang upon thy breast," notwithstanding my vileness and distance from God; but "to whom shall I go but unto thee? thou hast the words of eternal life." Lord make me more humble, more conformed to thy blessed image, that I may be better qualified for the important situation I am called to fill. O that thou wouldst keep the door of my lips, "that my conversation may be seasoned with salt." Since writing last I have been left to mourn the hidings of God's face, and have thought I tasted the wormwood and gall. I hope God has given me deliverance, though I many times suspect it, fearing it may be some of my own framing, by the insinuations of a busy adversary, who is always near at hand; I wish I could resist him more.

August 25.—The two last Saturdays and Sabbaths we were highly privileged in this place and the adjoining with conference meetings, and the preached Gospel, and sacramental seasons, and one day met around the banks of Jordan and witnessed a citizen of Zion obey the commands of heaven; but in all this my heart was 102
not right with God, or I could not have been so insensible to his goodness in providing such rich feasts and love tokens for his children in the wilderness. Texts as follows:—"Being built upon the foundation of the Apostles and Prophets, &c."—"Yet it pleased the Lord to bruise him; he hath put him to grief, &c."—Isa. 53, 10. It was the Gospel in its purity preached by my companion. Oh I wonder the infinite love of Jehovah does not dissolve my heart more into thankfulness and melt my eyes more into tears. Lord, when shall that dear day arrive that I shall have uninterrupted communion with thee, or at least in a degree, here on earth? The wanderings of my affections are so many, and my temptations so strong, that it seems impossible that any of my imperfect requests can reach the ear of Deity. Yet that I am a temple for the Holy Ghost to dwell in, I cannot doubt, from the rich manifestations of God's love to my soul in times that are past; but I cannot live upon this, I want a fresh supply.

> "I cannot live without thy light,
> Cast out and banished from thy sight!" 103

O make me, dear Jesus, a wrestling Jacob and a prevailing Israel! May I have skill to use the weapons of my warfare, which are not carnal, &c., that I may be useful to my fellow creatures, that I may pray much for the prosperity of Zion, and for the Gospel heralds.

November 11.—The faithfulness of a covenant-keeping God is still manifested towards me, a hell-deserving sinner; truly it is well for me that I have no might or merit of my own, for were I left to myself, I should be plunged beyond recovery if the Lord did not preserve me. I feel that I am a great debtor to grace, and I am willing that God should have all the glory of my salvation, and of that of the whole of his elect, which he will most undoubtedly. Many are the revolutions I witness daily. Oh that I could profit by all that is trying as well as all that is pleasing. I think I feel sensibly hurt when Christ is wounded in the house of his friends. Oh why are christians, and I among the rest, not living as we shall wish we had, when we come to die?

December 12.—Sabbath evening. I have spent the day at home and in considerable retirement, and although I cannot get that nearness to God I want to, yet I trust I have felt some repentings for my manifold transgressions and remissness in duty. O that I could forsake, as well as confess! Lord, thou alone hast power to enable me to do so, and O be pleased to make it known, for my will needs to be bowed and brought into subjection to the will of a kind and compassionate God, who daily bears more with me (it appears to me) than with any of his children. Another year has almost expired, and what have I done for my blessed master? I fear, nothing; I wonder oft-times the Lord does not cut me down as a cumberer of the ground.

January 1, 1830.—New Year's Day. Pleasant and delightful, but no snow to ornament the earth; and I am spared in health to behold it, while others are no more in this world. My obligations, how great, towards a covenant-keeping God! I trust I have felt some desires that it might be begun in the fear of God, and that I might have more grace, strength, wisdom, and humility, to govern my future conduct, that the present year may not be spent as the past, if my life is prolonged; and if not, I have a hope it will be spent better, yes, far better, in eternity, where no perplexing cares, and sin, my worst enemy, nor Satan's devices, shall vex my eyes and ears any more.

March 14.—Sabbath day. What shall I render unto the Lord for all his goodness manifested (O that I could say, *felt*) since I last wrote? The reason why I have not written before is, I have been waiting to have something interesting to notice, and sometimes my doubts would not suffer me, strengthened as they were by a perverse wretched will and heart, and by Satan's fiery darts; all helped to dishonor God and rob my soul of comfort. When I look back upon my past life, and particularly the few months past, I am filled with astonishment that my dearest Lord could bear with such a wretch, when in days and months that are forever fled, he has given me to feel so much of his coming nigh, of his supporting, soul-ravishing and heart-cheering grace. Happy for me that I shall live and die a debtor to sovereign grace. The little Zion in this place is not in as prosperous a state as it has been; the enemy has been suffered to make inroads among some of her members, and the love of too many is waxing cold. Lord, revive thy work in the midst of the years, and pour out upon us a spirit of prayer, that this Church may yet look forth, fair as the moon, &c. &c.

May 9.—How can I sufficiently admire and adore that hand that has upheld me and brought me through another scene of affliction (to enjoy almost my wonted health), while mercies are
mingled with it? I am now the mother of a fine daughter. My 104
obligations and responsibility to God are increased. O why am I such a dull scholar in the school of Christ? Why not more engaged to promote his honor and glory, instead of observing and talking about trifles?

> "Were half the breath thus vainly spent
> To Heaven in supplication sent,
> My cheerful song would oftener be,
> Hear what the Lord has done for me."

Dear Jesus, take me out of this lethargic state.

June 24.—Another Association has been attended to, but I did not enjoy the privilege of meeting with the goodly number, but understood it was a refreshing season; much union and harmony prevailed. This ought to be cheering to my soul, to hear that others enjoy a feast of fat things, while I am wandering on the barren mountains. It appears to me that I would be willing to make every sacrifice that lies in my power (but here I cannot trust my heart), if I could only enjoy the light of Immanuel's countenance, and have my affections raised from this sordid earth and placed on heavenly and divine things, have my whole soul deeply imbued with eternal realities and feel the worth of immortal souls lie near my heart, and see what an escape the ransomed of the Lord are enabled to make through the efficacy of that blood that was shed on Mount Calvary for poor lost perishing sinners. O Saviour, have mercy upon me, and raise me out of this miserable condition which sin has brought me into.

August 9.—My soul is pierced through with many sorrows (and yet I do not feel all I ought to); serious difficulties have arisen in the Church of which I am an unworthy and unprofitable
member. "The precious sons of Zion, comparable to fine gold, 105
are esteemed as earthen pitchers." I have reason to be thankful that I am not concerned in the difficulty otherwise than as a member of Christ's body, it becomes me to help bear the burthen; but there is so much contrariety in the human heart to the example our blessed Lord left us, that confusion and almost every evil work appears to be manifest. "O Lord, spare thy people, and give not thine heritage to reproach." "Oh that my head were waters and

mine eyes a fountain of tears, that I might weep day and night for the slain of the daughter of my people."

August 15.—Sabbath day. Not favored with attending the public means of grace, and my heart is very cold in attending private ones. Oh how often do I think I attempt to pray, only to still the roarings of a guilty conscience! How wretchedly depraved I am—only fit for the dunghill; if I am saved from the yawning pit at last it will be only through the mere mercy of God. Surely I do not glorify God in the present state of mind I am in, if ever I do. I could dwell on the dark side for hours, but I must forbear; but I plainly see where the death in my soul proceeds from,—want of love to God and communion with the ever blessed Three.

"O for a closer walk with God,
A calm and heavenly frame—
A light to shine upon the road
106 That leads me to the Lamb."

September 5.—Lord's day. Have been priviliged with hearing the Gospel delivered by a young servant of the Lord, from these words—"How shall we escape if we neglect so great salvation?" Our stated pastor (my companion) is now absent, and will be for some time, having gone on a mission to the destitute parts of the Province. O that his journey may be prosperous by the will of God, that he may be the instrument in the hands of God of awakening some poor careless sinners to a sense of their danger, and pointing them to Christ as a sovereign remedy, and of comforting the weary heritage of Zion. The Lord return him in safety in his own good time, richly laden with the blessings of the Gospel of peace. My own mind is yet in a state of commotion; no solid inward peace, on account of sin, and backsliding from God; how great will be my misery if I am only dreaming of heaven, while my soul is mistaken. O Lord, remove those doubts and fears, if I am a child of thine, and give me to enjoy the influences of the Spirit, that I may walk in the light as Christ is in the light.

November 28.—Sabbath evening. I have experienced many mercies (since writing last) amidst the afflictions of Joseph. The little Church here has truly been in adversity; nothing but rents and divisions appeared manifest for a time; the breach widened, till it was thought advisable to call a council from sister Churches. They came, and aided us all in their power, fully approving of the conduct of the Church towards the offenders, but the measures proposed, have not yet been adopted. Yesterday a few in number met in conference, and had a profitable season in confessing their faults. I was not there, neither have I enjoyed the privilege of meeting with them to-day, but my heart has been with them, I trust. I have had some severe trials of late. Satan has been very busy with me ; it appears to me he rallies all his forces. O Lord make me to feel that thou art able to conquer.

December 26.—Sabbath day. I have just returned from visiting the grave of my first-born child, who three weeks ago to-day was in the enjoyment of good health (excepting a cold), and a week after he was removed from time to a vast eternity, aged two years and nine months. Five days before his death he was severely scalded (by sitting down into a kettle that had about two quarts of boiling water). Although he had two severe fits caused by the worm fever setting in, and was extremely ill, yet some symptoms appeared favorable, and we were too much encouraged until the day before he breathed his last, when the mortification took place which ended his mortal career. God has seen fit in his wisdom to hand me the cup of affliction to drink of, in common with the rest of his intellectual creatures, and although I have found it, and do still find it hard to be reconciled to this my lot, yet I know my dear Redeemer has chastened me for my profit, for he scourgeth every son whom he receiveth, and he hath in faithfulness afflicted
me. I acknowledge that his strokes are "fewer than my crimes, 107
and lighter than my guilt." O, I needed it; I have been such a rebel against God; and though he has touched me in this tender part, and wrung my heart with sorrows, yet I feel to say, "I will bear the indignation of the Lord, for I have sinned"—and desire to say with the poet,

"Peace, all my angry passions, then—
And each rebellious sigh
Be silent at his sovereign will,
And every murmur die."

Yesterday I was favored with the privilege of meeting in conference with my beloved brethren after an absence of two months. 108
The dear people of God are still laboring under a burden. O sin, thou monster, what hast thou done! Will the Lord grant us all a more watchful and prayerful spirit, that we may be up and doing whilst the day lasts? May death, judgment, and a vast eternity, deeply engross our attention, that we may have our lamps trimmed and in bright burning! And oh that poor careless sinners would consider their latter end and prepare to meet God when he comes to be glorified and admired in all them that love him!

January 26, 1831.—My affections are yet pinioned to earth, and although the Lord hath solemnly reminded me that it is a fearful thing to love what death may touch, I cling to other affections, and others twine about my heart and around me, but one
tendril of the heart is torn away forever. My afflictions, which 109
are not joyous, but grievous, I trust will yield the peaceable fruits

of righteousness to my immortal soul; but I feel at present that I am too insensible, too stupid under them, and though I find my heart struggle amidst its fancies like a prisoned bird that would escape and cannot, on account of him that is no more, yet I do not turn my thoughts within, and viewing there the malady of sin, look by faith beyond it to the remedy provided, to the *Lord Jesus Christ, the Saviour of Sinners. Precious words!* I cannot deny that in him I have felt there was a balm for every wound, a cordial for every fear. "His name is a strong tower, whereinto the righteous run and be safe." O that I could feel it more sensibly, that "He is to his people as rivers of waters in a dry place, and the shadow of a great rock in a weary land." I desire not to "despise the chastening of the Lord, nor faint when I am rebuked of him." I need the supporting and enlivening grace of God to quicken me according to his righteous judgments. Lord, restore peace and union unto Zion in this and every other place where it is needed.

February 18.—My life is a chequered scene; only two months since the funeral of my dear child, and now a wedding (the daugh-
110 ter of my dear companion's first marriage) in the house: many things serve to remind me of the mournful scene that is past, but I desire a mind like the poet's:

> "Since all that we meet
> Shall work for our good,
> The bitter is sweet,
> The medicine is food."

O that I could feel the worth of religion as I ought to! how would I look away beyond these meaner things. O thou who walkest in the midst of the golden candlesticks, and hast so much against this little one, grant us all true repentance, that we may return and do our first works, that thereby thou mightest come to us in a way of mercy.

March 16.—The little Zion in this place is yet groaning under a serious burthen. What the result is to be, heaven only knows. Nothing can supply the place of union and brotherly love in the members of Christ's body. The Psalmist might well say, "Behold, how good and how pleasant it is for brethren to dwell together in unity." O that the God of infinite wisdom would condescend to direct this feeble band to adopt such measures for the removing of difficulties as shall be most for his glory! May everything offensive to his pure nature be eradicated, that this Zion may yet be "a quiet habitation, a city not forsaken." Grant us all, dear Lord, a praying spirit, for we are well assured that the effectual fervent prayer of the righteous availeth much. O the wisdom and goodness of the divine government! I sometimes get a little glimpse of it although it sees fit to tear my idols from me and leave me to mourn their loss. I would desire to call upon my soul and all that is within me to bless the Lord for the wonderful plan of salvation. O for a weighty sense of it, that it might stimulate me to acts of new obedience!

March 27.—I have not felt that assurance of an interest in the
Redeemer's blood that I have desired. I want to be led to greater
searchings of heart, and more close self-examination, to know how
the case stands between God and my immortal soul, that whenever
the summons come I may be ready to go in unto the marriage supper of the Lamb. O shall I meet my dear little Leander there? 111
I trust I have known what the faith of reliance is, through many
of my trials, particularly my sore bereavement; but for a length
of time I have not felt that assurance of my glorious inheritance
that I once did.

> "When I can read my title clear
> To mansions in the skies,
> I bid farewell to every fear,
> And wipe my weeping eyes." 112

But it is more than I deserve.

> "Let me but hear my Saviour say,
> Strength shall be equal to my day;
> Then I rejoice in deep distress,
> Leaning on all-sufficient grace." 113

May this be my happy case, that whenever the storms of life beat upon me, and at all times, I may feel my anchor cast within the vail. Lord, suffer me not to do anything that will dishonor thy blessed cause, that is bleeding around me, either directly or indirectly.

April 26.—A severe trial is presented to my view, and some
others, to engage in the important duty of uniting to commence a
female prayer meeting. I hope it is duty when I say so; I know 114
I do not feel as I ought to about it; but the fear of the rod being
laid upon me makes me desire to engage in it cheerfully, if it is
for the honor of God. I want to see the path plain.

> "Dear Jesus, steep this rock of mine
> In thine own crimson sea;
> None but a bath of blood divine
> Can melt the flint away."

Thou, blessed Redeemer, hast declared that "thou wilt keep him in perfect peace whose mind is stayed upon thee." O may this be my happy case; "work in me to will and to do of thine own good pleasure."

June 12.—Sabbath day. I am yet the spared monument of God's mercy, but am overpowered with deep insensibility. I know not but I am rightly punished for not making more sacrifices to get to the house of God. I plainly see I am indulging too much in sloth, and that an indolent christian never will prosper. I have not had it in my power to attend but two of the prayer meetings; the last time I offered my unprofitable gift among them, Satan, to human appearance, seemed to have me in possession. O that God would make a display of his Omnipotent power (both in my heart and in christians in general), and right up my mind in the truth. This is an important crisis with the Church in this place; she is indeed down to the bottoms of the mountains with the weeds wrapt about her; her harps are hung upon the willows, and she is in a strait to know what to do, or what course to pursue. If no reconciliation takes place between the parties, excommunication must inevitably take place, and then the difficulty is so intricate that it is hard to discern which of the parties is the greatest offender. Lord give them that wisdom which is profitable to direct, that thou mayest be glorified. O may all wrongs be rectified and forgiven, that God may again shine upon his weary heritage!

August 7.—Sabbath day. As no meeting is contiguous to us to-day, I spend the day as much in reading as my eyes will allow me; but it seems very strange to me that the precious word of God does not interest me more, and the blessed duty of prayer; but not strange, either, can it be, when I look at my wretched strayings and wanderings from God by sin. Shame and confusion of face belong unto me, and yet it is deeply mysterious that a heaven-born soul, whose chief delight in its earliest love is the privilege of prayer and praise, and reading thy sacred volume of divine inspiration, as also in times of affliction "when the Almighty troubleth him and maketh his heart soft," should be in such a state. I plainly see that prosperity will not do for the christian, unless wonderfully sanctified. Why hast thou cast me off, O Lord, and hid thy face from us, and left thy little Church (in this place) to grope her way in the dark? Sin, thou monster, what hast thou not done! Come, O come, precious Jesus, leaping over the mountains of our sins, and hills of our provocations, and once more shine upon thy bride. Where iniquity has abounded and the love of many has waxed cold, may a reformation be commenced in thy professing children; and O may it extend to ungodly sinners, that Zion may no longer mourn because so few come to her solemn feasts.

November 20.—How dull and reluctant am I in the duty of writing, as well as other duties, but the purport of the following verse is the cause:

"A wicked world and wicked heart,
With Satan now are joined;

> Each acts a too successful part,
> In harassing my mind."

When, O when, shall the day dawn, and the day-star arise again in my soul? O that I could have a spirit of prayer to plead with God to remove this deep insensibility and enlighten my mind in the knowledge of the glory of God! but while cast down, I am not in despair, nor destroyed. I know the government is on Immanuel's shoulders, and though he sees fit to give me and the members of Zion in this place a long winter season, yet spring will come in his own due time. May we have it to say—

> "The winter season has been sharp,
> But spring shall its wastes repair."

March 27, 1832.—I may truly say it is of the Lord's mercies I am not consumed, for surely I am a cumberer of the ground, when my opportunities are so many of shewing myself on the Lord's side and of recommending him to poor careless sinners. I think since last writing I have enjoyed some tokens of Jehovah's love, some very precious seasons, while sitting under the sound of the Gospel. What shall I render to the Lord for all his benefits? O give me, dear Jesus, a sensible thankful heart, and may I experience a fresh anointing from above, that will enable me to love thee more and serve thee better, and to plead more fervently for thy backsliding Israel.

July 3.—This is the twenty-fifth anniversary of my life, and how little (if anything) I have done in the service of my Lord and Master! Nearly twelve years since I have seen an end of all perfection here below, [She did not publicly profess religion until in her seventeenth year, as may be seen in the commencement of this Journal.—W. C.] and yet what poor progress have I made in my journey heavenward. The present time is in some small degree a time of lamentation with me on account of my little devotedness to the cause and interest of Zion, and that I so much of the time live at a poor dying rate. O Saviour, chase away the dark clouds of sin and unbelief, and O may I have grace to use the weapons of my warfare, that Satan may not be suffered to overpower me with his fiery darts. May a spirit of prayer be given!

September 22.—I am much disappointed in not being able to meet with the Church in this place, in conference, this afternoon; indisposition prevents, but it is all right, I trust. Jehovah Jesus will not pass me by at home in my dwelling. I have been indulged with many privileges of late, and have enjoyed some of them quite well, although the solemnities of eternity do not rest with that weight on my mind I wish they did. Yet I believe the person, attributes, doing and dying of the Lord Jesus have been and are precious to me.

> "His worth, if all the nations knew,
> Sure the whole earth would love him too."

O how much I need the teachings of God the Holy Spirit. Meet with thy people this afternoon, dear Lord.

November 25.—Sabbath day. In the providence of God I am deprived of attending public worship; but alas, how little of a worshipping spirit do I possess, notwithstanding judgments are mixed with mercies, and at all times a sufficiency to humble me and keep my mind awake to righteousness. My companion has for a length of time been in a poor state of health, and many things crossing to my wishes transpire; but I know in the school of adversity we are most likely to be taught useful lessons, and such I desire may be the case with me, for why should a living man complain for the punishment of his sins? O that God would in mercy visit this Church and people with his overpowering grace to unite their hearts in love, that each member may be as a city set on a hill. Lord, prepare the most unworthy of thy children for all the good pleasure of thy will, that whether living or dying she may glorify thee, the King of Kings and Lord of Lords.

February 15, 1833.—Many, very many, have been the changes of a kind Providence towards me since I last wrote. The God of heaven has laid me down upon a bed of sickness and raised me up again and committed to my charge a lovely babe (another daugh-
115 ter.) O how repeated are the obligations I am under to love and serve my blessed Redeemer, with all my *heart, soul, mind, and strength!* but, alas, alas, instead of living more devoted to God, I feel myself to be getting farther and farther from Him who is the chief object of worship. Would to God I could be more disentangled from earthly objects, that is, my mind less diverted with them, so that I might use them and not abuse them. O Jesus, suffer me not to cast off fear and restrain prayer.

April 27.—Conference day. I regret I am not able to attend meeting, owing to indisposition; may it be a refreshing season from the presence of the Lord. to those who are permitted to enjoy the privilege. O that my soul may receive a fresh anointing from above, for surely it stands in great need of it: why am I thus clogged down to the earth and the vain allurements thereof, when I have so much to remind me of the near approach of death and eternity?

> "My God, permit my tongue
> This joy, to call thee mine;
> And let my early cries prevail
> To taste thy love divine.
> Within thy temple, Lord,
> I long to find a place,
> To see thy power and glory too,
> 116 And feel thy quickening grace."

These lines are the language of my heart. O for the Spirit which searcheth all deep things to search me, that God the Father, through his Son and Spirit, would

> "Warn me of every sin,
> Forgive my secret faults,
> And cleanse this guilty soul of mine,
> Whose crimes exceed my thoughts."

O that spring-time may soon come in our Church, and the singing of birds be heard: may a spirit of prayer be given!

May 19.—Sabbath day. The two Sabbaths past I have had the privilege of attending public worship, but how have I to complain of a wretched wandering mind, that so diverts my attention from hearing and meditating upon the Gospel as I want to, applying and conforming to it, as I journey along through this dark vale. Oh to be more consecrated to God,—to have much of that mind in me that was in Christ Jesus,—to be ready at all times to perform what duty points out. I find the christian's three potent enemies, the world, the flesh, and the devil, to be very powerful; but I am satisfied that grace, rich, superabounding grace, is sufficient to conquer and bow down the loftiness of man. A crumb now and then, I trust, falls from my Heavenly Father's table, that enlivens and quickens my drooping heart; but ere I am aware, some sensual bait seizes my taste, and my joys are polluted. O for more of the Spirit's divine operation upon my soul, that it might transform me into the lovely image of Christ my Lord, that thereby I may live a holy, watchful, and prayerful life. Grant me wisdom, O God, to resolve, and to put in practice the resolution.

May 26.—Sabbath afternoon. What reason have I to bless God for permitting me to meet in conference yesterday, and to-day attend his public worship, and commemorate the sufferings and death of the once dying but now risen Jesus! Although I could have desired to have had more of a worshipping spirit, yet I desire to thank the Lord for what I did feel and enjoy. I think I felt deeply interested in the things of religion; the precious Lord appeared in his complex character as altogether lovely, as a God of love and infinite compassion. Though no rapturous feelings seized my mind, yet I trust it was stayed in some degree upon the living God, and the grace of charity being in exercise, I felt love to the brethren. O that my future conduct may be more as becometh the Gospel, the inward principle governing the outward walk. My companion, I trust, was assisted by God, the Holy Spirit; his text,—"That they may be one, as we are one; I in them and thou in me that they may be perfect in one." Oh may it not be a lost opportunity.

June 30.—Through the tender mercy of my covenant-keeping God, I was indulged with the privilege of attending part of the time at the Association, where I heard that Gospel dispensed which edifies and feeds the soul of the true believer. I must say, I took courage and desired to press on.

> " Though dark be my way,
> Since He is my guide,
> 'Tis mine to obey,
> 'Tis His to provide."

O, I would desire to be such a character as God would have me to be; but I need converting daily and hourly from the error of my ways, that the importance of religion may rest with due weight on my mind, that I may have my lamps trimmed and in bright burning. O for the Spirit's quickening influence to be felt upon my heart, that thereby I may serve God acceptably with reverence and godly fear.

August 18.—Five Sabbaths have elapsed since I heard the sound of the Gospel. My blessed Redeemer has seen fit to lay his hand of affliction upon one of my tender offspring and caused her to be entirely helpless, although much better on many accounts this fortnight past (her complaint the St. Vitus's Dance), yet the
117 cause is not removed. How it will terminate is known only to Him who "rides upon the stormy sky, and manages the seas." I can say, peace be still; a mixture of hopes and fears has often pervaded my mind, but I think I have as often felt desirous, and I trust willing that God should govern and do all his pleasure with us, and the language of my heart to the precious Jesus "be thou my King." I would desire to live in humble subjection to thee, and submit myself to thy control and direction, and to be enabled to say, "not my will but thine be done." O subdue every rebellious principle within and make me all resignation and cheerful obedience to thee. O the pleasures of humble submission! I think I have known something of it. How pleasant to lie as a subject at the feet of this mediatorial King, without arrogating the sovereignty to myself, for which I or any other creature am utterly insufficient. Blessed Jesus, thus reign in my heart. Some of the above remarks are extracts, but so fully coincide with my views that I
118 adopt them. And the following strikes my mind forcibly; a wise Minister when preaching and speaking of the beauties of Creation and Providence as being a faint transcript of the excellencies of Jesus, says, "If the copy be so fair and lovely, who would not love the Original, that has eyes to behold it? Believers see as much of the love of Christ as is sufficient to captivate their hearts and convince them of their guilt in loving him no more, and the clearer their views are of him, the more they are mortified at the

criminal defects of their love, for they see that he deserves infinitely more." I must say that I have had a feast to my soul this day, in reading a sermon preached from this text—"Unto you who believe, he is precious." Yes, I trust he is precious to my feeble helpless soul; but I have to say with the poet—

"My soul lies cleaving to the dust,
Lord give me life divine;
From vain desires and every lust
Turn off these eyes of mine." 119

The hymn is very sweet. O may I be content, my Father, with thy will, and quiet as a child, and let me and all thy blood-bought ones see more and more of thy glory. O remember thy Zion in this place for good. Build thou the walls thereof.

September 8.—Am still the spared monument of God's mercy, while the arrows of death are flying abroad. A near relation was yesterday consigned to the silent grave, having left a husband and four children to mourn her loss, with many friends; but our loss is her unspeakable gain. She is, I trust, beholding him face to face, for whose cause she suffered persecution and shame (at least for a time) when about to make a public profession of religion among
the Baptists. She evidenced the reality of religion at many sub- 120
sequent periods, and is now, I humbly hope, worshipping before the throne without any alloy. May it be sanctified to surviving friends, and be a salutary warning to us all to set our houses in order. O to be actually ready to meet the grim messenger (although to saints death is the gate to endless joy), is what I desire above everything else, so that that day may not come upon me unawares. How much have I to call up my attention to reflect upon the important concerns of the soul! The continued indisposition of my child (although appearances are favorable), with many other privations, ought to lead my mind from the objects of time and sense to Christ the pure fountain, for a right improvement of all his dealings with me. My companion is now absent on a missionary tour for six weeks among the destitute on Prince Edward
Island. I trust I do not wish him otherwise engaged, hoping that 121
his visit may be made a lasting blessing to some perishing souls, and that he may be the instrument of building up the spiritual kingdom of our God. O God, grant him thy special influence this day and at all times, that he may speak forth the words of truth and soberness, and teach transgressors thy ways! May we all be directed in the path of duty!

September 30.—Since writing last I have enjoyed unnumbered privileges, and some of them I think I did enjoy in reality. After an absence from the house of worship for two months (owing to sickness), my ears were again saluted with the cheering sound of the Gospel from the lips of my old pastor, Elder Manning. The following portions of Scripture were expounded—"Oh that the salvation of Israel were come out of Zion. When God bringeth back the captivity of his people, Jacob shall rejoice and Israel shall be glad." "Ye were once darkness, but now are ye light in the Lord; walk as children of light." The Lord's Supper was attended to—a solemn season. The day previous, conference, and an interesting season it was to many souls; I feel as if I could say with the poet, sometimes,

> "The christian would not have his lot
> Be other than it is;
> For while his Father rules the world
> He knows that world is his."

I trust I do not feel a disposition to murmur at my situation at present, although cares and anxiety weigh me down at times; but I hardly dare trust this deceitful heart of mine; it has caused me to be such a rebel heretofore, that I have great reason to adore the riches of free and sovereign grace that could and does bear with such a heaven-provoking sinner. O what unbounded love is manifested by Jehovah to man, the noblest work of his hands, and yet the most undeserving! it may well be said, "That God is love and he that dwelleth in love dwelleth in God and God in him." O may this ever be my high privilege, that this pure love may possess my breast, "where'er I rove, where'er I rest." I would fain hope my husband's absence would prove a good school for me, if I were not such a dull scholar. Do thou, precious Jesus, take the uppermost seat in my heart, and reign and rule there without a rival. O may I be crucified to the world and the world to me, that I may die daily unto sin, and live unto righteousness.

October 6.—Sabbath day. Am not permitted to engage in social worship this day, and the stupidity of my mind is so great that I am not prepared to engage in private. Alas, I am too much under the influence of the carnal mind, or I should be feeling the force of these words,

> "Well he remembers Calvary,
> Nor lets his saints forget."

Surely they never should forget the amazing blessings that were purchased by the sufferings and death of the sin-atoning Lamb. Thanks and praise be given to thy name, O God, for the restoration of my darling child to the use of her limbs and a good degree of health. May she be like Mary of old, who pondered all those things in her heart, and sat at the Saviour's feet. How much I feel these lines—

> "The fondness of a creature's love,
> How strong it strikes the sense!
> Thither our warm affections move,
> Nor can we call them hence."

I may well say that I am often present in spirit with my companion. O that it was a pure spirit at all times, that thereby our joint petitions might ascend the throne of God for all those things we stand in need of, (and for other immortal souls,) to direct us through every changing scene. I anticipated his return this week. O may our desires be realized if it is the will of the Lord.

November 16.—A variety of changes have taken place since I last wrote, while others have experienced adversity, mercies have flown unto me without measure, and among the number I am permitted to enjoy the society of my partner in life again, though led to anticipate to the contrary, as he did not return as soon as expected; but alas, I do not experience holy intercourse with my divine Lord and Master as I want to, owing to this depraved nature that so clogs me down. I have of late felt much concern about the state of Zion in this place; her ways indeed do languish. O that the mighty God would rend the heavens and come down, that the mountains of sin may disappear before thee,—that the cloud of mercy that is bursting about eight miles East of this, may extend to this corner of the Lord's vineyard,—that we may see a reformation in thy children, while sinners are made to discover their danger, and the remedy, sovereign grace has found, to heal diseases of the mind. O how seldom do we rise to God, or taste the joys above!

December 22.—Sabbath. It appeared duty for me to remain at home to-day, having had the privilege of attending conference yesterday, and to-morrow, if my life is spared, shall attend the funeral of an aged neighbor; there are some grounds to hope favorably concerning his future destiny. But the God of heaven will do him no injustice. O that the solemnities of death rested with due weight upon my spirits; then would my mind, I trust, rise superior to the objects of time and sense. The following passage has struck my mind with force to-day while reading, "I have blotted out as a thick cloud thy transgressions, and as a cloud thy
sins; return unto me, for I have redeemed thee." I plainly see I 122
need faith and a heart right with God to receive the invitation and promise. I think it exactly applies to me, for my sins have become like separating walls between God and my soul. Surely the God of heaven bears much and long with me. O help me, Saviour of sinners, to return unto thee, with brokenness of spirit, rending my heart and not my garments. O may I realize that all the fitness thou requirest is to feel my need of thee.

January 19, 1834.—Since writing last the year has closed and another one ushered in. Alas, alas, what progress have I made heavenward during the past year, as well as all my life? With gratitude and pleasure can I recount some of the mercies of God (and were it not for my amazing stupidity I might recount them all the time) towards me who am less than the least of all saints; but O what poor returns do I make! O God, enable me not only to confess sin, but to forsake it and cleave unto thee with full purpose of heart. I want to realize more and more that I am a sinner, and if saved it will be by free and unmerited grace,

> "O to grace, how great a debtor
> Daily I am constrained to be;
> Let that grace, *Lord*, like a fetter,
> Bind my wandering heart to thee."

There have some mercy drops fallen in this vicinity; may it only be a prelude to a plentiful shower.

March 2.—Sabbath evening. Praise and thanksgiving is due to thy name, Holy Father, for the marvellous change thou hast wrought many individuals (since I last wrote) within this vicinity. Thou hast indeed ridden triumphantly, O God, and made glorious displays of thy power; the inhabitants of the rock have been made to sing and to shout from the tops of the mountains, while many in the valley have found thee precious to their never-dying souls.—[The above language is very appropriate, inasmuch as the revival commenced on the Black Rock Mountain, and the ingathering was principally there. On the very day of the above entry there were eighteen baptized in the sea, and on the mountain in all fifty-three, and sixteen in the valley, and several of whom, Father John White, Brother Meryon, his two daughters, &c. have since gone home to glory, to meet and hail with welcome the author of this
123 journal.—W. C.] I have again been made to feel the rod of chastisement (though but light) in the sickness of my little daughter for this fortnight past, but hope she is recovering; may it yield the peaceable fruits of righteousness.

April 6.—Indisposition still hangs about my child; both she and the other healthy child are subjects of the hooping cough. I want a disposition to say and feel that all is well, whether life or death. I think I feel that I am at too great a distance from God. I feel more and more astonished at my own declensions, which make the stroke necessary.

May 6.—The thing which I greatly feared has come upon me. My dear little Mary Eliza is no more: her immortal spirit took its flight (we hope to a mansion prepared for her) this morning, aged
124 four years and nearly a month. Although this is what I have long looked for, and have tried to hold her as a lent favor, yet the bitterness

of parting is great, with one so dear; nature cries, forbear, "but faith disclaims the hasty plaint impatient nature spoke, and said the will of the Lord be done." I hope I feel to acquiesce therein, knowing that her judge will do her no injustice. But now I want the supporting grace of God, that will enable me to feel that it is a stroke of mercy instead of wrath; such I found the death of my dear Leander. O what wise purposes there are in the designs of Jehovah! Make me, dearest Saviour, to seek for comfort and happiness only in thee, who art the restorer of the breach.

May 9.—Yesterday the last duties of respect were paid to my dear deceased child. Elder Manning preached; text,—"For we
must all appear before the Judgment seat of Christ," &c. I hope 125
the occasion was solemn and interesting to all assembled. I desire to be thankful that my own mind was (dare I say it) stayed upon God; this I hope was in some measure the case, and I could say while standing by the graves of my beloved children, can I not trust my treasures to his arms, whose changeless care passeth a mother's love, and hope when a few hasty years their race have run to go to them, though they no more on earth return to me? Oh that this blank may be more than filled up by the sanctifying influences of the Holy Spirit! I am well satisfied that the Lord never takes any thing away, but what he gives some thing better.

"The dearest idol I have known,
What e'er that idol be—
Help me to tear it from the throne,
And worship only thee," 126

May the death of dear little Mary be the eternal life of some soul.

May 11.—Sabbath afternoon. After an absence of five weeks from the house of God, I was again permitted to enter his sanctuary, and hear these words discussed by my companion, "For our light affliction which is but for a moment, worketh for us a far more exceeding and eternal weight of glory." A deeply interesting subject to all the children of God; it is the word of inspiration, and therefore is truth. O what rich mercy and love, that ever devised such a well-constructed plan of life and salvation, so honouring to God and safe to man! What amazing stupidity pervades my whole frame!

May 18.—Sabbath morning. Alas, what I complained of when I last wrote, has been too much the case through the week. I was led to take the composure of my mind for it sometimes, until yesterday I began to feel more sensibly the repinings of nature for my lovely little girl, whose body now rests in earth—I would fain hope a soul gained through the Saviour's death.

"Her toils now o'er, her spirit fled,
Her mortal part alone is dead."

O may I again say—

> "Peace all my angry passions, then,
> And each rebellious sigh
> Be silent at his Sovereign will,
> And every murmur die."

O that the Spirit might help my infirmities by making intercession for me with groanings which cannot be uttered.

June 16.—Sabbath evening. Yesterday I again had the privilege of meeting in conference, found it a comforting, and I hope, profitable season. I seldom if ever felt the cross less in speaking, perhaps it was owing to stupidity, but still I cannot but think I enjoyed a refreshing season the evening before, when alone with my God. Time appears short with me. Oh that I could realize the great necessity of redeeming it! I find it good to be afflicted, if my heart does not deceive me; but I need to be transformed by the renewing of my mind daily.

July 3.—This day I am twenty-seven years old, and Oh, how does my past life appear *a blank indeed!* nothing, as I can see, done for God. I was led to say last night, while reflecting upon it,

> "Here Lord I give myself away,
> 'Tis all that I can do."

But alas, alas, through the prevalency of sin I fear there is some reserve; but turning from myself I can, I think, see that the hand of the Lord has extended goodness and mercy to me all my days. What a mercy that I am out of hell, and, in addition, that the precious Lord has set his love upon me, and made me to feel at times that he is the chiefest among ten thousand and altogether lovely! What obligations am I under to devote myself a living sacrifice, holy and acceptable in his sight, O for a full surrender of my all into the hands of my best friend. It may be the will of heaven that I shall not spend another birth-day on this earth. O that when the summons comes (let it be sooner or later) I may be in actual readiness to meet him, whom vile mortals shall be like in glory; and see him as he is. Lord, grant that all my afflictions may have the desired effect, that glory may be brought unto thy great name thereby.

July 11.—Have had a weeping time this morning in reflecting upon the subject of death; many of Watts's hymns upon the same
127 appeared very comforting. I begin to feel the strong tie of nature dissolving between me and my dear little Mary, although I have felt, I trust, to resign her into the hands of him who lent her to me for a short time. Yet the struggles of nature and yearnings of affection towards her, were strong, very strong at times; but I trust I can rejoice that the will of God is done, and hope ere long

to greet her on that peaceful shore where parting will be known no more.

> "Prepare me, Lord, for thy right hand,
> Then come the welcome day,
> Come death and some celestial band
> To bear my soul away."
> "Then shall I see thy lovely face
> With strong immortal eyes;
> And feast upon thy unknown grace
> With pleasure and surprise."

Lord, grant me the influences of the Holy Spirit that I may be led in a right path, for without thee I can do nothing acceptable in thy sight.

July 13.—Sabbath day. As my companion is absent to a remote part of the County, there is no meeting near our dwelling. May the influences and comforts of the Holy Spirit be his, with all the whole Israel of God this day. O that the ministers of Christ may stand between a living God and dead sinners in reality. What responsibility rests upon them! Well might the Apostle Paul say, "Who is sufficient for these things?" Their trials, O how great and diversified—particularly pastors of churches! but yet how sweet their comforts, when they can see the increase of their Redeemer's Kingdom. Many ministers and people, I trust, are worshipping God in spirit and in truth, through the wide extended globe; but alas, how many, have I reason to fear, are too much like myself, living beneath their privileges, not purified from earth, —their earth-born thoughts. Surely, when I am made to feel the force of words like the following, I ought to be on the alert:

> "O if my Lord would come and meet,
> My soul would stretch her wings in haste;
> Fly fearless through death's iron gate,
> Nor feel the terrors as she passed."

Precious Saviour, if thou art about to remove me hence, stir me up to greater diligence in obeying all thy commandments, and may my thoughts be more conversant with my great and last change, and the need of being in actual readiness to step over Jordan, that my lamp may be trimmed and in bright burning.

August 7.—Am yet the spared monument of God's mercy. enjoying a good degree of health while many around me are called into eternity. Last Sabbath an esteemed christian relative was interred in the silent tomb; she had been lingering with consumption for some time; her life was one of exemplary piety and usefulness; without doubt she has entered into peace; now her happy spirit is at rest, blessing God for the most distressing visitations while here on earth. O that I were more disposed to follow her in my imagination and meditation into that pure region, where this wicked heart will no more disturb the settled rest. Forbid, mighty God, that I should be impatient to follow her, fearing that I may have some wrong views in it; but may I be looking for the glorious appearing of my great God and Saviour, in humble submission to thy will. O that the graces of the Spirit may be more fully communicated to my immortal soul! O that I could realize more sensibly the worth of souls!

October 7.—What shall I render unto the Lord for all his benefits? he has again made me the mother of a fine son, and after a continued scene of suffering from a broken breast, I am now enjoying a good degree of health, though not fully recovered from the
128 latter. Here again (as well as every day), are my obligations renewed to devote myself afresh to God; but what a strange commixture am I of heaven, earth, and hell! I want to be useful, not only in temporal things but spiritual, and yet am shrinking from duty. Lord, grant that as I have desired (in a particular manner through my late confinement, which I trust I was enabled to endure with patience and some degree of resignation), my graces may not be only revived but added unto, that I may be enabled to go forward in the strength of the Lord of Hosts and be harnessed to the battle before me. O for heavenly wisdom to guide my feet, that I may not have a name to live and yet be dead. Lord purge me from dead works to serve thee the living God, that I may know what is duty and be able to perform it.

October 26.—

"My soul with various tempests toss'd,
Her fairest hopes and projects cross'd,
Sees every day new straits attend,
And wonders where the scene will end.
Through this wide wilderness I roam,
Far distant from my blessed home;
My earthly joys are from me torn
And oft an absent God I mourn.
Is this, dear Lord, that thorny road
Which leads us to the mount of God?
Are these the toils thy people know,
While in the wilderness below?
'Tis even so, thy faithful love
Doth all thy children's graces prove;
'Tis thus our pride and self must fall,
That Jesus may be all in all."

The above lines are truly descriptive of the state of my mind for several days. I feel the billows swell, and in darkness and distress do not seek my Saviour through the floods as I ought to, or as I sometimes feel a desire to. My nature would ask for smooth sailing to heaven, but it cannot be so. O that these inbred lusts and corruptions, which so perplex me, may be slain, that I may once more enjoy the light of Immanuel's countenance.

"O Lord the pilot's part perform,
And guide and guard me through the storm;
Defend me from each threatening ill,
Control the waves, say, peace, be still."

I have found the 62nd Psalm very comforting. 129

November 9.—After an absence of nearly five months, I was permitted this day to tread the earthly courts of the Most High, and hear a doctrinal discourse by my companion from these words, "But we are bound to give thanks alway to God for you brethren beloved of the Lord, because, &c. &c."—2 Thess. 2, 13. I think I can say the Gospel, the discriminating truths of the Gospel, were sweet to my soul.

"O for a heart to praise my God,
A heart from sin set free;
A heart that always feels thy blood
So freely shed for me." 130

I do hope the work of sanctification is going on in my soul, however depraved I am by sin, and alas, too much under its influence, when it disturbs the serenity of my mind and leads the rising passions of nature to irreconciliation at the dealings of Jehovah with me. I can say with a dear saint, "It is no easy thing to bring the like of me to reach the glory of heaven."

January 20, 1835.—Since writing another year has closed, and a new one has ushered in upon me. Such was my peculiar situation that I scarcely had time to think about it, and without doubt a proper disposition was wanting; but when I for one moment reviewed what the Lord has brought me through during the year, I was led again to exclaim as at a former period,

"Look back my soul, the Lord has been thy friend,
He's brought the last year's troubles to an end;
Then what's to come, Lord give me strength to bear,
And at thy feet to cast my every care."

O that I could more freely make a full surrender of myself and all my concerns to my God, and be willing to be at his disposal! This I find harder to do than formerly, though I have been called to pass through enough to wean me from earth; it must be owing to the carnality of my mind, whereas to be spiritually minded is life and peace. Were it not that God is good, a compassionate long-suffering God, I could have no hope. May the present year bring me nearer to the foot of the cross, that I may be led in that way that will glorify God and be beneficial to my fellow creatures.

February 1.—Another month has rolled away, and still have to lament my distance from God, notwithstanding all the means of grace I am favored with. A week ago to-day I was permitted to enter the sanctuary for public worship; I think in some small degree I felt the need of a worshipping spirit; it being our communion season, I felt to mourn over my unfitnesss for that solemn ordinance, but could say, I trust without presumption, "Behold God is my salvation." Bow this stubborn will, precious Jesus, and bring me into greater nearness to thee.

April 27.—Although I have to complain of much stupidity, yet I do feel at times that the Lord is good and gracious, or I, (that has experienced so much of the Lord's kindness in various ways and yet dares to rebel,) should not have a being on his footstool. I have of late felt much the necessity of resignation, patience and meekness, having had some severe trials in which I have needed the graces of the Holy Spirit, and indeed without them I should be but a sounding brass and tinkling cymbal. I have thought much on this passage, "Cleanse your hands, ye sinners, and purify your hearts, ye double-minded." Lord make bare thine arm, and strip and search me, and purify me unto thyself, and make me willing to be humbled. O make me prayerful.

May 31.—Unnumbered have been the changes since I last wrote, even within my own notice. The Lord is visiting his people with sickness, and in two instances in this vicinity the arrows of death have been felt,—one a very sudden death: an esteemed christian of the Presbyterian demonination, went to meeting last Sabbath, and on Thursday was conveyed to the narrow house of the tomb. There are others in a precarious situation, valuable friends, and this rebellious heart of mine cries, "forbear, thou mighty conqueror." The Lord has also laid me down upon a bed of sickness for a week, and raised me up again; it was a severe attack of the scarlet fever; but the stroke was light and fewer than my crimes. I think I feel to say, "The sufferings of the present time are not worthy to be compared with the glory that shall be revealed; but I greatly fear it has not as yet been sanctified, though it has given me a greater disrelish for the world, and I hope some desires to arise to newness of life. O for an overwhelming sense of divine things in this time of visitation, as well as all my life through, and this will lead me to view my vileness in a proper light.

July 31.—Although surrounded with company and confusion, I trust I feel the force of truth delivered in its faithfulness (I think) to-day by my companion from these words—"Neither is there salvation in any other," &c. Second text, "Now we live, if ye stand fast in the Lord." The latter discourse in particular exposed my errors. "Cleanse thou me from secret faults," precious Immanuel, and give me more love to thee, that it may crucify me to the world. O make bare thine arm, and cause thy work to advance in spite of earth and hell.

August 30.—Sabbath evening. My companion being absent to-day among a branch of the Church on the Mountain, I attended a prayer meeting; it proved interesting to me, in some small degree, but I well know the cause why it was not more so; my own state of mind is deplorable,—so much inactivity prevails,—so little as I ought to be. Oh, when shall that glad day arrive when I with all the members of this vine shall be roused to a weighty sense of our responsibility to our Maker and our Redeemer,—when our hearts shall burn with love to Jesus and one another, and all unkind feelings be removed as the leaven of former difficulties? A yearly meeting is expected to be attended to in this region shortly; may it be the beginning of good days among us!

October 4.—The anticipated meeting has taken place a week since, being held two and a half days, in which time there were six sermons preached at the Meeting House, with exhortations, prayers and praise (evening meetings elsewhere); the whole proceedings were of an interesting character. At the close of the meeting a fresh impulse was given, we can but think it was the work of the Spirit; such confessions of past transgressions among Ministers cannot be the work of proud nature. It was indeed a melting time. [The last sermon was preached by Father Theodore S. Harding from Ephesians 5, 25—27. His topics were, the internal, external, and eternal glory of the Church. The "doctrine dropped like the rain; the speech distilled as the dew, as the small rain upon the tender herb, and as the showers upon the grass": the effect was most powerful, as above remarked.—W. C.] I was led to exclaim, what cannot a God of sovereign power and love effect upon his creatures? but alas I did not feel that self-abhorrence that I want to. O to be more childlike, more willing to come to the feet of my friends and enemies! Not until there is such a feeling among us as brethren shall we arise to newness of life, I fear. The Lord has promised that his word shall not return unto him void; may it be the case in this instance; indeed we cannot but think it will.

November 1.—Sabbath day. Duty required me to remain at home to-day, but I feel so little exercise of mind upon the all-important concerns of eternity, that I am as it were a cypher in the Church and in the world, as it regards the life and power of religion. I can do my part in domestic duties to my satisfaction, at times, but seldom or ever do I fill that place in my family or elsewhere in performing those spiritual duties that are enjoined upon me, in the word of God and by the articles of the Church. I trust it affects my heart now while writing, that I am so sinful by nature and practice, and thereby dishonor my precious Redeemer so much. O for quickening and renewing grace, that will enable me to rise superior to the transitory things of time! And although my hands are necessarily much engaged at the present time, may my affections be spiritualized, and the love of God so possess my breast, that my right hand may scarcely know what the left doeth. May all the laborers in the vineyard be assisted this day, to honor God and benefit immortal souls.

November 16.—Many, very many, have been my privileges this fortnight past, in attending meetings; but alas, how have I to complain of the poor improvement I have made of them!—sometimes from drowsiness, and oftener from a stupid mind. Yesterday I had interesting interviews with some of the sisters, and to-day have felt some degree of solemnity upon my mind, viewing faintly the shortness of time, and our responsibilities to God as finite creatures. I was not privileged with attending meeting to-day, owing to the indisposition of myself and child, but hope I tried to improve the opportunities at home for reading and reflection; but this wretched, deceitful heart, and wandering mind, will scarcely allow me to stretch a thought towards God or anything good.

December 13.—Another year has nearly closed, and while I am spared many have exchanged worlds, and among the number is a beloved friend of mine, a brother's wife, who departed this life a
131 week ago to-morrow. It may truly be said of her that she lived beloved, and died lamented; but in her death we hope, in her last sickness, which was consumption, she was brought to yield herself, her husband and children, into the hands of God, to do what seemeth him good, (although not rejoicing as some are favored.) Yet there evidently appeared an humble trust and reliance upon the strong arm of Jehovah; she appeared perfectly willing to meet death, and we hope she is now spending her first Sabbath of eternal rest around the blissful throne of God; if such be the case our loss is her gain. May her death be the means of the spiritual life of the surviving husband (and friends, if it be the will of the Lord), that it may ere long be manifest that he is a living stone in the building of our God! May all the changes this frail, sinful worm meets with, tend to stir up her mind to pure devotion, that she may not have a name to live and yet be dead! O Saviour, give her heart-searching exercises, that she may know how the case stands between God and her immortal soul.

January 10, 1836.—Sabbath day. My frail life is yet lengthened ont to witness the commencement of another year; but alas, alas, how do I enter upon it? the same dull careless creature that I too generally am. O when shall that glad day arrive when my captive soul shall be set free, and made like the Chariot of Aminadib? As the last year has passed, and left the Zion of our God in trying circumstances in many places, may this year be one in which the Lord shall right up his people, and bring in his precious jewels into his blessed fold.

February 14.—Since writing last I have experienced much of the Lord's protecting care and mercy, having been a distance from home and escaped many dangers, that I was exposed to; but ah what poor returns do I make to my Heavenly Father for all his gracious dealings with me! I am yet a cumberer of the ground, yet living beneath my privileges. O God, purge and purify me by whatever means thou seest fit; only give me to view thine hand in it, and be reconciled thereto. I want to feel time to be short and the necessity of being actively engaged in the cause of the divine Redeemer while the day lasts. O for a weighty, an overpowering sense of eternal realities, that it might drive me constantly to a throne of grace to seek supplies of wisdom and grace for every time of need; for the promise is, "ask, and ye shall receive." May I ask aright!

March 12.—Sabbath day. Duty often requires me to be absent from the house of God; but I think I can say without dissembling before God, that I would always prefer going when my health would admit of it; but alas my gospel opportunities are too much abused. I feel sometimes a great struggle between duties spiritual and temporal, lest the latter should too much interfere with the former, which I am convinced does take place, and leaves my soul lifeless and barren, while the things of time and sense are often pursued with avidity.

May 15.—Since writing last a variety of changes have transpired within my own observation. My youngest child has been brought low by sickness, and his situation was precarious, but the Lord has in mercy raised him up again. In this visitation I have felt the necessity of "rejoicing in hope, being patient in tribulation." But I am so far from being what I ought to be, that I am but a cumberer of the ground; but I have felt of late to enter into the house of the Lord with thanksgiving and some degree of praise, after a season of cold winter. Naturally, how delightful is spring; just so with regard to our spiritual concerns, after the Church has had a long wintry season, how pleasing to see the hearts of christians warmed and revived, by the enlivening influences of the spirit of God. Such, I hope, is the case with this little vine, while the Lord is pouring out of his Spirit in the region near us, marvellously. We begin to feel desirous that the good work may be extended unto us and farther. O may we all be enabled to wait upon God, and to be of good courage, for he will strengthen our hearts!

June 6.—At our last conference we had an addition of two to the Church of God; it was pleasing to visit the banks of Jordan again, after an absence of seventeen months; one of them was a young man who married a pious girl two years since; her christian deportment had much influence upon his mind, but being of a hasty temper, it required the powerful influences of the Spirit to overcome him; yet he was brought to bow, and we hope in such a manner as will ever make him feel his dependance on God to bring forth fruit, and that it may remain. The Lord is still carrying on his work to the West of this, and we hope and trust it will extend unto us, and among all the Churches; there appears to be a spirit of supplication given unto many. I want to feel more of it in my own soul, that I may feel the worth of souls, and the great necessity of living anew for God. I would like to feel the force of the following words at all times—

> "My soul, come meditate the day,
> And think how near it stands,
> When thou must quit this house of clay,
> And fly to unknown lands."

I think I do feel to set to my seal that God is true; he has so wonderfully supported me in times that are past, and has assured me of my support in time to come, that I am ready to say, I can praise him for what is past, and trust him for what is to come. I sincerely hope I have known something of the meaning of these words of late, "Thou wilt keep him in perfect peace whose mind is stayed upon thee." O I trust I am not deceived in it; but O may it continue and increase, for I stand in much need of wisdom and grace to guide me through the erring paths of life.

June 26.—A prayer meeting is again attended to, at the Meeting House, owing to the absence of the pastor to attend the Association; a goodly number are collected here, and no doubt throughout the world, where there is a house for God, the day being fine. May the good Shepherd feed and refresh their souls! I have recently been reading a book,—"The art of divine contentment": it is a blessed work indeed,—it has led me to hope that I knew something of its meaning. I am also perusing another work (called "The Mother at Home"), a book of instruction in very deed. O may I be enabled more and more to evince that wisdom
132 and prudence that the Bible and other books point out. I feel at times my great deficiency, and long to be made what I ought to be. I daily feel the necessity of gratitude for the unnumbered mercies and blessings of the Lord, that he is smiling so far in the season upon the Creation. O how verdant do the fields and trees look, and the little warbling hosts sing forth their Creator's praise. May those lesser streams only lead my soul up to the fountain more!

July 23.—Three weeks ago to-morrow was safely delivered of a lovely little daughter; the Lord's goodness in this instance I feel (and O may I ever feel more sensibly), is not to be disregarded nor forgotten. I desire to thank and praise him, and to devote 133
the life which he has made his care to his glory. He has, I trust, enabled me to rise above my spiritual enemies so far that they have not been suffered to molest me with murmuring or repining, and having hard thoughts of God for the manner in which I have been brought so far on my journey through life. I also desire to be grateful for this, for I find the wide difference between looking on the bright side and on the dark.

July 24.—Sabbath day. Yesterday was conference; three persons related the dealings of God with their souls, and to-day are immersed in the liquid stream. A good degree of union appears to be reviving in the Church; prayer meetings are well attended, and a goodly number unite at a throne of grace. May this be only the beginning of good days among us! for my own part I want to have and feel more quickening grace to arm me for the duties of life. I think I in some measure feel that my own strength is but perfect weakness. O for a deep sense of obligation to God, and a greater confidence in him, that I may surrender myself and my all afresh into his hands, and feel safe under the shadow of his wings. I am distressed to-day with the fear that my late exercises, as it regards submission, are a delusion. O search and try me, Holy Father, and lead me in the way thou wouldst have me go. A host of immortal souls are assembled at the house of worship near us; may my companion be influenced by the pure spirit of the Gospel, that he may preach the unsearchable riches of Christ to his dying fellow men. May all the Ministers and people of God be led by his spirit now and evermore, and that will lead us all to feel for poor sinners, posting the downward road to everlasting ruin.

September 2.—Many, very many have been my privileges since I last wrote; but God has in his wise Providence appointed me another privation—the absence of my companion for seven or eight weeks, going as a messenger from this Association to the Baptist Associations in the State of Maine. I think I have acquiesced in 134
it, and hope I shall henceforward, for as the poet observes—

> "Good when he gives, supremely good—
> Nor less when he denies;
> Even crosses from his sovereign hand
> Are blessings in disguise."

I have always found that the Lord never removed any temporal good but what it was more than made up with substantial good. His cheering and supporting presence I have often found to be my stay and staff. O may it be the case in this visitation, for surely I need the plough of the Gospel to more fully root out the weeds of corruption in this perverse, slothful heart of mine. "O that my head were waters, and my eyes a fountain of tears, that I might weep day and night" for my own sins and those of others too! May the good Spirit of our God attend his servant on his journey and remove the fear of man from him.

September 26.—Sabbath evening. I have been highly favored
this day in hearing the Gospel dispensed by a young Brother—
McLearn—upon the subject of being careful to maintain good
135 works; a practical discourse indeed, and much needed; may it have
some good effect; but O I have to say with the poet—

"My soul lies cleaving to the dust;
Lord, give me life divine;
From vain desires and every lust,
136 Turn off these eyes of mine."

October 2.—Sabbath evening. Heard the subject of union
among brethren discoursed upon to-day by a young Brother—Por-
137 ter—the inferences drawn were very plain and true. The Lord is
very kind to us in sending his messengers when our pastor is absent. O that we might make a right improvement of those unmerited blessings. A mysterious Providence to human view has afflicted a brother of mine in the flesh and in the fellowship of the Spirit too, with a paralytic stroke (living a distance of thirty-five miles from me); he is, we hope, recovering from it. But O methinks what a loud call, should the Son of Man come at an unexpected hour and find us sleeping. O that his soul may experience nearness to God in this trying hour. Stir me up, blessed Lord, and all thy blood-bought children, to a deep consideration of our duty while passing from this to a world of spirits, that whatsoever our hands find to do, we may do it with all our might, that we may be divested of self and of a worldly spirit and be adorned with a spiritual mind that will enable us to look at things not seen, as being eternal, and to bear in mind that we must soon account to God for our transactions while here in this militant state. I feel to-night as if I wanted to be consecrated to God, that I might in some way be useful to my fellow creatures. May an abiding sense of this exercise my heart, that I may have no rest till I put on self-denial, take up my cross, and engage in some noble object for the welfare of those around me. May the corruptions of my wicked deceitful heart be slain, and a proper qualification granted me for whatever is before me.

October 30.—Thanks and praise is due to my Heavenly Father for returning the partner of my joys and sorrows for me and others to enjoy his society, and more than that, I hope, to be the means of comforting the saints and sounding an alarm in the ears and to the hearts of some poor perishing sinners. O God, condescend to make his ministry more and more effectual (whether we live to see it or not)! May we often plead thy promise, "My word shall not return unto me void": his visit was beneficial to his own soul, and I trust honoring to God, for unless that was the case it was of but little use for him to go. At our last conference, a few days since, and at the last communion, on Sabbath, the Lord was pleased to grant me a ray of light in my soul, that cast a veil over every earthly object, I do sincerely think, and led me to feel that I was personally accountable to God for all my conduct; and the solemn realities of eternity seemed very near, but only seen through a glass darkly. I desire to be thankful for this refreshing gale, that inspired me with fresh desires to be up and doing while the day lasts. O that I may not only watch opportunities when they offer, but seek them, of being useful to my fellow creatures, that my moderation may be known to all men in disposition and earthly desires.

November 2.—While contemplating to-day, on the possibility that I had never properly accepted Christ upon the terms of the Gospel, I was unexpectedly cheered with these lines:

> "The soul that on Jesus hath leaned for repose,
> I will not, I will not desert to his foes;
> That soul, though all hell should endeavor to shake,
> I'll never, no never, no never, forsake."

Yes, I think I can truly say it is unto him alone I can look for salvation; but alas, I do not give up myself, my all, to be consecrated to his service as I ought. But I can say with a pious saint, that has gone home to glory, "The older I grow, the more I feel the necessity of living nearer to God." O for the power of quickening grace to animate me in my christian life!

December 18.—Sabbath evening. Had the privilege to-day of hearing the Gospel preached from these words—"And it shall come to pass that the great trumpet shall be blown, and they shall come which were ready to perish in the land of Assyria." O that the application of this passage may be correct, as we may hereafter discover, that many perishing sinners may hear so as to live. The Church in this place have concluded to have a protracted meeting, to commence next Saturday evening, not only for our own edification, but for the benefit of perishing souls yet out of the ark of
safety. O may it not be in vain,—that God's Ministers may come 138
here, laden with the good news of salvation to precious souls; send, Lord, by whomsoever thou wilt send, only let there be a manifestation af thy mercy and our hearts shall rejoice! O make it truly manifest—"For the oppression of the poor, and for the

sighing of the needy, now will I arise, saith the Lord." May all thy children possess a deeper spirit of piety, that earnest supplication may be resorted to.

December 30.—The protracted meeting is now going on; the results, so far, are somewhat encouraging; it is to be continued two or three days longer. It will be a week to-morrow since it commenced, and we doubt not but seed will be sown, which will ere long spring up to everlasting life. Five Ministers have attended the most part of their time, and their preaching and exhortations are very alarming and powerful; many persons having had hopes they were christians seem much stirred up, and some unconverted souls appear anxious about their future state; but yet there appears too much coldness and insensibility among the Church. My own heart is not warmed and led out with such longing desires as the case requires, but still feel much anxiety that God would exert his own Omnipotent power and lay the aspiring rebel low.

January 8, 1837.—Another year has rolled into eternity, and a God of love and mercy has permitted this poor worm to enter upon a new one under favorable circumstances, surrounded with every common mercy which a contented mind can wish for; her body in health, and those around her; but though there is the same fulness of spiritual blessings treasured up in the Lord Jesus Christ for my needy soul, yet I am not so active in seeking supplies as need requires. O how precious to feel and say—

> "Lord, we are come to seek supplies,
> And drive our wants away."

How much have I to deplore the misimprovement of my time and advantages the past year (as well as all my life through)! O that I may be more roused up to action the present year, if my life is spared, be more engaged to promote the glory of God and the good of my fellow creatures. May the Zion of God in this place (as well as many others) receive fresh strength from God, to be active in every good word and work. The above meeting has, we trust, been instrumental of good to a number of souls; three or four seem deeply impressed. How many solemn considerations there are to arouse every dormant feeling of the soul! O may it truly be the case with me!

January 20.—A number of deaths have taken place of late, within my hearing. One man dropped dead in the street, leaving a wife and several children to bemoan their loss; this is a most solemn warning to the living; surely it may be said, "in the midst of life we are in death." Oftentimes the awful realities of another world seem very near, and the solemnities of passing through the dark valley and shadow of death are in a degree full

in my view. I know that if I am a child of God death is only the
gate to endless joy, but still the great importance of being actually
ready is what appears to me to be of the utmost importance. O
may I have my spirit so awed with a weighty sense of my accountability to God, that trifles may not find a place in my heart ; may
the soul that never dies, so absorb my thoughts that I may view
my fellow creatures around me in their true state, hastening to
the impartial bar of God, there to give an account for the deeds
done in the body, and not fail to warn them of the danger of
appearing there without the robe of Christ's righteousness. "Take
up the cross, despise the shame," are words that often come into
my mind. I do feel at times lately as though I wanted to go without the camp, bearing the reproach of the despised Nazarene, and
in some way to be useful to my dying fellow men. A Sabbath
School has for some length of time much occupied my mind. I
have hitherto felt that I had so many other duties to perform (too
many of them temporal), that I could not attend to it, but I feel
disposed now to try to surmount those difficulties (hoping the Lord
will provide a way for me, if my motives are pure), and to cast in
my mite in such a laudable undertaking; but when I look at my
want of proper qualifications I am ready to shrink from the important work of instructing little immortals in the things pertaining
to godliness. O God, stir up thy children to view the importance 139
of this most noble object, that has effected so much good in thy
hands throughout the world. May we all feel more and more our
dependance upon thee, and if we can say "Whom have I in heaven but thee, and there is none upon earth that I desire beside
thee"—O help us to be more actively engaged for the promotion
of thy glory. O give us right views and motives, which are the
dictates of thine Holy Spirit.

January 22.—Sabbath evening. Yesterday this Church had quite an interesting conference. There appears to be some waking up among the members to their own spiritual wants and the wants of others. Lord, increase the love and zeal of us all! May we truly exemplify what the Apostle enjoins, "Be ye followers of God as dear children, and walk in love, even as Christ hath loved us and given himself for us." This has been rather a day of trial with me. I can say with David, "My soul melteth for heaviness, strengthen thou me according unto thy word; I will run the way of thy commandments when thou shalt enlarge my heart." It was not my privilege to attend public worship to-day, but this did not make the trial, wholly; my proud deceitful heart aims to shun the cross in many ways. When, dear Lord, shall this rebellious, stubborn will, be brought to bow more fully to thy righteous commands? An inmate of our family was buried in baptism to-day,—

a young woman that has had hope in God for three years or more, but for want of strong faith and decision for God, has conformed to the world (as she expresses herself,) in a manner unbecoming the christian character. May her future life truly evince her sorrow for the past, and her zeal to glorify God henceforward; may her influence be of a most salutary kind wherever she goes. As she has friends and connections at a distance of a worldly character, may she not shun the cross, when meeting them. Here again I ought to be a nursing mother, particularly when I reflect that my influence is to be felt upon future generations in a religious
140 and moral point of view. O Saviour, grant me strength equal to my day.

January 29.—Sabbath evening. It was my privilege to hear the word of the Lord dispensed to-day by my companion from these words—"Let thy work appear unto thy servants, and thy glory unto their children, &c." It was truly interesting to those who stand in a capacity to receive the truths of God, in the love of them; whoever is willing to be reproved by the faithful preaching of the cross, thinks no admonitions too close; such I would fain hope was the case with all the members of the Church at least to-day. How responsible the situation of being an under shepherd (so many capricious humors to suit)! but he that is disposed to seek the honor of God and not of man, must expect many frowns. My feelings and trials are often indescribable in reflecting on our situation; not that we have more trials than other Ministers and their families, have, nor so many; but the situation is peculiarly trying when the mind is not borne above it. O may we never be given up to sinful despondency on any matter. O for more of a spirit of prayer and strong faith, that we may believe that God will yet revive his work amongst us.

March 12.—Sabbath evening. Heard my companion speak from these words—"God is faithful, who will not suffer you to be tempted above what ye are able, but will with the temptation make a way for your escape." I felt the subject to be adapted to the state of my mind for some time past, in a peculiar manner, but I do not see so clearly the way of escape as I have done in days gone by. I feel the necessity of more of the strength of Israel's God to be made perfect in my weakness, so that I may be able to do duties, to bear burthens, and resist temptations. O that God would quicken my perception and grant me clear discriminating views of divine truth, that I may have true spiritual discernment to distinguish between gracious exercises and counterfeit; and O may I be led to deep contrition for past offences. Lord, I want more conformity to thee and thy blessed ways, to arm me more for the duties of life in this state of trial. May heavenly wisdom direct all my future steps, that as I have had much forgiven I may love much, and come boldly to a throne of grace, that I may obtain mercy and find grace to help in time of need.

April 3.—I trust I am feeling the force of the following words
in some degree—" But it is good for me to draw near unto God."
For some time past, have felt renewed desires to awake from the
state of torpor that I have been in for months and for years; have
felt more determinations to make sacrifices of worldly pursuits, for
I plainly see that worldly ambition is taking the lead of spiritual.
How many christians are wearing themselves out in the service of
the world, to heap up wealth and honor, that is fading in its use,
and doing nothing, comparatively speaking, for the honor of God,
and worse than nothing, for " they that will be rich fall into many
hurtful snares." O for a lighting down of thy power among christians who have not just views of the religion of Jesus, to crucify
them to the world and mortify the deeds of the body. I have
already found the beneficial effects of reading the Bible and other
valuable works, but yet, owing to a variety of cares and the duty
I am trying to aim at, the training up my children in some measure
in the way they should go, I am prevented from enjoying such
repasts, or the pleasure of retirement, as I would desire. I some- 141
times feel as if I never wanted any more worldly things to attend
to, but to be given up and devoted to a missionary life; but I am
but little acquainted with the treachery of my heart, I fear. The
more I discover pride and unbelief and aim at the opposite, the
more the enemy sends his fiery darts; he will try to worry " whom
he can't devour:" well, let him worry, if I am only one of those
he cannot devour; God is more than a match for him and for all
the rest of my enemies.

April 18.—Was again permitted to enter the sanctuary and
heard from my companion the accountability of the stewardship
spoken upon; a solemn and impressive discourse; were we anything
but stocks and stones we should feel it. My soul has been tossed
with various temptations of late; I can discover pride under many
forms, and the awful depravity of my nature shows itself in many
ways. Last evening when reflecting on the buffetings of Satan, I
was somewhat consoled with these words—" Behold the Lamb of
God which taketh away the sin of the world." I think they never 142
appeared so beautiful before.

April 23.—Through the goodness of God I have had a little refreshing to-day and yesterday, but particularly to-day, when these words were spoken from by my companion—" O Lord, I am oppressed; undertake for me." Although I only heard the first part expounded, it was deeply interesting to me, and I doubt not it was so to many others. May poor sinners feel the awful oppression they labor under; the power and tyranny of sin and Satan is hard bondage. I had for a length of time felt oppressed in body and mind, and it was a very seasonable time to me. Felt very loth to be absent when the bright side was brought to view, but the indisposition of my children prevented me, together with a wish that others should share in the provisions of the Gospel. O may the provisions of God's house be more abundantly blessed, and her poor be satisfied with bread! But my exercises are so transient, that I have many reasons to doubt whether they are of the right kind. Purge me, precious Jesus, from filthiness of flesh and spirit, and let melting and stripping work take place with me, and a proper reconciliation to the ways and means to accomplish it. O Lord, undertake for me, and all thy tempted, tried followers, and if any souls are seeking thee sorrowing in this congregation, lead them to thy finished work for acceptance with thee. Help all to wrestle more perseveringly against the powers of darkness, that beholding the excellencies of thy character we may be changed into the same image from glory to glory. O Lord, revive thy works in the midst of the years; remember mercy, make thy children more watchful and prayerful.

May 9.—My mind, O how dormant in considering the one thing needful! as it is again necessarily involved in much care, owing to the absence of my companion for three weeks, who left rather unexpectedly for Prince Edward Island (with another ministering brother, namely J. E. Bill), to see to the affairs of Christ's kingdom; may their mission be owned and blessed of God, that it may
143 be the means of settling difficulties instead of increasing them. O when will the pure Spirit of our God exercise the hearts of his dear children, (yes, dear-bought by his own blood,) that their hearts may be knit together in love? O Lord, support thy sinking cause in many places, while thou art making marvellous displays of thy power in other parts of thy vineyard.

May 14.—Sabbath evening. Heard a young Brother—Rand—preach this afternoon from these words—"Whatsoever is born of
144 God overcometh the world." The practical part was the subject; O may it be truly sanctified to the congregation. I feel to say with an eminent saint, "It appears to me I have been asleep all my days"—as though I had only gone round the margin of God's works and my own misery and helplessness. O that I might from henceforth wake up to acts of new obedience and devotion; may I strive more against the workings of sin and Satan. Had some disposition this morning to examine myself; hope it was profitable, though I could not find that I had that love to God I ought to have, yet I could not find it in my heart to hate a God of spotless purity. My mind has been in a good degree solemn all day, and

feel a longing desire to be more Christ-like, to be actively engaged in his blessed cause.

June 4.—Sabbath evening. The Lord has mercifully returned my companion again to preach the word of truth and soberness unto us. Text to-day—"Knowing the terror of the Lord, we persuade men." A solemn and impressive discourse, urging motives upon us to induce us to live a life of piety. I think, if my heart does not greatly deceive me, I feel more and more the importance of it, and to have more of the Spirit of Christ. I read, "If any man have not the Spirit of Christ, he is none of his." O how much I need his powerful influence!

June 14.—The Lord has again visited us with a light affliction,
the sickness of my little son; he is a very delicate child, and the
slightest cold subjects him to disease on the lungs; his case has
many times seemed almost hopeless, and in this instance symptoms
were alarming. A kind Saviour has in some good degree restored 145
him to health. My exercises through this scene have not been
very comforting. I have felt something of Job's mind—"Wherefore is it that thou contendest with me?" But I tried to check
this, for his strokes are few and light to what my crimes are, and
merit. I would desire to feel gratitude to God for his kindness,
without selfishness. I had anticipated attending the Association
at Yarmouth, but the indisposition of my child seemed to deny this
until these two days past; still if it is not the Lord's will that I
should go, I desire to be still; but whether I go or stay, I hope I
may enjoy some of the shinings of God's face, for I think I can
safely say, nothing looks so desirable. Meeting with friends, and 146
christian friends too, will be rendered doubly interesting if we can
feel the weight and importance of being in the exercise of true
grace and a lively faith, glorifying God in every movement. O
that I may have a spirit of prayer, wherever I am, that God would
pour out of his Spirit upon Churches and people, that we may see
God in every thing.

July 4.—A kind Saviour has permitted me to perform the anticipated journey, and returned me with my companion in health and safety. Found our dear family enjoying much better health than when I left them. My debt of gratitude is greatly augmented: I may well "call upon my soul and all that is within me to praise the name of the Lord and forget not all his benefits," not only in temporal things but spiritual. I trust my soul was more than once satisfied as with marrow and fatness; the Gospel of the grace of God was never more sweet to me than during this session; but when I realize what a heart-searching God has and does view in me—how much sin—I feel as if it was almost presumption to hope that I had gracious exercises; but if the season has a salutary effect upon me in having an influence upon all my conduct, what reason shall I have to bless God for the precious privilege! It was indeed a precious season to many souls; there were upwards of thirty Ministers present.

July 8.—Sabbath evening. Had the privilege of hearing the
Gospel preached in the fore part of the day by a son of my companion, who in early life, at the age of sixteen, embraced the cross
of Christ, and three years after entered more extensively into the
work of God, the ministry of reconciliation being committed unto
147 him. O Lord, make him an active and useful servant in thy cause.
His text, "Come, for all things are now ready." My compan-
ion's text—"But the God of all grace, after that ye have suffered awhile, make you perfect, establish, strengthen, and settle you." The duty of prayer was much insisted on. The Sabbath School has at length commenced, but we hope to have a still greater ingathering to it. My adamantine heart needs to be melted to view the importance of this and every other work, where the value of the soul is concerned. O for a view by faith of the work of redemption!

July 18.—A regular Sabbath School was formed last Sabbath by the exertions of the beloved Isaac (the son spoken of above), and I consented, I hope not altogether thoughtlessly (although I do not feel those vivid impressions that I did in the winter), to become a teacher, and to my surprise a class of young women fell to my lot, those for whom I have felt deep anxiety in time past, and several of whom have had their minds seriously exercised, and three or four entertain hope in the pardoning blood of the Saviour. May this training be the means of bringing them into the fold of
God! But O, how shall I, who am but a child, be able to instruct
148 those interesting females in the pathway of life? I feel indeed
(I think) that I can do nothing to profit without divine influence. O that I felt this still more powerfully, to lead me continually to seek for a spirit of prayer, and to watch and pray with all diligence!

August.—Sabbath afternoon. Had the privilege of hearing
a Presbyterian Minister deliver a discourse from John I. 11th,
149 12th, 13th verses. It was truly evangelical. Our Sabbath School
is prospering, we trust, although I do not feel as I ought to, or want to. I want more spirituality of mind, so that I might be led fruitfully into the word of God, that as I freely receive, I may freely give, and be the means of affording instructions to those more immediately under my charge. O may we all be enabled to use the means put into our hands in the fear of God, that God's children may be enabled to work more effectually in his vineyard, that our imperfect works may be accepted for Christ's sake. My

own exercises of late have not been very profitable; too mnch unreconciliation prevails. I know I have need of much humbling (yes, very much humbling), but I am not satisfied with the way my God takes with me. O what a base, vile, unholy creature I am, when the God of the Universe has dealt so tenderly with me, and does at times give me to feel that I am adopted into his family; when I am enabled to chide myself and chide down unbelief, I am ready to say,

" O what are all my sufferings here,
If thou but count'st me meet,
With that enraptured host to appear,
And worship at thy feet." 150

September 26.—Such a variety of engagements have fallen to my lot of late, that I had but little time for writing or reading, and alas, too often have neglected bowing the knee at a throne of God's rich grace, through indisposition and fatigue; but I hope the Spirit has made intercession for me with groanings which cannot be uttered, and I sometimes have felt that free uninterrupted intercourse with God was more than everything else beside. Our last Sabbath School lesson has been in some measure useful to me; a part of it was, the two men possessed with devils coming out from among the tombs. The illustration of it by my companion, who superintends the School, led me to view more clearly the legion of devils that is in every human heart. Were it not for the restraining grace of God, how like devils men would act,—and indeed many do—and what a mercy that God undertook our cause, and humbled himself even unto death for our sakes, that he might restore us unto our right mind. Heavenly Father, help me to feel the necessity more and more of being conformed to thee; O for faith and patience to be in exercise!

November 12.—Little did I think when my mind was forcibly struck with the foregoing ideas, that I should have to experience the overwhelming affliction of a child of my companion's being deranged, and in such a degree that were it not for the liking he takes to one of our neighbors who has him completely under his control, we should all be in danger of receiving harsh usage. [He, 151
however, in the kind Providence of God was soon restored to the use of his rational powers.—W. C.] Now is the trial of our faith and patience. And in addition to this severe trial my own little daughter has been brought very low, with inflammation of the lungs, and is now too feeble to raise her head; but we hope her case is favorable, unless she relapses. O that I felt more nearness to God in these trying visitations; but I am sensible that my sins have separated between God and my soul, and that I am now made to feel the smart of the rod. O that it may have its purifying

effect, that I may have true godly sorrow for sin, that will work repentance unto life, may be prostrated in the dust at the feet of my insulted God, and be willing that he should reign and rule. My companion is now preaching for the first time since the foregoing circumstances have so changed. Heavenly Father, grant him strength and grace to bear up above the feelings of human nature.

January 1, 1838.—New Year's Day. My unprofitable life is yet lengthened out, to close another year, and commence a new one under favorable circumstances, considering the many afflicting incidents to us in this short life (my children are not well, but nothing alarming in their case at present.) This day has been appointed as a day of fasting and prayer by the Church: may it indeed be profitable and salutary to all; there is great need of our being more humbled, and the great principles of christianity more fastened upon our minds; I feel myself the need of the love of God dwelling more abundantly in my own heart, to burn up the dross and tin of my corrupt nature, and to enable me to set out anew to win the prize, for I have loitered too long.

January 24.—I have spent much of my time of late in solitude, as it regards the company of mortals, and alas, alas, I blush and am ashamed before God that I have so wickedly departed from him and caused the hidings of his face; and the worst of all is, I do not feel it as I should. I am not awake to the all-important concerns of the soul in the manner I ought to be; no, far, very far am I from it, or I should not be living at this poor dying rate. Even when I had cessation from worldly cares, I had no mind for reflection on those points. O how wretchedly depraved from the crown of the head to the soles of the feet! but notwithstanding all my darkness I desire to trust in God, knowing that it is He that can clear the darkest sky. O may I yet praise Him, who is the health of my countenance. Lord, prepare me for every changing event.

February 18—Sabbath evening. It has not been my privilege to attend upon the public means of grace to-day, and but very little upon the private; my little family takes up my attention so much that I can find but little time for reading, and when the closet is not visited I feel awfully guilty, and more or less guilty when I do, duty is performed in such a lifeless manner. I find it is highly necessary to leave all my trials at the foot of the cross. Some of the trials connected with the pastoral relation have burdened my mind of late; amidst them all may I be enabled to say with the poet—

> "Lord, draw my heart so near to thee,
> While through this world I rove,
> That I may always be
> Transported with thy love."

Be not far from me, O God, for trouble is near. O help me to pray for the outpouring of thy Holy Spirit upon myself, this Church and congregation, that my own heart may be set right, that I may be enabled to plead earnestly for those who appear alienated from their pastor. How long will cold-hearted professors be Achans in the camp, and yet the cause remain undiscovered? 152

April 29.—On the 22nd day of March I was again made the mother of a fine little daughter, and have been mercifully preserved through many dangers since, even when my eldest daughter was very ill. I was carried through it beyond my expectation; 153
although I have heaped up mountains of sins by my continued rebellion, I have to say, what shall I render unto the Lord for all his benefits? O Lord, reconcile me to thy will, and make me humble and mild.

June 1.—My mind is yet low and depressed, mourning at times over my real state and standing, for "unto him that knoweth to do good, and doeth it not, unto him it is sin," and "the thought of foolishness is sin." Then, O how much have I to mourn over and repent of! O that I possessed the grace of repentance, whereby I might find life! I feel so destitute of the fruits of the Spirit, that I am often ready to sink when I view the responsibilities of my situation, the charge of souls, and so much depending, with the blessing of God, upon a mother's influence. I begin to know a little about the mental anguish of a mother's heart. Precious Saviour, abundantly qualify me for the work of training those dear children temporally and spiritually. O remember thy cause in this place, and let the Day-Star arise.

July 14.—Sabbath day. I have again had the privilege of hearing the Gospel preached, but with what dulness and insensibility! O how much do I feel the want of the cheering operations of the Spirit to raise my mind above the affairs of this transitory world! I often adopt the hymn,

> "Come Holy Spirit, heavenly dove,
> With all thy quickening powers, &c." 154

Can I be a child of God, and live at such a distance from my best beloved?

September 22.—Self-righteousness and unbelief cling to me more than I am sensible of, though of late I have sometimes felt to say, "Lord, I believe, help thou mine unbelief." Were I to say that I have no relish for divine things, feel no interest in the prosperity of Zion, I should say wrong. I fear they are not more to me than my meat and drink, or I would often loathe and abstain from food for the enjoyment of them; but I find it difficult to

know exactly the right path; this I know, had I that trust in God
that is necessary, everything would bow to the cross. Those words
almost invariably strike my mind, when tried to know what course
to pursue with my children in the government of their disposition,
155 "This kind cometh not out but by prayer and fasting." The former I am vastly deficient in, but the latter I have not yet made
trial of. When, O when, shall I in this mortal state be thoroughly
drenched in the love of God, to consider my obligations aright, to
devote myself and my all a living sacrifice unto God? Lord, help
me to be more in earnest about my own salvation, and that of
others.

October 29.—Not long since I had the unspeakable privilege
of attending conference meeting, and the next day commemorating
the death and sufferings of the once crucified but now exalted
Lord. I must acknowledge (however far I fell short of being in
a proper frame) the season was refreshing to my soul. I could
almost say, "My beloved is mine, and I am his." Appearances
in the Church are more favorable than for a length of time; the
chastening hand of God has pressed sore upon some of its members, in the sickness and death of their children, and when one
member suffers, they all mourn, and we fondly hope the set time
to favor Zion will soon arrive. This I think would afford me more
156 happiness than anything else on earth. I think I can often adopt
Paul's words to the Philippians—"For God is my record, how
greatly I long after you all in the bowels of Jesus Christ," and
apply it to saint and sinner.

December 20.—Sabbath evening. To-day heard a young
Brother—Beckwith—preach a preparatory sermon previous to the
holding of a series of religious meetings, from these words, "Pre-
157 pare ye the way of the Lord." It really appeared to be well
appropriated to the present arrangement, as the Church have felt
the importance of using some extraordinary means to benefit souls
among us; they have concluded to have another protracted meeting, and have sent for several Ministers to attend. God in his
Providence directed the above named Brother among us a fortnight
since (he is a native of Cornwallis, or of this Province, but has
been absent for several years in the United States); he has been
in a number of revivals, and seems ardently desirous that the work
of God should revive and flourish in this place; he has been
preaching frequently in this place in connection with the pastor, to
very good acceptance, and will continue through the meetings;
but in vain will be the coming of God's Ministers, unless Jesus
comes with them, and opens the hearts of men to receive the word.
There still appears much solemnity upon the minds of many, but
the Church needs a thorough breaking up, or I, as an individual;

it will apply pretty generally, for we are all too much asleep. I feel great need of a spirit of supplication; O that this may be the favored time when God shall make bare his arm, and convert souls to himself, and enable his people to be laborers together with him. "Arise, O God, and plead thine own cause." O may we all feel right and do right.

January 2, 1839.—How can I sufficiently bless and adore the Almighty that has showered salvation down upon precious souls in this place! the results of the meeting have been most favorable; the Church in general is aroused from her slumbers; backsliders are returning; numbers that have indulged hope years gone by, are now making it known publicly, while the stout-hearted sinner is made to bow to the mild sceptre of King Immanuel. A number of the young Ministers have remained among us a week longer; the labors of all seem to be owned and blessed of God. The meetings begin to be powerful. God is manifestly pouring out of his Spirit. "And yet my heart unmoved remains insensible to love or pain." But I would desire to trust in God, as the prophet Isaiah hath declared. I am obliged to be in Martha's place, and I seldom or ever get Mary's. [Our dwelling house being near the Meeting House we necessarily had much company, which unavoidably occupied much of my beloved companion's time and attention; and such was her benevolence that she greatly delighted always in making her friends comfortable.—W. C.] 158

February 23.—Sabbath evening. "Bless the Lord, O my soul, and forget not all his benefits." The Church is coming up out of the wilderness, leaning upon her Beloved: additions are made to her of such as we trust shall be eternally saved. A host have come up to the help of the Lord against the mighty; nearly one hundred have put on Christ publicly. 159

March 31.—Sabbath day. Had the privilege of attending the public means of grace, and with some profit, I trust. Text, "denying all ungodliness," &c. How delightful is it to look around and see a host of the youth solemn and attentive hearers of divine truth, whereas they were not long since listless! may they not only be hearers of the word, but doers. O get to thyself, Holy Father, a great name and praise in the earth; and may this church contribute to it much! the number is increasing; bless the Lord, O my soul, that I have lived to see this day.

"Wonders of grace to God belong,
Repeat his mercies in your song."

April 20.—Sabbath morning. As a branch of this Church had a conference yesterday about six miles from the meeting House, public worship is attended there this morning. O may they indeed worship God in spirit and in truth! Come down among them, precious Saviour, by thy divine influence, and let their meeting be for thy glory; and not only their meeting, bnt all the assemblies of thy saints throughout the world. My own exercises of late have not been such as I wish they were; but I feel more the importance of fervent prayer mixed with faith, if possible, than ever before. My mind, for a length of time, has been pondering upon the subject of female prayer meetings; my better feelings say, "promote it and engage in it;" but proud nature shrinks. I trust my desire is that God would direct; my past life ought to reprove me, that there has much been left undone that might have been done, and these words often present themselves—"Whatsoever thy hand findeth to do, do it with all thy might; for there is no work nor device found in the grave whither thou goest." O for a right sense of eternal things, that a solemn weight may rest upon my spirits! I have lately read a tract upon growth in grace; it gave me some hope, but occasioned much fear.

May 17.—Sabbath evening. Had the privilege of hearing a young brother—Elder—[Samuel Elder, who afterwards became pastor of the Church in Fredericton, N. B. and is now, we doubt not, in glory.—W. C.] preach to-day (one of the fruits of the revival; commenced preaching in connexion with the Church here about a month since). Text, "Thou God seest me." His mind was fruitful, and he spoke interestingly. What a wonder God hath wrought for this youth! five months ago he was strong in the Uni-
160 versalist doctrine, and a stranger to grace. Our Sabbath School is again in operation (it is discontinued in the winter); what a mighty work, I hope and pray, may be wrought by it.

June 14.—Sabbath evening. Our conference meeting yesterday was very refreshing to almost every individual present; it was indeed good to be there. O may the spring that it hath given be abiding, that our fruit may be unto holiness, and the end everlasting life. To-day I remained at home, rather at a loss to know what duty was, being communion season; my seat should be filled when health and circumstances will permit, but a desire to accomodate others often takes the lead.

July 2.—This is the eve of my birth-day: thirty-two years of my frail life are fled and gone, rolled back into eternity. Solemn thought! and most wonderful that amidst all my strayings and wanderings, I am yet permitted to enjoy the feeble hope of entering that rest that remains for the people of God. O that I were more anxious to be up and doing while the day lasts, that there might be within my breast a continued reaching after the things that are before. It has been my privilege of late to attend an interesting Association; the season was truly refreshing to those who took a deep interest in the concerns of Zion, and the welfare of im-

mortal souls around them. I have to say, confusion of face 161
belongeth unto me, for my indifference to all that is worthy of an immortal soul to feel. The preaching at the Association was of the right kind; the promise stands good that it shall not be lost. O for faith and prayer!

July 24.—Sabbath evening. Yesterday was favored with attending conference: an interesting season to many; and to-day heard a salutary discourse by my companion, "And Barnabas exhorted them all that with purpose of heart they would cleave unto the Lord." I have recently been absent from home for several days; it has been my privilege to mingle in the society of many sincere christians. I indeed felt much united to them. I hope I was led to reflect on the discharge of duty to my fellow creatures.

September 29.—Sabbath evening. Many, very many have been my privileges and mercies since I last wrote; and to-day heard our young Brother—Elder—preach from these words—"A new commandment give I unto you that ye love one another." A profitable sermon I hope it may prove to all of us who heard it. My companion is now absent to attend a yearly meeting in Newport, and a protracted one also in Onslow, which commenced yesterday. I do indeed, I think, feel much interested for the welfare 162
of Zion in that place, as it was one of the places I visited before I last wrote. O may the Holy Spirit be shed down with power on the inhabitants of that region, and everywhere else; for without it vain are the efforts of feeble man. As it regards my own prosperity in the divine life, I can say but little; I am awfully insensible to my own best interests and to the honor of God; but still am enabled to repose an humble trust in God for all the future (but sometimes fear it may be a careless trust). O for a cheerful resignation to all hls will, concerning me and mine.

New Year's Evening, 1840.—I am truly astonished when I see such a length of time has elapsed since I last wrote. I have indeed been much enveloped in cares and pursuits of this life, but worse than this in clouds of darkness of mind. I am too well convinced that the energies of my soul are paralyzed by the neglect of the private means of grace; I justly deserve the hidings of God's face, and a wonder of wonders is it that I am favored with so many mercies and scarcely an affliction of any kind for a length of time, except what is common to all. I am, it is true, put to my wit's end to know what course to pursue with my children. I discover so much corruption in myself and them; but I know it is my desire to do right by them, but in how many instances, alas, do
I leave undone the things that ought to be done! What reason 163
have I to adore the patience and forbearance of God with me, that I am spared to enter upon another year, when I have so sadly

misimproved the past! O for strong desires to dedicate myself and all I have and am to God! The Church observed this day as a day of fasting and prayer; too few broken and contrite spirits, I fear; I know it was too much outside with myself.

"Wretch that I am, to wander thus
In chase of false delights."

March 10.—Much sickness and death has prevailed in our
neighborhood of late: many solemnities to arouse my attention.
My own family have been the subjects of disease, but as yet
nothing very alarming in their case; these words have seemed very
164 precious—"Rock of ages cleft for me," &c. I think I feel sometimes (when I have any religious reflection) to trust my all in the
hands of a faithful covenant-keeping God: how necessary this in
life or death! O for actual preparation for my great and last
change!

April 6.—The return of spring is truly delightful; appearances are very encouraging for the husbandman; still the hopes may be blasted. I have still to complain of the dormant state of my religious feelings, and I may well know the cause,—too much inattention and indifference to the means of grace. My mind is too divided; I do endeavor to examine myself, to try my motives with regard to having my hands so much employed with time's things; but after all the search there are deficiencies of every kind; but my mind is for the most part calm.

May 31.—I am again and again laid under increased obligations
to God for his kindness and mercy towards me. He has made me
the mother of another little son, now six weeks old, a promising
child to all appearance; but oh how soon may the fond hopes be
165 blighted! I do indeed feel the need of an increase of patience. I
feel that I am placed in an important field of labour, surrounded
with five small children (the survivors of seven), and to train
them up in the way they should go is a difficult task for one who
is so deficient in all the necessary qualifications. I am encouraged
to ask for that wisdom which comes from above; but here again I
am deficient. O my God, forgive my past offences and lead me in
a plain path; grant unto me a constant spirit of prayer, that I
may never cease to look upwards.

July 8.—So many are my engagements, and my love so cold, that I seldom take my pen to notice what might be worth looking back upon. I have been much comforted with the following beautiful remarks:—"But is it not sweet to think our Heavenly Father has surely seen our affliction, that he knows all its aggravation, is intimately acquainted with our peculiar temperament, and discerns exactly what nerve the thorn pierces,—that he sees the conflict of contending duties, sees our efforts to leave and to forbear, the struggles we have with our spirit, the taunting word suppressed, the indignant feeling quelled, the tumultuous agitation hushed, the anguish of fond regret calmed down, the tears which flow in secret. All are seen by him; He knows the full dimensions of our sorrows, come they whence they may; the weakness of our faith, the coldness of our love cannot be estimated by any but God himself; language cannot convey to another the real degree of deficiency. A naked human heart can be tolerated and compassionated only by the God of all grace, mercy, and love. Oh consoling thought! Such is the being with whom we have to do." I know something by experience of every point mentioned. Such are the trials of my mind with regard to the way that I should take with my children, that I hope I do not apply the promise wrong—"They that sow in tears shall reap in joy."

September 30.—I am ashamed when I look back and find this small common sheet [Having for the thirty years from the time of commencement of her Journal to the end, for the most part wrote it on one single sheet of paper folded into eight small pages at a time; this will account for her observations here.—W. C.] commenced more than a year ago and not written through. Conscience tells too plainly what it argues. O for deep repentance for past omissions and commissions; now justly might the passage be applied to me, "Cut it down, why cumbereth it the ground?" How much I need a thorough breaking up! I find such a lingering of affections around earthly objects. My companion is now absent upon a mission. I think much about him, but cannot enjoy that spirit of prayer that I want to, and fear the case is too plain: I do not receive because I ask amiss.

November 1.—Sabbath evening. I see so little in me and about me that looks like the christian, that I am strongly inclined to give up all pretensions to religion, and seek for new hopes of salvation. I do for the most part of the time keep my head above sinking in deep water (or rather the Lord keeps me), but so much pollution is manifest!—and yet I know but little of myself.

"My God, permit me not to be
A stranger to myself and thee." 166

I feel an insupportable weight of responsibility resting upon me with regard to my duty towards my children. I am so inadequate to the task of training them, even temporally, my heart often sinks within me. I think it is my sincere desire to train them up for God. Will these dry bones live before God? No joy can equal that. O may I be more decidedly engaged in this good work! 167

November 15.—"Long do I neglect to record my religious exercises, and long have I lived a formal professor of religion. I have forgotten my Saviour, wandered from his sheep fold, and

rown unconcerned about my danger. While writing I fear I have no true penitence, all is cold indifference and dead formality. The word of God is not to me a delight as it once was; its beauties are hid, and its promises and threatenings glided over unheeded and unapplied. I fear and believe too many of my Sabbaths have been improved to no spiritual advantage: thus pass away my days, beclouded with sin, without engagedness in Zion's cause, without gratitude to my Saviour, or obedience to his precepts. O thou blessed Jesus, I have forgotten thy love, have strayed from thee; I desire to humble myself with true repentance before thee; help me to return from my backslidings; quicken me in duty; show me my ingratitude and my sins. May I fear to offend thee and live henceforward to thy glory." The above is the exercise of an eminent Deacon, but so fully agrees with mine that I could not for-
168 bear to notice it. I have been much cast down for several days, but many precious promises encourage me to hope in God, for I shall yet praise him who is the health of my countenance.

January 24, 1841.—Sabbath evening. My frail life is yet lengthened out to enter upon a new year, and I might with propriety say an unprofitable one. I feel that religion is at a very low ebb in my soul: I can truly say—

> " How seldom do I rise to God,
> Or taste the joys above ;
> This mountain presses down my faith,
> And chills my flaming love."

O, I want the power of God to come down upon me, to stir me up to a consideration of the duties I owe to him and my fellow creatures. Yesterday was our conference: nothing very special, as it is a mourning time; this indicates some life in individuals. To-day is our communion season. I do think I felt some gratitude for the institution of this divine ordinance to bring to our remembrance our obligations to God, to honor him in our day and generation. I feel increasingly desirous to hold the Saviour continually up for an example of meekness and patience. I desire to hold earthly things more and more at loose ends, to die daily unto sin, and mortify the deeds of the body.

May 16.—Sabbath afternoon. Can it be possible that nearly four months have elapsed since I wrote on this sheet? The want of retirement [Having contrived to keep her Journal a secret from every one, I conclude is what she here means principally by retirement.—W. C.] sometimes is the cause, and at other times the want of spiritual life; the winter has been spent in a too dull and inactive manner by me in matters of religion, and the darkness is so general that it may be felt, at least in this Church. Many parts of God's vineyard have been watered of late in this Province.

In Horton, where an institution for education has been got up,
many of the scholars in the Academy, and students in the College,
have shared in a blessed revival in that place. It evidently
appears that the powers of earth and hell are against the prosperity
of that institution with regard to getting aid from the Legislature;
great opposition to it at the last session. It has been about fifteen
years in operation; several revivals of religion in the Baptist
Church at Horton since, in which the inmates of the above institution have shared, evidently shewing the manifestations of heaven
in its favor. God will never leave himself without a witness, and 169
very many are rising to call him blessed; but how small the number compared to those going the downward road! I feel increasing
need of pleading for the prosperity of Zion, and for a clean heart
and right spirit for myself.

June 20.—Sabbath evening. As this is the usual period for
the Association to convene, my companion is absent at Onslow,
where I trust by the blessing of God much good may be done. 170
We had a prayer meeting here to-day, and a sermon read—one of
Payson's, upon the punishment of the wicked—very striking—I
hope will not be in vain. I want my hard frozen heart warmed 171
with the pure principle of love to God and my fellow creatures,
that we as a Church may no longer slumber.

> "Nothing has half thy work to do,
> Yet nothing's half so dull."

August 4.—Again after a lapse of time I am permitted to write
and record the mysterious dealings of Providence with us. But
why should I say "mysterious" when so many of God's children
have been stripped of their earthly goods? My companion (and
two others of his family) having been bondsmen for one of his
sons, who has failed in business under heavy liabilities, is now
called upon with the others concerned with him to meet a large
demand. The effort to meet it will leave us entirely dependent. 172
This indeed is a powerful trial for the faith of reliance, and I desire to bless the Lord that he has enabled me more sensibly to
repose my trust in him, and to feel that he will never leave nor
forsake me. O support me in every time of trial and difficulty.

August 26.—Such have been the circumstances of the case above mentioned, that I have had much more to take my attention than usual, and have not been able to notice some of my feelings in this trying affair; but I do feel of a truth (if my heart does not greatly deceive me) to believe and say, "The Lord is good—a stronghold in the day of trouble"; "his ways are past finding out, his paths are in the great deep." My mind as yet has not sunk very low with fears of support. I think for the most part of the time I can bless God for what is past, and trust him for what is to come. I often fear something more will befal me to rouse me up more to engagedness to duty.

September 10.—Sabbath day. My companion is absent on the Mountain to-day, and a Presbyterian Minister preaches in our Meeting House. The past week has been one of deep trial to me, proceeding from a variety of causes—my own sin and corruption producing the most. I am beginning to feel the effect of our recent trouble. As we have not been dependent on the Church alone for our support, a removal from this place will probably follow, as they are not able, as might appear, to sustain a Minister with his family. The idea of separation from long-tried friends seems painful, but these lines often meet me—

> " Though dark be my way,
> If he is my guide,
> 'Tis mine to obey,
> 'Tis His to provide."

December 20.—Time is rapidly passing away; soon another year will have rolled back into eternity. Many have been the new and fresh trials in my breast the past year. I have been led to say to-day, " I sink in deep mire where there is no standing"—when I look back, and when I look forward. But with regard to looking forward to the future, as regards pecuniary matters, I have no business with it. Our Heavenly Father knoweth that we have need of these things, and will no doubt open such a door in Providence as will most glorify his holy name, and be for our best good. O reconcile us to thy will, dear Lord, and make us humble and
173 active in thy cause.

January 16, 1842.—Sabbath day. Heard my companion preach from a passage in Jeremiah—" For these things mine eyes weep." O that the Church generally could adopt it! but alas, alas, insensibility prevails to a great degree, I fear, at least I judge from my own knowledge of myself and some individuals. " By whom shall Jacob arise?" should be our daily cry. I too well know I am awfully deficient with regard to secret prayer and retirement. I well know that this is the life of the christian.

February 14.—Enjoyed the stated means of grace to-day, or rather attended upon them, for want of spiritual life too little enjoyed. Text—" And he shall be lifted up as an ensign of the people." My own exercises for the few weeks past have been truly painful; distressing doubts about my interest in the Saviour, and such darkness enveloping my mind. Yet am often invited, as it were, by the sweet promises of Jehovah to cast myself on his kind arm; but this seems like presumption for a wretch like me. Still I desire to cast my care on Jesus, and not forget to pray. I fear my views of myself and of the awful nature of sin, are too indistinct, too much upon the surface. I beg the trial of thine eyes; come over the mountains of my sins, dear Lord, and let me have unfeigned repentance therefor, and experience thy delivering power from this state of insensibility and stupor of mind, that in thy light I may see light.

April 1.—What a variety of scenes and conflicts have I passed through since I last wrote! God has laid his afflicting hand on my beloved companion, and brought him down to the gates of death. For four weeks he scarcely left his room, and the greater part of the time was confined to his bed; his complaint partly the effects of severe colds repeated; having for fifteen years been very much troubled with dyspepsia, his constitution was enfeebled by it, and hence was brought very low with the pleurisy, and had symptoms of typhus fever; but amid it all his mind was in a very happy state; the Lord was indeed very near and precious to him; he was ready to say at times, it is enough, the clayey tabernacle can bear no more. What a mercy this, that when his body was suffering acutely, his soul was feasting on angels' food. But alas, alas, my mind could not share with him. The fearful forebodings of my future situation, which seemed at times to threaten very seriously when violent fainting fits came on (and indeed there seemed but a step between him and death frequently, but he is now fast recovering), caused my stubborn heart to rebel, and as I had for some time endured the hidings of God's face, the conflict was sore. It appears like presumption for a wretch so vile, that has hoped to enter heaven through the merits of the suffering Saviour, and yet lives at such a distance from him, so regardless of his commands to expect much of the joys of salvation. I may truly say,

> "Here on my heart the burden lies,
> And past offences pain my eyes."

I fear I am looking too much to myself and not enough to the sin-atoning Lamb, "who of God is made unto us (such rebel worms)
wisdom, righteousness, sanctification and redemption." The follow- 174
ing words came very forcibly to my mind to-day—"In the Lord have I righteousness and strength": but my faith is so weak, I hardly dare to apply it to myself. O when will the clouds of darkness be chased away, not only from my mind, but from the Church in this place? Zion mourns because so few come to her solemn feasts. Pour out of thy Spirit, dear Lord, upon the weary heritage, thy backsliding children. O rend the heavens and come down.

June 7.—Sabbath evening.

> "What shall I render to my Lord
> For all his kindness shown?
> My feet shall visit thine abode,
> My songs address thy throne." 175

I know it is the duty and privilege of God's children to be offering up praise to the everlasting Father for what he is in, and of, himself; but I am led to conclude it would not become me. I live so much below my privileges (if a child of God at all) that I go mourning the greater part of my time. When, O when shall I be able to rise superior to those my doubts and trials, and move forward in the strength of the Lord God of Hosts, experiencing the pure joys of salvation? O that I had faith as a grain of mustard seed, to lay hold of Christ as my chief good, as just such a Saviour as I need; may the veil of darkness be drawn aside that I may be enabled to discern clearly my real character. Heard these works spoken from to-day by Mr. Obed Parker—"And that,
176 knowing the time that it is high time to awake out of sleep." Many excellent remarks made. God is pouring out of his Spirit to the Westward of this marvellously. O that it might reach us, that we may rouse up to action. I have taken a class in the Sabbath School, and hope it may prove a benefit to myself and the precious souls I endeavor to instruct. How much I feel the want of a spiritual mind in this undertaking, as well as in all the duties incumbent upon me as a mother and Minister's wife in particular. Have mercy, have mercy upon me, O precious Saviour, that I may be clothed in my right mind sitting at thy feet. [How lamentable that any one possessing the true marks of evangelical piety, should so indulge in evil forebodings and thereby really occasion unnecessary distress of mind. "Blessed are they that mourn, for they shall be comforted." "Blessed are they that hunger and thirst after righteousness, for they shall be filled." Why not believe the Lord Jesus Christ, and rely upon the fulfilment of his divine and immutable promises? It shows, too, how wrong it is to keep the mind locked up from those who might be the means of relieving
177 them.—W. C.]

August 14.—Sabbath day. Very rainy. It seems almost incredible that so much time has elapsed since I last wrote, and so many things of importance have transpired to notice. Much sickness and death have prevailed among us for several months past; not uncommon for two in a family to be removed within a short time. Although six of our family had the measles, yet all were mercifully preserved, which calls loud for gratitude and a dedication of all our powers and faculties to the service of Jehovah. For nearly a year I have been much deprived of the faculty of hearing, I think I may say with propriety, one of the greatest afflic-
178 tions that ever befel me,—so wounding to my pride, and distressing to all my feelings, and perhaps a judgment on me for past neglect in hearing the word of God; for the admonition is, "Take heed how you hear"; but as a natural cause to be assigned, my

head from childhood has been easily affected with cold, and has now become so weak that I am scarcely a day without cold in it. [Perhaps erysipelas in the head, common to her, was a more natural cause.—W. C.] I desire to bear it with submission, as well as many other cross Providences, and have faith to believe that promise,—"That all things shall work together for good to them who are the called according to the purpose of God," and who love him with an undivided heart. My evidences of this are so dim, so inconclusive, that it seems not much to be wondered at, that I have for a length of time been wandering on the barren mountains of sin and unbelief; and yet it is far from the course a helpless worm should pursue. A needy dependant beggar seeks for relief, and in some measure I hope I have, but yet it has been with so little fervour, so little anxiety to what the case demands, that I often conclude I shall never again see the light as I fondly hope I have seen it.

> "It is wondrous how God, when we wander from him,
> Our fears and afflictions can double;
> And comfort impart to the sorrowful heart
> That we never could know but in trouble."

My fears have indeed been many, and yet not of the right kind, I judge; but for a few weeks past my mind has become more calm (I fear more supine), [No doubt that Satan has much to do in preventing or occasioning our want of the exercise of faith in Christ, and humble dependance upon him in darkness as well as light; but a deep sense of the nature and consequences of sin, and an exalted view of holiness, and viewing ourselves as it were enveloped in the one and very deficient in the other, will often lead to fearful agitation and distress of mind. Yet where a deep sense and abhorrence of sin, and an ardent desire after holiness exists, there true piety is implanted in the heart; in such cases the christian should endeavor to trust in God, look upward, and strive to walk by faith and not by sight. It is evident this course would contribute to much more comfort in the soul, and be more pleasing in God's sight.—W. C.] and anxiously desirous to throw myself at the feet of the Saviour, believing that "He is able to save unto
the uttermost all that come unto God by him." O for the Spirit's 179
teaching, without which we cannot do anything aright! What a dwarf in religion have I been all my days, and how unprepared to lead my children in that straight and narrow path which leads unto eternal life! We have had some encouragement of late, that our God has not wholly forsaken us as a Church; two young females have professed hope in the Saviour, and we hope will ere long make it manifest publicly; a number of young persons seem anxious about their state. The Church is too much asleep.

October 23.—Sabbath evening. I have this day had the privilege of sitting at the table of the Lord, and commemorating his death. His precious language to his followers was much in my mind—"As oft as ye do this, do it in remembrance of me": but alas, I could see plainly that my thoughts were upon my own sins and sufferings, more than upon the sacrifice made for them. I could truly say, "O Lord, I am oppressed, undertake for me." I live at such a distance from glorying in the cross of Christ, being crucified to the world and the world to me,—live so little by faith on the Son of God, that I have great reason to fear I shall yet be a cast away. My mind is so harassed with past and present delinquencies as it regards the training of my children, which course is best to pursue I cannot all times judge; though I well know I do not pray enough; for a length of time such darkness has veiled my mind, that I am truly groping my way unprofitably. I felt a little encouraged to-night in reading these words—"O thou afflicted, tossed with tempest and not comforted, behold I will lay thy stones with fair colors, and lay thy foundations with sapphires." "And thy children shall be all taught of God." Can it be possible? O for strong faith to carry them in the arms of my desires to the Saviour, and entreat him to subdue their stubborn wills, and bring them into subjection to his easy yoke and reign. "They that trust in the Lord shall be as Mount Zion, which cannot be removed." Grant that it may be my happiness, precious Saviour.

November 18.—Sabbath evening. My companion spoke under many discouragements to-day from "Unto you that fear my name will the sun of righteousness arise with healing in his wings, &c." The attendance small, and so much apathy and worldly conformity abounding! I have myself been an eye-witness of much levity and trifling for the week past, and that too much encouraged by those who ought to reprove such unfruitful works of darkness. Observing the influence it is having upon my children, I am truly pained at heart, and feel that I need special wisdom to enable me to do what I can to suppress it. O that the fountains of the great deep were broken up in my own heart; then should I feel more anxiety about those nearly allied to me. I do hope I feel desirous of redeeming the time, knowing that the days are evil. O for more real piety towards God; then should I be able to discharge the duties of a christian mother. How true is the language—

> "To spend one day with thee on earth,
> Exceeds a thousand days of mirth."

January 10, 1843.—My frail life is yet lengthened out to enter upon another year. O how little I know whether I shall live to see another or the end of this! The great point is, to live every day as though it was my last. I well know I should be loth to be summoned out of time into eternity in the present unfeeling state of my mind; for I feel, while a protracted meeting is in operation among us, so very little like what I ought to, that I am ready to conclude I never knew what the power of religion was; but alas, I too well know the cause of death and darkness; my Bible, my closet are neglected,—my increasing cares and privations press heavily upon me, and I am too ready to make excuses, and think it is principally for want of time; but this will not always do. The meetings, so far, have been somewhat encouraging, but we want to see a greater breaking up among the Church, and in my own heart, and then we might hope to see sinners alarmed at their danger.

January 15.—This has been, we hope and trust, a week of God's power amongst us as a Church and congregation, excepting some individuals like myself that are dark and stupid. O, I want a thorough renovation, that my soul may be set at liberty, and a spirit of prayer granted, that I may plead for myself and family and all around me. Some are now relating what God has done for their souls.

February 4.—The work of God is still progressing gradually among us; a number of the youth seem to think they have experienced a gracious change, while others are not satisfied, but are seeking for something greater; among the number is my eldest daughter, ten years of age, whose attention was arrested more powerfully during the protracted meeting, but owing to the natural
temperament of her mind she has manifested at times but little 180
concern. During the last week she hopes her sins are forgiven, and is more intent upon reading her Bible and retirement, and to-day wants to tell her exercises to the Church. Shall I say this has brought an inexpressible trial upon me? (indeed I feel it to be so,) her childhood, &c. &c. together with an awful deficiency on my part of instruction from the holy precepts of the Bible, not reading, studying and praying over it with her, as much as I ought to have done. O, I awfully fear, when I look back upon my past life, that the fruits of the Spirit have been but little in exercise, to what the case demanded, and to have this lamb (if one) suffer on that account, brings poignant sorrow. O may I be forgiven by him "with whom is forgiveness, that he may be feared," and henceforward be enabled to redeem the time.

April 23.—Sabbath day. Since writing last I have passed through a greater variety of changes than usual. Some sore trials have been inflicted by enemies to the religion of Jesus. I have also been made the happy mother of a sweet little daughter, on the
twenty-fifth of February; but the young plant was only lent me 181
seven weeks and four days, to spring up and bud a little while; my Heavenly Father saw fit in infinite wisdom to take her to himself,

to dwell, I hope, where no mortal can conceive what he hath prepared for them that have been washed and made white in the blood of the Lamb. 'But the parting scene was made more tolerable than I could have anticipated, owing partly to my own illness, which was occasioned by the sickness of the dear babe, my physical powers getting out of order through loss of appetite and rest, together with anxiety and distress at seeing her suffer (the complaint was inflammation on the lungs). I endured excruciating pain for the greater part of two days, and nearly all this time the little sufferer was struggling with the king of terrors, though sometimes apparently asleep: but she is gone, and I think I have been enabled by supporting grace to adopt the language of the following lines—

> " Farewell sweet babe !
> Thou art no longer mine ;
> Thy pulse has ceased to beat,
> Thy spirit's gone.
> The stroke is heavy, but I'll not repine,
> My soul exclaims, Thy will, O God, be done."

I have been satisfied for a length of time that I needed the rod of affliction to bring me to consider; and my greatest desire is now that it may be sanctified, that my mind may be aroused to healthful action. If I am not deceived, the precious Saviour has already enabled me to look on him whom I have pierced and mourned, and has encouraged me to exercise more faith on him. O that I could say, I must, I will, I can, I do believe. The word of God seems very sweet, and the promise—" Thou which hast shewed me great and sore troubles shalt quicken me again," meets my wants.

May 8.—Our family, or four of the children, are now exercised with the whooping cough, but not yet very severe. O may I and they be prepared for whatever awaits them in the journey of life, whether it be long or short! I think I am sincere in the desire and request that their souls may be saved from everlasting burnings, whether they possess much of this world or not. I do hope I have had some gracious exercises, since God has called me to resign some of my earthly comforts. This passage was very sweet to me this morning—" In whom we have redemption through his
182 blood, even the forgiveness of sins." But I want to live nearer the fountain, to be enabled to impart wisdom and instruction to my children and others before the streams lose any of their healing qualities. O may I draw near to God, for he has promised to draw nigh to such; but without thee I can do nothing.

183 *June* 27.—My companion is now absent to the Association. I trust it may be a refreshing season, not only to his soul, but to many others, that the kingdom of the dear Redeemer may be

advanced. In looking back upon my past life I see much to deplore, but yet much, very much of the Lord's goodness to record. I find that I am often the subject of sore conflicts, but I am warned "not to think it strange concerning the fiery trial, as though some strange thing happened unto me": but if I only could make my way to God "through dismal deeps and dangerous snares," I should be better satisfied; but I awfully fear my besetting sin is impatience and fretfulness, and I thereby lose sight of the meek and quiet spirit which is in the sight of God of great price. O for a coming down to the feet of the Saviour, and a disposition to follow his blessed example!

July 3.—This is the thirty-sixth anniversary of my life, and it seems like a dream. How true is the scripture—"Our life is even as a vapor, that appeareth for a little while, and then vanisheth away." O how necessary to feel the worth and nearness of eternity! O that my mind was more forcibly impressed with its solemnities, that I might realize how fast souls are hastening to the judgment seat, the tribunal of the Most High God, and use my best endeavors in the strength of Almighty grace to save them from going down into the pit. Lord, revive thy work in this place and everywhere. The intelligence from the different Churches of revivals of religion is truly gratifying; may they be praying energetic characters in the kingdom of Christ. For a length of time I have found these lines very sweet—"Cast thy burden upon the Lord, and he shall sustain thee."

"Accept the trust, accept the care,
O Father, which I bring to thee;
And let this holy act of prayer
Exert its soothing power on me.
This burdened heart, this throbbing breast,
Would fain discharge its heavy load;
But where can it securely rest,
Save in an all-sufficient God?

I dare not sink, I dare not weep,
Beneath the chastening of thy hand;
Yet unsustained I cannot keep
My spirit girt to thy command.
Assist me, then, assist me now
To cast my weight of care on thee;
Submissive at thy feet to bow
And hear what God will speak to me."

NEWTON.

The principal burden that lies near my heart now is the charge of my children, although I suffer in many ways from the disadvantage of not hearing as well as formerly. "Blind unbelief is sure to err," &c. &c. O that I were more diligent in applying to the fountain for the supply of all my wants, and enter upon another year of my life more devoted to the best interests of my own soul and those around me. Grant it, precious Saviour.

August 23.—I have to complain of very great insensibility to the all-important concerns of religion; one cause perhaps is, I am so much of a Martha. Necessity seems to demand it; the support we receive is so limited, that we are obliged to carry on farming pretty extensively; this I cannot think belongs to a Minister of the Gospel; it not only secularizes his own mind, but if his companion has a spiritual mind it must tend to paralyze it; such I awfully fear has been the case with me.

September 6.—For a length of time it has been a rare thing to hear of a death in this vicinity; but in an unexpected hour the head of a family, a neighbor of mine, was laid upon a bed of sickness, where she lanquished for nearly a fortnight, and then fell asleep in Jesus, leaving a most affectionate husband and six children to mourn their great loss. I would fain hope this visitation has led me to feel more sensibly the necessity of being in actual readiness to die. O for greater reconciliation to the dealings of a Sovereign God with me, that I may continually sit at his feet and learn of him.

December 31.—It seems incredible that almost four months have elapsed since I noticed any of the exercises of my mind here, especially when I have passed through so many different scenes. I have been called to experience a new scene of affliction, in personal illness. Nine weeks of debility and weakness, though not suffering much pain; time often appearing very short, and the necessity of having my lamps trimmed and in bright burning, of the greatest importance; much of my time, when my mind was awake at all, was spent in mourning over my mispent life,—so little done for him who I trust has done so much for me. I hope I enjoy some of the passive graces, and through the unbounded, unchanging goodness of God I am now so far recovered, that I can attend to some of the concerns of my family. I may well say, "What shall I render unto the Lord for all his benefits?" Surely I have the most reason to bless and praise his holy name of any of his tried children, and yet alas how little of it is manifested! the enemy still keeps me in bondage with too much of a closed mouth upon those most interesting subjects. I think I can safely say—

"Here I raise my Ebenezer;
Hither by thy help I'm come;
And I hope, by thy good pleasure,
184 Safely to arrive at home."

And were it not for unbelief, which the Saviour whispers "begone,"

I would take the cup of salvation and call upon the name of the Lord more fully than for some time back.

> " This year is just going away,
> The moments are finishing fast;
> My heart, have you nothing to say
> Concerning the things that are past?"

Yes, many things of a public, trying nature, affecting the Baptist denomination, have transpired, but the government is on Immanuel's shoulders.

> " Though men of spite against me join,
> They are the sword, the hand is thine."

The great wheel of Providence is moving round, accomplishing the perfect plan of God. O make me like a weaned child, that I may acquiesce more cheerfully in all thy dealings with me, especially in the partial loss of my hearing, which I find to be often a sore trial. Grant me wisdom and strength the coming year, if life is spared, to honor thee in my family, in the Church, and in the world, precious Saviour.

January 1, 1844.—This day as usual is observed by the Churches of the Baptist denomination as a day of fasting and prayer. May it indeed prove a salutary season, that sorrow for past wrongs, and holy desires for future reformation, may evince itself hereafter. O that the children of God were more diligent in studying the Scriptures as the rule of life, and I among the number, that our humility and faith might be more apparent. Grant us, Holy Father, a spirit of grace and supplication.

January 7.—My companion is this Sabbath day addressing the youths more particularly; they appear to be getting on from one degree of vanity to another, and while the Church is so little conformed to the requirements of a holy God, we cannot expect much else. O may not the word be as water spilled upon the ground. Have mercy, have mercy, dear Lord, and appear for the deliverance of Zion and enable us to say—

> " My spirit glows in Faith,
> My heart in strong desires;
> And God will come, will come,
> Ere the lamp of life expires."

January 15.—Sabbath day. Being at home, alone, except my little son, I have more retirement than through the week. Being afflicted with sore eyes, I cannot sit up late at night, and my health is not fully recovered to rise early; hence my mind becomes too much absorbed with the temporal concerns or wants of my family, and is exercised too little with an imploring spirit, that while my hands are employed my desires may be ascending upwards. I often feel that I have great need of learning again which be the first principles of religion. O may an earnest desire for the salvation of the youths and others around us characterize our proceedings. Death is making breaches among them. A young man was buried the past week not far from us, and at the next house one is fast sinking into the grave with consumption, and several others are on beds of languishing. O may they be prepared for their great and last change!

February 19.—Lord's day. Last Sabbath I went to the house of God for the first time for four months. My companion preached; text—"He was despised and rejected of men, &c." I felt the want of my hearing very much; did not enjoy myself as I wanted to, though I felt somewhat grateful that my health permitted me to attend, and to-day fear that I conferred too much with flesh and blood; my health will not permit me to do as I have done. O, I hope I may be kept from dishonoring God by indulging in inactivity or fears of venturing too far. There is variety of schools in which it seemed needful for me to be taught, I want to be improved aright, so that the work of sanctification may be going on, and I be prepared for a seat at God's right hand. O make me such an one as I ought to be, Heavenly Father. May my children manifestly be brought within thy covenant. The Church have so much revived as to establish prayer meetings; it rejoiced my heart to hear of them, may good result from them.

March 3.—During the last week I have passed through an almost overwhelming affliction. My dear and honored father has gone the way of all the earth,—has passed from time to eternity, has put on immortality in the regions of glory and happiness, and will be forever satisfied, because he has awoke with the likeness of his Saviour and God. We cannot doubt of this, if a holy life and conversation, with every other incontestible evidence, are marks of acceptance with God. I feel the loss most sensibly, for he was one of the best of fathers, but I quite forget my own sorrow, when I think of an aged and infirm mother, and a lone sister, that has so long experienced his tender care and attention; but were it not that the Gospel has made such provision for human weakness, and given such great and precious promises, not only to the widow and fatherless, but all others, I might have reason to sink and be cast down. O help us all as a family (four brothers and two sisters, only three of them public professors), dear Lord, to apply to thee, the overflowing fountain, for the sanctification of this severe bereavement, so sudden and unexpected—only three days illness; I did not get to see him while sick, the physician and family not being alarmed (he died with inflammation of the bowels), but our great loss is his unspeakable gain. May we prepare to follow, believing "that the Son of Man will come as a thief in the night," and "blessed is that servant whom his Lord, when he cometh, shall find watching." Such has been the case with the dear parent now gone; his mind for a length of time seemed to be dwelling upon the shortness of time, and the happy state of the believer after death. O Saviour, support the new-made, feeble widow. We have long been looking for her departure; but God's thoughts and ways are not as ours.

March 23.—My sorrow of mind at times has been almost insupportable, upon reflection that I did not get to see my dear departed father on his sick and dying bed. Although many things were wanting in kindness and attention on my part through life, yet we have always lived in the most sincere friendship; but I should have been glad to have been the means of leading his mind away from his sufferings, to tell of the preciousness of the Saviour in the dark valley; but that God whom he delighted to serve on earth did not forsake him, although he said but little upon any subject, his sufferings were so great, and not being apprehensive of such speedy dissolution. O how great the necessity of actual readiness to go out to meet the bridegroom. Alas, my mind is not dwelling upon death as it ought to be; the concerns of this present life too much take my attention, together with our trying situation; but it might be worse. O for submission and contentment.

April 15.—Sabbath day. My companion is absent on the Mountain to-day, baptizing and preaching, and a young Minister preached here to us in the Valley acceptably. There is mercy in store for us, I cannot but hope; yet my own mind is awfully stupid. I want more of a spirit of prayer for those nearly allied to me, and for the whole world. The week past I visited my widowed mother, living at the distance of thirteen miles. She evidently appears to be declining, with a variety of complaints, but the loss she has sustained wears upon her; I felt as if I could hardly endure the loneliness occasioned by the removal of one so dear, the short time I was there; and what must it be to those residing in the old mansion house! O thou who art the widow's God, sustain and bear her mind above her sufferings and sorrows, and all in similar circumstances, and pity fatherless children.

May 5. Sabbath evening. A week ago to-day I had the privilege of commemorating the sufferings and death of our risen Lord. I found it refreshing to my mind to think that my beloved father would no more drink of the fruit of the vine on earth, but was enjoying it forever new in the kingdom of his God. I have been enabled, I trust, more fully to let go my hold of him since then. For the week previous to this I was rebelling, I fear; I miss his society and counsel so much. O for greater submission to the will of heaven! I may well compare myself to ancient Israel, who often displeased God, and brought down misery upon themselves. I desire to bless the Lord for all the way in which he has led me; but this perverse will needs more humbling, so that in poverty's vale I may be content, as well as in every other situation.

May 26.—Sabbath day. Owing to rain and other circumstances I did not go out. I would wish to do what is right, and not confer with flesh and blood too much, but I often find too much exertion injurious; hence I need prudence and wisdom. I want a disposition to murmur at nothing, realizing that nothing befals me but what pleases my Heavenly Father, and He will prove me with no affliction that resignation cannot conquer. O that all my privations and difficulties might drive me more earnestly to a throne of grace, there to pour out all my complaints, and have my strength renewed by waiting upon God.

"I dare not sink, I dare not weep
Beneath the chastening of thy hand;
Yet unsustained I cannot keep
My spirit girt to thy command."

And where there is much rust it wants a rough file; but I must not think it strange concerning the fiery trial as though some strange thing happened unto me.

July 8.—I have recently passed another birthday; and O my soul, how far short hast thou come of holy self-denial and of a close walk with God the year that is past! Although one change after another has taken place to wean my affections from things below, I am still leaning too much on an arm of flesh, still trusting to my own strength too much. O may I experience deliverance from this henceforward, that God may be all in all.

August 11.—Sabbath day. The past has been a sorrowful week to my poor troubled breast, owing to a variety of causes; but more particularly the want of my usual hearing has produced many sore conflicts; no doubt the enemy has made use of many things to disturb my settled rest, but alas, I do not enjoy my settled rest as in days gone by. I have many times thought I had no daily cross, but I do not think so now; the responsibility of a parent's situation rests with almost insupportable weight upon my spirits. I want to pursue a right course, to use the powers God has given me, and yet not to be deficient in casting my care on Jesus, saying with the poet,

"Accept the trust, accept the care,
O Father, which I bring to thee;
And let this holy act of prayer
Exert its soothing power on me."

O that I possessed more of a spirit of prayer and holy trust in God where the proper settled rest lies.

September 7.—Sabbath evening. My companion is now absent on a visit to Windsor, to preach for an afflicted brother who has been deprived of his voice. O, I hope the Spirit of the Lord dictated his work in the hands of earthen vessels this day, that much glory may redound to Father, Son, and Holy Ghost, through the labors of finite creatures. I have of late taken some encouragement from these words, "The Lord will not suffer the soul of the righteous to famish." I justly deserve desolation in my soul as one that dares insult the majesty of heaven as I do, by neglecting a throne of grace, or set times for the duty; true it is that I desire to look up to God every hour or moment, for wisdom to direct in my responsible situation; and sometimes in the night seasons, when sleep departs from me, my soul (if I dare say so) enjoys communion with God in his word and promises; but alas it is seldom: no wonder I pine away and nearly die, for as the natural body cannot be sustained without food, neither can the immortal part be in health without daily supplies from him who is the bread of life. I love the privilege of prayer, but oh what backwardness to pray! Surely I may write bitter things against myself, and exalt the mercy of God above all other.

October 6.—Sabbath evening. A few days since, while reflecting on the scanty knowledge I had of God and his divine attributes, I was led to conclude that few had more experience of the mercy and love of a covenant-keeping God than poor unworthy me, and I do hope my stony heart was somewhat softened with the view (at least for a time). Were it not that Jehovah is a God full of compassion and long-suffering patience, I should ere this have been cut off as a cumberer of the ground. O that I could say more fully—

> "My spirit looks to God alone;
> My rock and refuge is his throne.
> In all my fears, in all my straits,
> My soul on his salvation waits." 185

My companion is now supplying a neighboring Church, occasionally, and will, it is expected, if life and health is spared him, for several months. I sincerely hope it is of God. I want to be quiet and submissive, and to say,

> "But to thy guardianship I trust
> Earth's dearest things to me;
> Befal what may, most wise and just,
> My soul confides in thee."

October 27.—Sabbath evening. My companion spoke from these words to-day—"Behold he cometh with clouds, and every eye shall see him," &c. &c. I was not present to hear the discourse, but from the natural tendency of the text, if managed judiciously, I concluded it must be very solemn and interesting, and such it appeared to be to a numerous congregation. No doubt there were many listless hearers to a subject of such overwhelming importance. Lord grant that it may not be as water spilt upon the ground, but the effects be seen after many days hence; O may my own mind be roused up!

December 8.—Again have I experienced the faithfulness of a
covenant-keeping God in making me the mother of a fine daughter,
186 and restoring me to a good degree of health. I may well say,
"Bless the Lord, O my soul, and forget not all his benefits": but
to my shame and confusion I fear I have not manifested my love
and gratitude to my gracious benefactor by seeking him with my
whole heart, and daily surrendering myself and all my concerns
into his hands. I feel indeed that I am following the Saviour at a
great distance,—so little of a spirit of prayer, and hence too little
interested in the advancement of the Redeemer's kingdom. The
Baptist denomination in this Province and New Brunswick are
raising funds to send a Missionary to Burmah; he is now preaching in our Meeting House, and will have a Missionary Meeting
187 to-morrow evening. I hope the hearts of the people will be
opened to contribute largely for such a noble object. Death is
making many ravages within our knowledge; in the course of a
few months two brothers of mine have been called to part with
188 their companions; both died in hope of a glorious immortality. I
regret that it has not as powerful effect upon my mind as I could
wish, to enable me to be in readiness to go out to meet the bridegroom.

December 29.—Another year is nearly come to a close, and I am, with my family, all spared, but may not see the close of it. My mind is much exercised about my children. I feel the want of a spirit of prayer, but still am desiring and hoping that God will open their eyes to see their danger; they are surrounded with temptations, but the greatest danger lurks within. O stretch out thine arm of delivering power, thou eternal Jehovah. I do hope I have had some little godly sorrow for my coldness in religious things. Oh may my repentance be such as needs not to be repented of. A naked human heart can be tolerated and compassionated only by the God of all grace, mercy and love, and O, consoling thought, such is the being with whom we have to do; but let me not presume too much upon the goodness of God—his justice must be satisfied; and here again our glorious intercession has made ample satisfaction. O my soul, wonder and adore, and seek to honor such a Being.

February 24, 1845.—Yesterday had the privilege of attending conference, after an absence of several months; my feelings were very much moved while speaking of the Lord's kindness to me; I hope I do sincerely feel at times that there is life in a holy God, a fountain that cannot fail, "a gentle hand that can wipe the tear, and soothe the contrite wail." But while I may appear to my fellow creatures to have strong faith in God, and to be living near to him, I cannot deceive the searcher of hearts; he well knows the awful deficiencies daily manifest. Oh, it is one thing to appear pious in the view of mortals, and another to be really so in the sight of God.

"This mountain presses down our faith
And chills our flaming love."

I want to be more awake to the necessity of agonizing in prayer (and of wrestling hard with sins and doubts and fears) for the Ministers and Churches and all flesh.

June 8.—A variety of scenes have taken place since writing last, within my knowledge, worthy of noticing, did time and space permit. There has been a quarterly meeting of Ministers with this Church; it proved to be a refreshing season to many souls; nothing special to appearance as yet with regard to the unconverted. The promise is—"My word shall not return void": but Zion mourns because so few come to her solemn feasts. A short time since my expectations were somewhat raised with the simple account my son, ten years old, gave of his exercises to me; it might be said of him, "Behold, he prayeth." I feel the need of being duly qualified to instruct and lead his tender mind, but I find it necessary to try to put my shoulders to the work; for a few weeks past his mind is too much asleep, and oh, I awfully fear
my own want of spiritual life and delinquencies may be the cause. 189
O the anguish of spirit I oft times endure on account of my deficiencies! My prayer often is, wherein I have erred in any respect, or with regard to training those precious souls committed to my care, Lord forgive, forgive, and grant me strength and wisdom to do my duty in future. What a consolation that there is a God in heaven who knoweth the conflict of contending desires, sees our efforts to leave and to forbear (the thoughts of a child suffering through life for want of the parent's doing their duty is most distressing to me); and I often fear I have left undone those things in many respects that ought to be done. I well know that I do not pray enough for this and every other object.

July 1.—My companion is now absent to attend the Association at Amherst; may it prove to be an interesting and profitable season. Time has appeared short to me of late. Not long since the following words struck my mind forcibly—"The Lord whom ye seek shall suddenly come into his temple." It has impressed my mind different ways, but not half so much as I want it to. My attention is so divided, and not enjoying very good health, I can say with the Psalmist, "I am shut up that I cannot come forth." "O may I feel submissive at thy feet to bow, and hear what God will speak to me." My temporal duties are so burthensome, on account of small means, and my aim and desire is to owe no man anything. When will the Churches feel the importance of supporting the Gospel properly? Oh how many gloomy hours might they dissipate were they disposed to make more sacrifices in dress and at their table! O how much better do I find it to fall into the hands of the Lord than into the hands of men; but I am truly a child of Providence, fed and clothed, particularly the latter, in an unexpected way. God is good, forever good, "a strong hold in the day of trouble." Let me take shame to myself that I abuse his mercies so, and do not seek for daily communion as I ought.

August 1.—Sad and sorrowful have I passed many hours since I last wrote; the reasons are too obvious—all the graces are too dormant; faith is weak, and love cold, though I cannot but think I love the Church in adversity as well as prosperity,—but here again this is defective. This Church has been involved in difficulty for a length of time, and has been obliged to withdraw fellowship from some of its members. Ardently have I desired that its officers and leading men, as well as all the members, might be under the influence of grace, cultivating much of the graces of the Spirit, that spiritual strength and discernment may be granted. It is written—"The joy of the Lord is your strength." O may we all be found waiting upon God, that our strength may be renewed daily.

October 19.—Sabbath evening. This has been a very quiet day with us, as my companion is absent at Windsor; no meeting—not even a prayer meeting near us; the Church is in a lamentable state, I fear. "O the hope of Israel, the Saviour thereof in time of trouble," do thou put to thy helping hand, and rouse thy children up to duty, to make sacrifices to send the Gospel to the remote parts of our own Province, where many are perishing for lack of knowledge. Alas, my own mind is too earthly, too little under the influence of that love that caused the Saviour to bleed and die. O may eternal realities appear nearer to me!

December 7.—My companion is now attending (and has been for nearly a week) the sick and dying bed of his aged father, now in the eighty-ninth year of his age, but who has enjoyed uncommon good health of body and soundness of mind, and has been a great blessing to society,—a member of Parliament for twenty-one years, where he contended for the rights of the people with undaunted firmness and zeal—a person of uncommon benevolence and kindness in aid of the cause of God, education and every benevolent object which called for his assistance (his mind was very much immersed in worldly concerns the greater part of his life, consequently not so actively engaged personally for the salvation of souls as we could have desired), but is now going to his reward, we trust. His mind is composed and happy in the prospect of death. 190

" Then oh may those who have gone before
Welcome him to the happy shore."

May the scene be truly sanctified to all present, and be a faithful monitor to relatives and friends. O Lord, revive thy work, in the midst of the years make known, and in wrath remember mercy.

" Saviour, visit thy plantation,
Grant us, Lord, a gracious rain ;
All will come to desolation,
Unless thou return again." 191

February 10, 1846.—Since I last wrote, death has deprived us of near and dear friends; my husband has lost one of the best of fathers, and I am bereaved of my widowed mother; the second of this month she was relieved from a suffering life, we trust, to join
the companion of her joys and sorrows in a better world. Mr. 192
Chipman's father was buried New Year's day. He was sweetly resigned to the will of God, and patient in his sufferings, yet preferred to depart and be with Christ whenever the Lord was pleased to call him hence. His hope was firm, resting on the merits of Christ's death; nothing intervening to disturb his settled rest, and we doubt not he fell asleep in Jesus. I have for some time felt that I was preparing for the rod; so much worldly-mindedness, and so little of a spirit of prayer,—this being occasioned too much by the neglect of it. And now my companion is laid aside from his labors with a glandular swelling under his arm; what the result will be, we know not. O prepare us all, dear Lord, to endure chastening whereof all are partakers. May it be our ultimate aim to glorify thee, as we sensibly feel to say with the poet—

" What shall we wish or wait for then,
From creatures, earth and dust ?
They make our expectations vain,
And disappoint our trust."

March 4.—My dear companion is again measurably restored to his usual health, but rather languid at times; in how many ways the mercy and kindness of God is made manifest, in the midst of clouds and darkness, and as one and another of our dear friends and relatives are leaving us and causing a great blank. O may we daily feel that we too must soon follow them into a world of spirits! It is high time to awake out of sleep, for the day is far spent, and

the night is at hand. Solemn and weighty considerations—upon which the most intense solicitude is necessary, and indifference thereto the most absurd. O Lord have mercy upon Zion, and may the set time come speedily to favor her; and shew us our duty, and give us strength to perform it, as members of churches, parents and neighbors. Change the hearts of my children, dear Saviour, and make them mild; and as I trust I have devoted them
to thee in infancy (though not with sprinkling), dare I say with
193 my prayers and tears (O, I hope so!)? Grant to clothe them with
the garments of salvation, and make them the honored instruments of promoting thy glory.

Mxrch 15.—Many have been the changes with me since I last wrote. In addition to some outward afflictions, the subtle foe has aimed his fiery darts to wound me to the heart; I have been under strong temptations to look upon the dark side of almost everything, and this no doubt is the effect of wandering from a God of spotless purity; possessing but little of a spirit of prayer, I have not obtained grace to help in every time of need, I fear. How true do I find that passage—"They that sow to the flesh shall of the flesh reap corruption." For a few days past I have felt more than usual anxiety for the souls of my children; I witness some of them to all appearance becoming hardened in sin and folly—no fear of God before their eyes, and every moment exposed to be sentenced to everlasting misery.

"And fain my pity would reclaim,
194 And snatch the fire brand from the flame."

O that I could say with David with regard to them—"But I give myself unto prayer"—knowing that the effectual fervent prayer of the righteous availeth much; but here is my great deficiency. Lord of glory, have mercy upon us all, and clothe us in our right minds.

March 22.—Yesterday attended conference. Although few in number, yet it was better for that few to disappoint the enemy than to have remained at home (if the roads *were* bad). I still feel (in a small degree, I fear,) anxious about my children more than others, and this is selfish, I know. We are all reading James's "Anxious Inquirer," and I am very desirous that it
should be made a blessing to us all, that the Spirit may set it home
195 upon the heart of old and young, or whosoever may read it. It
seems like a messenger from God to awaken our drowsy powers; it is like standing beside the dying bed of one of our fellow mortals, solemnized by the exercise of religious emotions; the feelings are elevated, and we feel as if there was but a step between us and death. This is the birthday of one of my daughters—eight years old. O that she may never experience another, with her heart

opposed to God. I feel daily the great loss I have sustained in the death of my parents; but I shall soon go to them, I trust; no wonder affection lingers about such departed worth. O sanctify it, dear Lord.

April 16.—Death and funerals are becoming very familiar to us. One of our valuable Church members was carried past our dwelling last week to the tomb (his name, Mr. John Meryon); he has been a doubting character, and fearing to sin against God in any form through life; hence he lived the life of the righteous, and eminently died so. Several months previous to his death he attained to the faith of assurance, and was as happy as an angel; his wife wrote to me that she had sat by him night after night (and they were precious moments), trying to instruct herself how to live and how to die; and the parting struggle was hers, but she had no wish to retain him here, for he seemed like an inhabitant of heaven. O the goodness of God to such worms of the dust! Help me to praise thy precious name, dear Redeemer, and trust in thee for dying as well as living grace. May the bereaved widow be strong in the Lord; about four months since she buried one of her daughters, and has but one child living now, and she is in delicate health: all will be well concerning her and all of us. To-day a funeral of a very different kind: a man living about two miles from this, being pressed for the payment of a debt, it so weighed upon him that he became deranged and cut his throat. He lived about ten days, and died begging for mercy in the exercise of his rational senses. He has left a wife and ten children to mourn their loss. May the sad circumstance be a solemn warning to all, that the sorrows of the world may not work death in such a way.

June 8.—As usual I have been the subject of much conflict (since I last wrote), but my religious feelings are at a very low ebb, partly owing, no doubt, to the want of the use of the means of grace, both private and public; so many temporal duties engross my attention, that my Bible and retirement are too much neglected; the worth of souls does not appear so weighty as a few months since. The God of heaven will not approve lazy dull seekers of the heavenly rest; then how much reason have I to fear I shall fall short of it. My companion is again absent to supply a neighboring Church a part of the time, which leaves us much at home. O that God might bless his labors there, as well as here, that the Church may revive and flourish.

July 12.—I have just passed another birthday, and one of my
children born the same day of the month, too. I am now in my 196
fortieth year, going down the declivity of life (in the afternoon of
the day); that passage struck my mind with force the past week,
"The night is far spent, the day is at hand." This life may be

well compared to a wet night of affliction, after which the birthday of the resurrection will arrive or follow to the christian. The weather has been extremely hot of late; the elements are all in commotion; no doubt many parts of the world experience tempests of thunder and lightning; but what is that to the judgment of the great day—"when tempests of angry fire shall burn, to blast the rebel worm?" O why am I not more anxious about my fellow creatures escaping the wrath of God! his justice must be satisfied. "Oh that they were wise, that they would consider their latter end."

August 4.—How needful are trials! and it matters little what kind of trials, so that they are sanctified. I sincerely hope they are weaning me from creature dependance; I do feel in some degree—

> "That life without thy love
> No relish can afford."

I trust I am not deceived in my exercises the past day, and at different seasons. Yesterday morning I awoke with these lines on my mind—

> "Behold the glories of the Lamb,
> Amidst his Father's throne;
> Prepare new honors for his name,
> 197 And songs before unknown."

The whole hymn was very sweet. The following night I had much satisfaction in being encouraged, I trust by Omnipotence, to cast my burdens on the Lord, feeling that he would sustain me. Have mercy, have mercy upon us, O Lord.

August 15.—Sabbath day. Quite alone again—my companion
198 absent, and the family gone to Methodist meeting. Through the past week I have had much to remind me of the goodness and forbearance of God; have felt some disposition to praise God for his wonderful works to the children of men; no wonder the Psalmist calls upon all things to praise God. A few days after the Association one of the aged fathers of the Baptist denomination, (namely) Joseph Dimock, "fell asleep in Jesus"; "he rests from his labors and his works follow him." The account given of the funeral and the mourning of the Church, by my step son, Professor Chipman, breathes consoling sentiments indeed; it is printed in the Christian Messenger, so that it is not confined to a few. May
199 it be the means of doing much good!

August 30.—The past week has been one of trial and sorrow, owing to a variety of causes; but the principal one is, the charge that devolves upon me with regard to my children, and the many fears that I have, that in days past as well as now, I do not discharge my duty. I know that I have not prayed with and for them as much as I should have done, and it is altogether probable I suffer in many ways on account of it. O what a fountain of iniquity the human heart is! I am more and more confirmed in the doctrine of total depravity every day of my life, and instead of dwelling on its darkness, I ought to look more to the remedy provided in the Gospel that is able to remove the veil of sin and unbelief from all flesh. Lord, lift upon us the light of thy countenance, and prepare us for whatever awaits us.

September 20.—Sabbath evening. I trust my soul has been refreshed and strengthened this day, especially while sitting at the table of the Lord. "Thanks be unto God who always causeth us to triumph in Christ, and maketh manifest the savor of his grace to us." None but Christ can do helpless sinners good; nothing but the stability of that covenant that is "ordered in all things and sure" is worth giving much attention to. I was thinking to-day I should like to have the same text preached from at my funeral, that was at my father's—"Thanks be unto God who giveth
us the victory through our Lord Jesus Christ." Yes, I feel to-day 200
that—

"Grace will complete what grace begins,
To save from sorrows or from sins;
The work that wisdom undertakes,
Eternal mercy ne'er forsakes."

Suffer me not, dear Lord, to deceive myself, but enable me to trust in thee at all times, for thou art a shield to them that do. But when I look at the weight of responsibility that hangs upon me, I cry with the prophet, "O Lord, I am oppressed, undertake for me," in the guiding and instructing my children as well as all other duties. O make bare thine arm and rescue those precious souls from the jaws of the devourer, that they may feel of a truth that none but Christ can do them good.

September 30.—Since writing last I have enjoyed a rare privilege in visiting dear relatives in Annapolis County. I took four of my children with me, and desired to journey by the will of God, and the good hand of God seemed to favor us. O how much cause for gratitude! for many go from home and never return. I often find the enemy coming in like a flood in many ways, and sincerely desire the Spirit of the Lord may lift up a standard against him. I find myself often exclaiming, "O land of rest, for thee I sigh;" make me patient and active, dear Lord.

January 3, 1847.—Sabbath evening. My frail life is still lengthened out to enter upon another year, with my family also in health and strength of body. "Bless the Lord, O my soul, and forget not all his benefits." I trust I have not altogether been a stranger to gracious exercises the past year; but alas, alas, how much have I to deplore, on account of my remissness and short comings. I have not grown in grace so much as I might have done; but I do hope Christ and his cross appear dearer, and he is my all-sufficient friend, to look to for succour and support; but O how deficient am I in this! I desire to praise my dear Redeemer for inclining the hearts of some of his children in this Church to unite in a prayer meeting. O may great good result from it, that sinners may be converted to God.

January 17.—Various are the scenes of conflict I pass through daily. Sometimes I hope I am not ignorant of Satan's devices, knowing he will worry those he cannot devour. I trust it has been my happiness for some time to enjoy a steady fixed trust in the divine arm, and to feel in some small degree "the joy of the Lord to be my strength," to enable me to bear burthens and to do duties. I feel the need of prayer daily, and I long to be more under its divine influence, for "only while we pray we live." I want more sensibly to realize that sinners are hastening to the judgment seat, and my dear children among the number, and to be agonizing in prayer for them.

January 24.—Lord's day. For the sake of having all my family attend meeting (except the youngest), I often remain at home, hoping those who have their hearing may hear to profit. (O may the word spoken by my companion and all others of God's Ministers this day reach the hearts and conscience of saints and sinners!) I do endeavor to fill my seat in the house of God whenever I consistently can, notwithstanding the great privation I endure, although I often hear considerable; the sight of mine eyes often is a comfort to me, setting aside the obligation I am under to my Maker; but I have become rather more reconciled to the affliction, realizing that there is a need-be for it, and knowing I shall ere long bless God, amidst the ardours of infinite gratitude, for even the most distressing visitation. "No affliction for the present is joyous but grievous, yet afterward it yieldeth the peaceable fruits of righteousness to those who are exercised thereby." O may this be my happy lot, and sometimes I hope and trust it is in some small degree. My children are enjoying the advantages of instruction at home by an excellent teacher; how numberless are our blessings! May they too be sanctified!

May 9.—Often would I have been glad to have put some of my thoughts on paper (since writing last here), but the multiplicity of avocations has prevented my having much retirement; but I do hope I have enjoyed some precious moments in reflecting upon the glorious plan of salvation and my interest in it; I trust I have seen more clearly than for some time past; have felt to say—

"My willing soul would stay
In such a frame as this;
And sit and sing herself away
To everlasting bliss." 201

We have also been called to mourn again in the loss of a grand-
daughter, aged fifteen years; we have not heard the particulars of
her death; O may it be sanctified to the family! The mother 202
(Mr. Chipman's daughter), as well as father, were much, very
much exercised in their minds about her future welfare. May my
dear children listen to the admonition! Many deaths around us of
late.

June 25.—My companion is now absent attending the Association; and I have, as is generally the case, a burden of care, but
I will not repine, as I humbly trust I have an High Priest touched
with the feeling of my infirmities, and I have come to the conclu-
sion to endeavor to bear whatever burthen is laid upon me with
meekness and patience; for where is peace but in trials meekly
borne? O that I might stand in my lot towards all my fellow 203
creatures! Help me, O help me, precious Saviour, to discharge
my duty to my children; and whatever trials I may have to bear
with them, that the discipline I use may prove beneficial. My
eldest daughters are absent at school; I feel very anxious about
them, surrounded as they are with temptation. May they cleave 204
unto that which is good! May the breach made by death upon
their number in school, deeply affect them, and all the children
connected.

September 20.—I find, by daily experience, this life to be a vale of tears. Scarcely any cessation (indeed I may say more) of anxious care and toil for a mother, morally, set aside the great exertions that ought to be made spiritually for their eternal benefit. I have to lament that I have not enjoyed that prayerful frame of mind of late, that I trust has been my privilege in many seasons of my life; but still I find no other resting place but to endeavor to cast my weight of care on Him who I trust careth for me. But how criminal to insult such a God (of whom we cannot have any adequate conception), by presuming to depend upon our own strength to walk this dangerous road! and such is too much the case when we neglect to seek supplies from the overflowing fountain, a throne of grace and the precious Bible. O Lord of glory, incline the hearts of my children to read thy word and reduce it to practice, and to feel the need of seeking a throne of mercy, realizing their true situation,—dead in trespasses and sins. O do thou quicken them by thy Spirit, and aid them by thy power and grace to life divine. How long O Lord, how long, ere thou wilt revive thy work among us?

October 1.—Sabbath evening. As is frequently the case of late, no meeting at our Meeting House near us; but my family sometimes attend Methodist Meeting. My companion still administers to a neighboring Church a quarter of the time, and a branch of this on the Mountain a quarter, which leaves him but half of the time at home; and so many, from political views, have wandered from their brethren in the Church, that support from the Gospel is withheld, and we are struggling on amidst wants and trials and much fatigue (but yet having much more than we deserve), often realizing how good it is to trust in Him who has said, "Your Heavenly Father knoweth that ye have need of these
205 things."

November 21.—My eldest son has now gone from the parental
206 roof, and entered upon his arduous duties of seeking knowledge. O may the eternal God create within him a clean heart and renew within him a right spirit, that with all his getting he may get wisdom and understanding. I have felt much comfort and satisfaction in commending him to God, to keep him in all his ways, and preserve him from yielding to temptation. O that I had more faith to believe that whatsoever I ask, not doubting, I shall receive. I feel more and more the value and efficacy of prayer, but so much latent evil remains within, that spiritual vision is very much dimmed. Shew me, precious Saviour, what my duty is, and help me to perform it. O search and try me, and whatever evil way is in me, do thou remove it, and may the love of God chasten and subdue unhallowed feelings. When will the wilderness and solitary places be made glad for us?

December 12.—Sabbath evening. No Meeting near us to-day, but we enjoy our solitude very much; the family all love to read, and we have a variety of good books, beside the Bible, which is always new, when any one can say, "Open thou mine eyes, that
207 I may behold wondrous things out of thy law." The past week has been one of severe conflict to my soul; many inventions have been sought out to disturb my peace and tranquility, which I fondly hoped I had enjoyed for some days, and hoped I was in the way of duty, but after all some wrong motives might have prevailed too much; was led to say—

"But pricking thorns through all the ground,
And mortal poisons grow;
And all the rivers that are found,
With dangerous waters flow."

Yesterday, my feelings became overpowered for a time, which is for the most part unusual for me, for I try to put a cheerful courage on, come what will, and bear up under trials of different kinds, principally the affliction I labor under for want of hearing quickly, which lays the foundation for numerous trials, and in a thousand ways: [Her feelings were so acute, that oft times she would be grieved, when on the part of others there was not the slightest intention of wounding her; and yet in general, as she remarks, her cheerfulness was such that no one would suspect it, nor yet know of it, until seen here.—W. C.] but I am often comforted with this promise—"Cast thy burden on the Lord, and he will sustain thee." O were it not for that, I should sink altogether, I fear. I have been somewhat consoled of late by these words—"For Israel hath not been forsaken, nor Judah of his God, of the Lord of Hosts; though their land was filled with sin against the Holy One of Israel." I can but hope it is the case amongst us; while hopeless despair seems to have seized the minds of many of the Church, others on sick beds, and elsewhere, are giving their testimony to the value of that religion which can support the soul amid all the trying scenes of life and death: but alas, iniquity abounds among us. O when will Zion's captivity be turned?

January 28, 1848.—My dear son spent a fortnight with us the last of the month of December; he has since become quite thoughtful and much concerned about his soul. This is another manifestation of the Lord's goodness to me, who am so undeserving. O if thou hast begun a good work in his soul, precious Saviour, carry it on; suffer no by-ends to hinder his determination to seek the Lord,—which do thou strengthen and increase. I would rely upon thy promise—"That thou wilt carry the Lambs in thy bosom." A blessed revival of religion is going on in Lower Cornwallis; about thirty have already united with the Church. To God be all the praise. "O bend thy chariot wheels this way, that we may see thy power and thy glory."

February 13.—Probably at this moment, or near this time, my highly-favored son may be going down the banks of Jordan, to be baptized as Christ was. A glorious revival of religion has commenced in Horton, in the College (that has been blessed with nine other revivals in about twenty years): every student now in the College, but one, has professed religion, and a large number of the boys in the Academy; among others is my son; although a trembling believer, yet it is manifest to all that he has received the grace of God in his heart. O that he may not grieve the Spirit 208
by rejecting the comfort which it gives! May he continually say, "Lord, I believe, help thou mine unbelief." The blessed work is still continuing in Lower Cornwallis and Horton: a host are expected to be baptized to-day. O may the blessed work extend and extend, East, West, North and South. We as a Church are experiencing much affliction in the sickness and death of some of its members. A valuable brother was buried last Sabbath; he has

left a wife and six children to mourn their loss. Another family of the Methodist order have buried two children in less than a week. O may it be sanctified to us all, young and old, that we may all feel that we too must soon give up our accounts to God.

March 12.—Sabbath morning. As this may be the last time I shall ever put pen to paper for this purpose, life being uncertain at all times (but especially in my present situation), I here want to record again and again the faithfulness and love of a covenant God,
209 when I so strangely revolt from him. * * * * * * *
I desire to feel thankful that I have learned in some small measure St. Paul's lesson—"In whatsoever state I am, to be content," although I would very gladly have my hearing again. The next consideration is, is my lamp trimmed and in bright burning, waiting to hear the call, "come up hither?" This is not in as lively exercise as I could wish. I find I am setting my temporal house in order, and I fear neglecting the spiritual too much. I can truly say—

"I leave the world without a tear,
Save for the friends I held so dear."

March 23.—I am still this side a boundless eternity, still on praying ground and pleading terms with the Lord of life and glory; but I have not that spirit of prayer that I wanted, or ought to have for those entrusted to my care; but when thinking of the absent, and those present too, my prayer is,

"Jesus and his salvation be
All to my child,
And all to me."

My impressions of short life are often vivid, and as such I see much to do while the day lasts; for oh what are all mortal charms compared with leaving a right impress upon those around us.

May 7.—Sabbath day. I have just been thinking where shall I begin to recount the Lord's goodness to me and mine, these few weeks past? Language fails me. While almost every family in the community have been visited by sickness and death, mine as yet have escaped the disorder prevalent (scarlet fever), and although I became the mother of another little son the last day of March, yet special mercy from day to day from the giver of every good and perfect gift has followed me, and restored me almost to
210 usual health. O Lord, how excellent is thy loving kindness; suffer me not to be unmindful of it, that as strength of body increases I may be guided afresh for the warfare yet assigned. O that I might apply more diligently to the fountain for wisdom to train those precious souls committed to my care. O may thoughts like these "take this child and nurse it for me," be resting with weight upon my spirit at all times.

May 23.—My companion is now preaching the funeral sermon of a female member of the Church who has been out of health for near twenty years, and the last six years has not left her chamber; she has glorified God, we humbly hope, by acknowledging his hand in her affliction, and at different periods has rejoiced in it. May the death and funeral services be sanctified! I do hope the Church here is about to revive and come up to their duty. O that I could say with the poet—

> "My spirit glows in faith,
> My heart in strong desire;
> And God will come, will come,
> Ere the lamp of life expire.
> Thou wilt not desert, I know,
> The heart that clings to thee;
> Oh no, the blessed will not go,
> Until he blesseth me."

May the people of God everywhere be wrestling Jacobs and prevailing Israels!

June 20.—My companion is now absent, with three children,
attending the annual Association. O may not only the power of 211
the Holy Spirit be felt in their hearts, but by all who may be present, and throughout the world. My desires are imperfect, and my efforts feeble, for the salvation of my own children, and O how far short do they come for the benefit of my neighbors and friends, and the world at large; but sometimes I would hope they are sincere, especially "when languor and disease invade this trembling house of clay." I can but cry, let thy light and thy truth shine into this dark and benighted understanding of mine and in all others.

October 1.—It seems strange indeed that I should let such a length of time pass, without writing some of my thoughts; but I am overwhelmed with cares and toils, and often my toil-worn frame is so disordered that I have no heart to engage in anything spiritual; still I hope I have not been without some right feelings in the midst of a great many wrong ones, and sometimes though far too few, hope I have enjoyed communion with God in his word and prayer (I have not been able to go to the house of God but four times this summer): the Bible seems very precious. Our Sabbath School furnishes an excellent library of books for old and young; at times I feel strong desires that the rising generation in this place especially, may no longer be suffered to pursue the paths of sin and folly. My anxieties are great about the young converts at Acadia College and in the Academy connected with it, where a most powerful revival of religion took place last winter, and nearly all at one time were hopefully converted. It has now greatly increased in numbers and efficiency.

December 31.—This is the last day of another year; I with all my family are spared in health to behold it. Oh how many mercies have I experienced the past year. I must again and again say—

> "Look back, my soul, the Lord has been thy friend;
> He has brought the last year's troubles to an end.
> Then what's to come, Lord give me strength to bear,
> And at thy feet to cast my every care."

But yet how awfully deficient I am in driving a trade with heaven, in living in daily and hourly communion with my God! True, I feel the necessity of preserving a constant disposition to look up to God in all my fears and straits; but alas it is often with so much coldness and stupidity that it seems like mocking God. "For God abhors the sacrifice, where not the heart is found." I am for the most part of the time taken up with cares of my family, and do not get much food for my mind by reading; but sometimes I hope my heart meditates right things, and I have a great favor conferred upon me in the rich communications of dear sisters in Christ, which I receive by letter, and a thousand ways in which I am favored to what many of my fellow creatures are, that are far more deser-
212 ving. O grant me thy direction, great God.

February 15, 1849.—Very many have been the exercises of my mind the past day and week; trials of a complicated nature almost overpower me. Were it not that I am convinced my blessed Lord knows the full dimensions of my sorrows, come they whence they may, and can enable those who have erred in spirit to come to understanding, I should be wholly discouraged. I know we are told "not to think it strange concerning the fiery trial as though some strange thing happened unto us," "but to count it all joy when we fall into divers temptations." Many of our trials doubtless are caused by our own deficiencies in duty. O what a perilous voyage is life, and O what a solemn charge are our dear children; in my view it is crucifying work to be a mother:—how much of a
213 spirit of grace and supplication is needed!

April 14.—About six weeks since the Church concluded to hold a series of meetings, and although the roads were very bad they were well attended by Ministers and people; and more than this, the Great King and Head of Zion met with them and poured out a blessing. A number of the Church were broken down and mourned over their departures from God; many of the young that had been stumbling over professed christians, became aroused to the duty of repenting and believing on God; the consequences are that a goodly number are rejoicing in hope, and to-day *twenty-two* were buried with Christ in baptism; last Sabbath, seven, and a large number more are expected to come forward next conference

(I have now three children public professors; O may they indeed be genuine professors, and may I have wisdom to instruct and guide them!) I feel as the Psalmist expresses it—"When thou turnedst again the captivity of Zion, we were like them that dreamed." It seems as if I could scarcely realize what wonders God has wrought. I have still not been without my trials from different causes, but I look for them, and I want the joy of the Lord to be my strength.

May 15.—The work of the Lord is still going on in this vicinity; above forty have been baptized; another little daughter of mine, eleven years old, is among the number. We have a little Church in our house; persons employed by us are also professors. O may they truly belong to the Church triumphant, and be clothed with humility! How much we need reviving and strengthening grace every hour! Enable us all, precious Saviour, to lay aside every weight, and the sin which doth so easily beset us, and to watch and pray that we enter not into temptation. The work is principally among the young. O may they be patterns of piety!

May 24.—Sabbath day. Twelve more are baptized to-day—the trembling widow, but not very aged, and eleven youths, and one lamb, seven years old among them. I feel to-day as if I could say, "Oh that men would praise the Lord for his great goodness to the children of men." O Lord, help thy servant, (my companion, who is now preaching for the first time for several weeks, in this Meeting House, as so many Ministers have come to his aid) to preach the unsearchable riches of Christ to his dying fellow men; his labors are very arduous.

July 15.—I have long omitted writing, waiting for something special to impress my mind, feeling that I have backslidden from God in heart, in murmurings and complainings, when I have so much cause to rejoice. Yesterday I attended conference, where about one hundred spoke of the goodness of God to them; truly it was a delightful sight to see so many youths among the number. Strengthen, O God, that which thou hast wrought for us.

August 20.—Sabbath day. A prayer meeting here is now going on near us to-day. May those who engage in it have the spirit of prayer! My companion is on the Mountain, where a number of this Church reside, and where appearances are favoring a revival; some are baptized to-day. The God of love is at the present time displaying his power in the restoration of sinners from the ruins of the fall, with many Churches in this Province, and throughout the world, bringing about his own designs and purposes by fire, sword, and pestilence. Who would not fear thee 214
and give glory unto thy name? Alas, how contracted are my views of such a God! How much happier should I be, were I

contemplating the character of God instead of complaining of my wants; whereas my great want is, want of contentment. "For godliness with contentment is great gain." During the aforesaid revival, up to last July 14th, there were *ninety-two* added to this Church by baptism. I have too much reason to fear I have fainted in the day of adversity, and I have not kept as near the throne as I should have done, as prayer "makes the christian armour bright, gives exercise to faith and love;" but for these few days past I have felt the need of returning unto God, I hope with purpose of heart, bewailing my unnumbered sins, and entreating forgiveness for Christ's sake. I can truly say with the Psalmist—"Bring my soul out of prison." Many are the words of encouragement which come to me from the Bible and precious hymns. As I awoke one morning—

"Come let us anew
215 Our journey pursue"—

With such passages as the following—"Wait upon the Lord, and be of good courage, and he shall strengthen thine heart"—"Draw nigh unto God, and he will draw nigh unto you"—and many similar ones, that ought to encourage such weak ones as I to put their whole trust in God, and be constantly at the foot of the throne. Last night I had some unusual views of this throne of mercy, for such rebel worms to be permitted to approach. "Sure we must fight if we would reign; increase our courage Lord." O make me faithful to all around.

September 16.—I am so overwhelmed with cares and company at this season of the year, that I have but little time for feeding the mind by reading or retirement. How often am I assailed with the thought that my profession is a mere name! I have so little of the life of religion in my soul, so little disposed to make sacrifices, and with zeal and energy promote the welfare of my dying fellow men. Dear Lord, suffer me not to live at this poor dying rate; lift the clouds of darkness, and enable me to go on my way rejoicing, having right and consistent views of all earthly things, and ravishing ones of heaven, that I may be a living example to the flock, in my family, and in the Church.

November 15.—Sabbath evening. My companion's text,—"If so be that ye have heard him and have been taught by him;" good attention, and I hope it will have a good influence. There is much of the evil effect of sin manifest in the Church already since the revival last spring; too many, no doubt, were too much under the influence of mere excitement, and did not give due consideration to the important step of uniting with a Gospel Church. Precious Saviour, grant to strengthen the things that remain which are of thine own right hand's planting. O may thy servant feed the sheep and lambs of thy fold with thy word, that God may be glorified by us. As regards my own exercises, I am yet wandering upon the barren mountains, so many hindrances to prayer and reading; but yet I do love wisdom's ways, and long more fully to deny self and take up my cross daily.

January 20, 1850.—Sabbath evening. I went to the house of God to-day, and returned with painful feelings, because I could not hear much. O how hard do I find it to be reconciled to this my loss! but I had the privilege of reading a skeleton of a sermon upon glorying in the cross of Christ. I trust I know something about that deadness to the world which it explains. I think I feel the most part of the time that I wish to use the world and not abuse it; I am necessarily much engrossed with its cares and anxieties, or the latter more than the former, on account of my children—what foundation is laid for their future usefulness. My heart often sinks within me when I realize my own deficiencies as a parent, and then that I cannot always understand their communications when not addressed to me. I do indeed feel that life is a fearful thing to all, but especially to a parent. O may we all possess more of a spirit of prayer, for without this we shall soon go astray. I feel my own want of it very much. We anticipate having a school in the house soon, and many will be the sacrifices of tranquility I expect to make, so many things often occur to disturb my peace. O suffer us not, dear Lord, to dishonor thy precious name!

February 24.—Our school is now in full operation, with the addition of two others to my family, and they seem to be making rapid progress to fit them for stations of usefulness. God grant to
adorn their minds with a meek and quiet spirit. I have felt con- 216
siderable anxiety of late about dying, but not half what I should. These words have been some comfort to me—"What time I am afraid I will trust in thee." O may it be the case at all times, that I may praise God more and complain less, for "He giveth power to the faint, and to them that have no might he increaseth strength." O how beautiful did the 40th Chapter of Isaiah appear to me this morning; the greatness of the majesty of God is set forth with much force and beauty.

March 10.—Very many are the conflicts through which I pass:

"The foes that furious rage without,
  The foes that lurk within;—
Temptations strong in phalanx fierce,
  That rush the heart to win.
But the precious Bible tells
  Where fit weaponry for such a fight is stor'd,—
The shield of faith, salvation's helm,
  The conquering Spirit's sword."

These lines are sublime, and convey a world of meaning to me, as
well as others, no doubt; they are taken from the "Messenger,"—
217 the title, "Paul's warning." I trust I find the word of God very
sweet to my taste of late. O help me, dear Lord, "to endure as seeing him who is invisible." How unworthy the notice of such a God have I appeared to myself—"whose eyes are as a flame of fire," who fills immensity and comprehends eternity. O may I not add to my sin and guilt by not trusting my all in his hands for time and eternity, when it is such a signal mercy that he has bid us draw nigh to him. I have felt the importance of salvation to dying men and women considerably of late (O may I still more). I often wonder I can be careless of those around me.

June 27.—With what sad feelings do I now pen a few thoughts,
the cause of which is the absence of my two eldest daughters,
beyond the time of attending the Association, one being taken sick,
218 and the other stopping to take care of her. Though they are with
their half-sister and kind friends, yet their parents' home would be more pleasing. When their brother left them yesterday, they were encouraged to hope she would soon be better, but a state of anxious suspense is most trying to human nature; yet I believe God will not prove me with any affliction resignation cannot conquer. It is a fresh trial for faith and patience. Since I heard of her illness my fears have been strongly excited, but yet have felt to say, even if she should be removed by death (as I hope she has a mansion prepared for her in heaven), *He doeth all things well;* but for a few hours past hope predominates over my fears, and looks upon the bright side; yet should the Lord see fit to take her to himself, shall I wish to retain her here among sorrow and tribulation? O may the affliction be sanctified to all of us as a family, and to the family where they are stopping, that humility and gratitude may characterise all our conduct! It has been an interesting Association: many difficulties have been settled. It is now divided into
219 three.

July 18.—Great are my obligations to infinite goodness in restoring and returning my daughter, the sick one. They were obliged to stop nearly a fortnight, but she is quite well now. O may the life which thou hast made thy care be more entirely devoted to thee. Rouse us up, dear Lord, to a weighty consideration of eternal things.

August 3.—Sabbath day. My companion is absent to minister to a neighboring Church that he has the pastoral oversight of: his labors are very extensive for his time of life, but he possesses a good degree of mental energy, with tolerable health; above all, his prevailing desire is to glorify God while life and breath remains. But he is necessarily considerably absorbed in worldly matters (as well as myself); yet repeated afflictions warn him of the danger of trusting to an arm of flesh; not long since he heard of the death of his youngest son, of the first family. He died among strangers, though kindly cared for and tended; but we can learn nothing at present very satisfactory of the state of his mind (this being the fourth son he has lost after they were grown up to manhood, and all absent from him when death came. 220

September 30.—I have experienced a long night of darkness, and cannot now say that a bright day has succeeded it; but for a few days I have felt my interest in the word of God, and the soul somewhat renewed, and the anxieties for my children's future welfare in this and another world increased, especially those who are yet in the gall of bitterness and in the bonds of iniquity, when I consider that it may be but a very little while I shall be with them, or spared to them, and so much devolves upon me.

November 3.—During the past month our house has been a thoroughfare: a great variety of company, and the attention to a sick person, for three weeks, who came to visit us (a dear friend and one of our former school-teachers, namely, Miss Elder), has tended to absorb almost all my attention and that of my daughters; she is fast hastening to the grave, and I trust is prepared for her great and last change. My body is so worn down with fatigue 221
and care that I get no time for rest or reading (except sleep, and I ought to be thankful for that), but I have had at times some solace from the reflection that there is help laid upon One that is mighty to save from all sorrow and sin, and He will finally bring me off conqueror, and all the redeemed.

November 10.—We have become rather more quiet from the bustle of company, still have many secular employments, which absorb too much of my time and attention, my head being very weak; but I have very many mercies to be thankful for; among the rest my children all in health; but unbelief—what clouds of darkness does it bring over my mind, what forebodings of the future—what evils does it pourtray! O precious Saviour, save my children from dishonoring thy precious and holy name. O may their minds be more solemn when God, heaven, and hell, and everything around us is serious.

December 1.—Sabbath day. A most lovely day; the sun is shining and warm like September, and my companion is now breaking the bread of life to many souls. O that they may have an appetite for spiritual food! May all Ministers of the sanctuary this day feel that they are standing between a living God and dead sinners. The past week a dear friend of mine (namely, Mrs. Alfred Skinner), a member of the Church, was committed to the silent tomb; she had been a subject of delicate health for many

years; and I firmly believe she has fought a good fight, and has
entered into the joy of her Lord; grace has subdued perverse
nature in her case: her work on earth was done, and she has com-
222 menced her Sabbath of rest. O blissful thought, concerning her
and the innumerable company which does and shall surround the
throne of God! and shall I be there to behold the triune God?
Alas, my evidences of it are not as bright and clear as I could
wish; I feel indeed that life is fast receding, and perhaps the next
grave dug near us may be for me. All day yesterday these words
were in my mind—"Reflect, thy end is nigh"—and in some measure could say, "I know that my Redeemer liveth." I want to
be led by the teachings of the Holy Spirit, in that way that will
most glorify God, whether it leads me into deeps of sorrow, or
pours the consolations of the Gospel into my heart.

December 15.—I have nothing very special to communicate of a
spiritual nature concerning myself or those within my knowledge,
excepting that in some Churches in this Province the Lord is pouring out his Spirit, and is present to heal the wounded heart. In
Yarmouth, a very extensive work of the Lord is going on. My
anxieties are unceasing for my children's welfare (how apt we are
to be selfish!); my desire is, that they may be kept from all idola-
trous associations and influences, and not have their hearts hardened through the deceitfulness of sin. O prepare us, precious
Saviour, for whatever awaits us in life, whether short life or long.
It is mercy, mercy I implore, for all our wanderings, and forgiveness through the blood of the Lamb. O may the light of divine
grace irradiate the dark clouds of sin and unbelief at all times!
How much sorrow have I had the past week on account of the want
of my hearing! To be such a rebel as to need such an affliction,
harrows up the inmost recesses of sorrow (at times, but for the
most part I try to be a better soldier), when I give vent to my
feelings; but that passage of Scripture has of late been a stay to
me—"Be not weary of the chastening of the Lord, for whom he
223 loveth he chasteneth." What sorrow should we not be willing to
endure for the love and patience of such a God toward us? And
when sorrow is not occasioned by immoral conduct in those around
us, we ought to strive to bear other petty trials with fortitude. O
for a closer walk with God!

February 8, 1851.—Since I wrote last I have become the
mother of another son, and have been surrounded with every temporal mercy a thankful heart could desire, though extreme cold
weather the most of the time (the son was born the twenty-second
day of December last), and very many spiritual mercies, all pur-
224 chased by the death of Christ. My exercises have not been what
I could wish, but have sometimes felt a spirit of prayer, though

often interrupted with wandering thoughts. The following words express too fully my case,—"If a man's prayer moves upon the feet of an abated appetite, it wanders into the society of every trifling accident, and talks with every object it meets, and cannot arrive at heaven, but when it is carried forward upon the wings of passion and strong desire, it passes on through all the intermediate regions of clouds and stays not, until it dwells at the foot of the cross, where mercy sits, and thence sends holy showers of refreshment." Too seldom is the last part of this the case with me. I oft times think I never knew what the spirit of prayer was. I have indeed been the subject of sore conflict for some time past, and fear I seldom know what true peace is, though I know where it is to be found. O help us, dear Lord, to move forward in the right way; and O help my children (two of the daughters are expecting to leave home soon for school,) to acknowledge thee in all their ways, to be more humble and solemn.

July 20.—My dear children have all been at home for some weeks, but expect soon to leave again, and I would be often overburdened with care and toil were I to allow it to weigh me down; but the conviction that I am submitting to many privations for their future usefulness (should their lives be spared), prompts me onward to endure hardness in many ways. I desire to be patient and hope for better days, even here on earth, when I shall have more time for reading and retirement; but while performing the temporal duties of my station, O may I walk by faith and not by sight, be looking and longing for that blessed hope and the glorious appearing of our great God and Saviour Jesus Christ. O rouse us all up to right considerations and just views of the present life, and that which is to come, so that we may feel that every action of our life has a bearing upon eternity. O suffer us not to be stupid and careless. O take this veil of darkness from our eyes, that so inclines us to conform to this world and its maxims.

July 28.—As usual I have to be very much engaged, but when very much cast down the past week on account of the trials by the way, my weak faith was enabled to lay hold of this promise—"Fear not, I am with thee; be not dismayed, for I am thy God; I will strengthen thee, yea I will help thee, yea I will uphold thee by the right hand of my righteousness." O that I had a fuller 225
realization of the worth of this and all the promises, that I might take unto myself the whole armour of God and fight manfully.

> "My faith would lay her hand
> On that dear head of thine;
> While like a penitent I stand,
> And there confess my sin."

December 28.—Another year is near its close, and we are all as a family spared in health, and are now all at home, but expect soon to be separated. My oldest son as heretofore, and my two eldest
226 daughters anticipate spending the winter at school at Wolfville. O precious Saviour, shield them beneath thy shadowy wings; O suffer them not to restrain prayer, but enable them to look to thee for strength and wisdom in all their engagements; may they listen to reason and make passion submit. O crown the undertaking with thy blessing, dear Lord, that glory may redound to thy name by it. We have recently had our hearts cheered by the announcement of the determination of one of the young members of our Church to sacrifice all worldly interests, to preach the everlasting Gospel; he is a son of one of our Deacons—another Deacon has also a son studying for the Ministry, the fruits of the last revival; they have both made rapid improvement in their studies and knowledge every way, we trust; may they both, as well as all others, be humble and sincere, and rely upon the promises of God, and be harnessed for the battle before them. O may this Church and all Churches pray much for the increase of laborers in the Lord's vineyard. We expect a number of Ministers to meet with us next Sabbath, and for some days, to hold a quarterly meeting; may much good result from it to saint and sinner! I am almost overwhelmed with care, the children planning to leave directly after the meeting; but I try to hang upon the promise—"As thy day is so shall thy strength be."

February 26, 1852.—Although five of my children are almost constantly at school (in this district and in Wolfville), I am more confined to domestic duties than ever for want of usual help, but my health is excellent, and living upon hope and faith makes toil pleasant. O that I had more of a spirit of believing prayer, to pray for all men, and all institutions connected with the glory of God. I trust my chief desire is to be preparing for the great change that will soon overtake me. O that I could discharge all the necessary duties incumbent upon me to my younger children as well as elder ones, and in every relation of life.

March 20.—Two very sudden deaths of late have, I trust, had some effect in quickening my mind to more deep reflection upon the fleeting nature of time and all that pertains to this life, below the salvation of the soul. I do feel as if I wanted to be more actively engaged in the duty of prayer and every other one that comes in my way. I have felt very anxious about my children of late, one and all. I have so much to be thankful for in the opportunity they have of getting knowledge (set aside everything else), that I feel ashamed of my past misgivings. O may I ever give thanks unto the Lord, for he is good and his mercy endureth forever, and again and again feel the force of these lines :—

> " Waken, O Lord, my drowsy powers,
> To walk this dangerous road ;
> And if my soul is hurried hence,
> May it be found with God." 227

May 9.—Lovely spring has again returned, though cold and backward until a few days past. Often have I desired that it might be spring-time in the Church generally. It has been a long winter season with too many in this Province; but some in the Eastern part are revived, refreshed, and added unto. I have had considerable variety of exercise of mind since I last wrote; some that have caused searchings of heart, and some that have led me to cry mightily to God to avert evils and cause reform. I have also felt more and more anxious about my children, but my seasons of retirement are so few, to what they once were, that I miss them exceedingly, and I often fear I shall be one of those of whom it shall be said, "Cut it down, why cumbereth it the ground,"—were it not that I have at times some scanty views of the way of life and salvation, and such a glorious Mediator to make reconciliation for his people who when iniquities prevail against them, will not suffer them to be overcome.

May 24.—Sabbath morning. I have again and again been disappointed in my absent children not coming home upon a visit during the lovely weather we have had this spring. I do not allow myself to be too anxious about it, for I know the motive that governs them, and in a few weeks they will be home for the summer and attend school near, if all is well. I often wish I thought as 228
much about the Saviour as I do about my children. To have them God-fearing characters, and well educated, is my highest wish. I have only two little ones at home during the week, out of eight; all at school the most of the time. I have been reading the past week a book entitled, "Sunny Side: the settlement of a pastor and family." It is like living my life over again. Many of the 229
circumstances are very similar to the trials and hard times we have had to grapple with, in keeping up an establishment upon a flimsy foundation for a number of years, though we have not been wholly dependant upon the people (for we had to expend our own means which God in his Providence placed in our hands), and so much the worse, for the honor of God, and the good of the Church and the rising generation. O I hope, wherever the sin lies, it will be forgiven. In my opinion, a Minister should be wholly devoted to his work, and sustained therein, and not have to toil and labor on a farm, or to look after it for his and family's support, in whole or in part: but I have mourned over it, until I have found it was no use: I might as well give it up in our case, and make the best of

230 it. I can say with "Sunny Side," "a busy life enough have I found the life of a pastor's wife, but I can truly say that it has fully recompensed me. If I could feel that I had met its claims to the best of my abilities, I should look back upon it with great satisfaction." I have greatly to lament that I have not prayed more for Zion's peace and prosperity, for I have not spent twenty-three years in this place without feeling deeply interested in the marriage and settlement of individuals; and when I see a host of young people coming up to fill the place of their parents, one cannot be insensible to the influence they will exert. O help us, precious Saviour, to redeem the time, for life is fast receding.

> "Our wasting lives grow shorter still,
> As months and days increase;
> And every beating pulse we tell
> 231 Leaves but the number less."

June 12.—Words are inadequate to pourtray our present feelings under the visitation of God in his divine arrangements concerning us and many others. On the seventh of this month, the beloved son Isaac (though but a step-son to me, yet as dear as my my own), a Baptist Minister from St. John, Rev. Mr. Very, with four students from Acadia College, two of them Ministers of religion, Grant and Rand, went to Blomidon, and on their return, when within a short distance of the shore, the wind blowing a gale and a heavy sea, the boat upset, and seven men were drowned (all
232 those mentioned, and one of the boatmen). Such unexpected and startling news has caused us to say with David, "I was dumb, I opened not my mouth because thou didst it." We believe it to be in accordance with God's unchangeable purpose, and therefore endeavor to be still and know that he is God, and has a sovereign right to do all his pleasure. But poor nature, ever weak, would shrink from the afflictive stroke. Our beloved son was nearly thirty-five years of age, a highly talented and useful Professor of Mathematics, a Minister of the Gospel also, and a devoted martyr to his country, in the cause of education especially. He went to Wolfville in July, 1829, a scholar under the ever to be remembered Mr. Chapin, Principal in the Academy, being then twelve years of age, and continued there at Wolfville as a scholar in the Academy and College, and as Teacher (with the exception of two years at Waterville College, in the State of Maine), until his sudden demise. The deep interest which he always felt in the institutions there, and the immense amount of labour and toil he went through, both mentally and physically, was only known to himself and God; a part, a small part of which was manifest in securing materials from all parts of the three provinces and other places for and in building the noble structure under his own superintendance,

besides the untold amount of cares other ways,—the business more or less of the Church at Horton, to which he belonged,—the business connected with the denomination in its various departments,—together with his labors also for the public good, &c., &c.,—all tended to wear him out (with other trials also). His health the past winter had been failing, but he was gradually recruiting at the time of his demise, though quite feeble. His precious and useful life was cut short. He has finished his work, and gone to his precious reward, where no more sorrows nor conflicts await him. Happy spirit, dwelling in that society where all the region is peace. Now, precious Saviour, what wait we for? Our hope is in thee. O sanctify it to our own souls. It is indeed a heavy stroke. The aged father bows under it with quiet submission. He was a friend and counsellor to us all, but he has left no wife or children, like Mr. Very. But this is only a small part of the ways of God: how many throughout the world meet with similar trials. O may more have the enmity of their hearts slain (by the law) at their deaths than by their life, that the cause of religion may be greatly advanced by this dispensation of Providence.

August 30.—Very many have been the different scenes through which I have passed since I last wrote; the astounding blow then seemed but the beginning of sorrows. Hardly had we recovered from the shock when sickness entered our dwelling, and five, for a few days, myself being one of them, were prostrated: three of the children were seriously and dangerously ill with the dysentery; they however all recovered, and their health was restored sooner than could have been expected, with the exception of the youngest one, who lingered along for five or six weeks in a miserable way, but is now upon his feet again. And now I fear I have a most sad account to give of the state of my mind through these afflictions; various indeed have been the trials, known only to God, on account of the rebellion of my heart; I dreadfully fear being hardened in the furnace instead of softened. The fiftieth Psalm is the language of my heart, I do hope. (I do not pray as much as I ought). 233
Alas, too much apathy and indifference, and unreconciliation to our loss, though I know it is his gain. O for more love to God and man!

October 17.—I still am the subject of severe mental agony, procured often doubtless by my own deficiencies and affliction, and sometimes by the proceedings of others. Yet I find the Bible more and more precious, and a throne of grace a sweet and sure refuge, though I have too much reason to fear I receive not because I ask amiss. It is not the "effectual fervent prayer," I fear. O may the falling leaves, with other appearances of autumn, remind me of my own declining, and the worth of souls around me. O

help me to use my tongue and strength for thy glory while this
short life remains.

March 24, 1853.—Seldom have I allowed such a length of time
to pass without penning a few thoughts, especially when under the
hand of affliction. It is now nearly four months since my eldest
daughter has been confined to her room with various complaints;
but she has been patient and resigned to her suffering, which has
been very acute, and feels that whether it ends in life or death, it
234 will be well. I trust I can say for the most part of the time, "It
is the Lord let him do as seemeth him good," but I want more of
the quickening and enlivening influences of the Spirit to enable me
to say, "It is good for me that I have been and am afflicted."
Many have been the trials I have passed through the past winter,
but hitherto God has helped me.

April 6.—Yesterday was a day of much weeping with me
(though unseen by mortals). I have increasing fears respecting
my dear daughter's health, and although for the most part of the
time I can leave her at the disposal of Omnipotence, yet nature
shrinks from seeing her pine and suffer. No wonder I weep, when
I reflect on the many deficiencies of my past life, with regard to
discharging my duty towards her and my other children, the
Church to which I belong, my acquaintances, saint and sinner. O
when will Zion arise in this place, and shake herself from the dust
of the earth? When will her members be more faithful, and
watch over one another with godly zeal? Hasten the time, dear
235 Lord, and grant us a spirit of prayer.

April 20.—No change, we fear, for the better in my child's
health, and I often imagine separation is not far distant; and truly
it will be so, for this life is short to all, but a hand breadth. I
have just been reading the last hours of Doctor Arnold, and a
short diary that he kept; seldom have I seen communications that
so interested me; it greatly strengthened my hope, when I read
236 such things. He says, "I am now at that age, forty six, to know
what this life is;" and then his anxiety to be more humble and
gentle to all around, and his views of the uncertainty of life,—
such desires to be sanctified throughout soul, body and spirit—and
be ready to meet death, let it come in whatever form it might,
which event was very sudden with him, his complaint being of the
heart. I feel daily that life is short with me, and I have to be such
a Martha that I seldom get Mary's place, or devote the time I
237 should to my little ones. I want more of the grace of the Spirit.

May 14.—Yesterday I was permitted once more to attend conference. I always find such opportunities refreshing, if I cannot enjoy them as I once did. I feel to lament the low state of Zion, and grieve for the afflictions of Joseph. O may we all arise to newness of life, more zeal and energy, wisdom and faithfulness, to look after the scattered flock. We have had a fresh demonstration of the kind feeling of the Church and others, the past winter, in a donation visit: it was truly a pleasant interview to us all, proving, I trust, that it is more blessed to give than to receive. Surely the receiving on our part of about thirty pounds in money and useful articles, could not fail to excite our gratitude. The address has been a great relief to my mind in strengthening the bond of union that has so long existed, though not always felt in its full vigor, owing to many difficulties which often arise in a Church. My dear daughter is not much better, if any. O Lord, prepare us to suffer and do thy righteous will. One of our mothers in Israel (namely sister Hannah Calkins) is fast hastening to her eternal rest; she is so peaceful and calm, waiting for the summons to call her hence and safely land in those mansions above. She has been one of the gentle, influential mothers, and has done a great work in her family, being left a widow with seven children; she has buried four. Happy woman! Well might the infidel envy her. 238

June 20.—Have just returned from the annual Exhibition at Acadia College, where my dear son (with his room-mate, who went to the Academy the same time he did,) delivered an Oration
for the first time. My nervous feelings were a good deal excited, 239
as they are generally of the fearful kind, but to the praise of God's grace and upholding power, he was enabled, with the other, to go through with composure, giving credit to the teachers and themselves (the subjects were, "the Duke of Wellington," and "Science in the Nineteenth Century"). I endeavored to make the occasion a matter of prayer for sometime previous, that all the faculties of the mind might be strengthened, and that he might depend on God to help him (and for others too); and when I surveyed the past and thought of the anxieties of mind I had in reference to his going there, I could but say, "Bless the Lord, O my soul, and forget not all his benefits." To those who could hear all, the occasion was highly satisfactory. My dear sick daughter is still languishing and no essential change. I strongly fear the result will be the sinking of nature, but God can overrule and bless the means for her restoration.

August 6.—Sabbath afternoon. Seldom do I have opportunity for writing here, and too seldom feel that glow of holy love and zeal which would be worth noticing; and I do not think it best to dwell too much upon the dark side of any matter here though these lines may be the revealer of thoughts and feelings when this poor body rests in the grave, for I do not feel disposed to burn them for my own satisfaction. And although many parts of them may go to shew a low standard of christian principles, yet I have never studied to dress up my feeble exercises with unmeaning language, for this I could not do, for want of more knowledge; but should these lines ever meet the eye of any mortal, and be the means of affording the least satisfaction, to God be all the glory. I have found them often a comfort to myself, for I am exceedingly fond of reading journals. My dear daughter is some better than she was, but nothing permanent to hope upon yet, as to her health, but everything strong and immortal in God. O what a Being of infinite perfection, filling immensity and comprehending eternity! How scanty are my views! But ere long I hope to see him as he is, without a dimming veil between, when this mortal shall have put on immortality.

[This is the last entry she ever made in her Journal, and hence it seems remarkable that it should have been so appropriate to her speedy and sudden demise.—W. C.]

CHAPTER III.

LAST ILLNESS, DEATH, AND CHARACTER.

Mrs. Chipman's last illness commenced on Thursday, the 6th of October, 1853. At first it appeared to be an attack of indigestion, and was so treated. But the symptoms became more severe and alarming during the next three days. Though there seemed to be but little fever or inflammation, the digestive organs were in a state of entire torpor, and no relief could be obtained. The medical attendant employed the most powerful means, day after day for a fortnight, but without success. Yet hopes were entertained, even till within two days of Mrs. C.'s decease, that she would rally and recover. Her own impressions, however, were different. On Lord's day, Oct. 16, she intimated to Mr. C. her opinion that she would be soon removed, and said that during the preceding night many beautiful passages of Scripture had occurred to her mind, from which she had derived much comfort. She particularly mentioned Psalm 17, 15—"Then shall I be satisfied, when I awake, with thy likeness." That expectation cheered her abundantly.

On Tuesday morning, the 18th, she again referred to the probability of her death. In conversation with Mr. C. she remarked, "I want you to forgive any improprieties you have discovered in me?" He replied, "I have much more reason to adopt Dr. Judson's remarks to his second wife, under similar circumstances, 'that he had much more cause to ask her forgiveness.'" "Oh," she said, "there are none of us but what have our petty foibles, but I ought to have forborne more." Then followed an affecting scene with two of her children. Embracing one of them she said, "My dear A——, I may be soon removed from you, and you will be left motherless. I want you to be a christian, to love and read your Bible, to pray to God to forgive your sins. Seek the Lord; seek him now; delay no longer; pray this night. I should be more willing to leave you all if I was persuaded that you were all born into the kingdom of Christ. I hope the elder ones are; but I want *you*, my dear, to be a christian." Some time after, she addressed him again, in the most solemn and impressive manner. At different times through the day she exerted herself much to speak to her other children, as well as to friends who came to see her. To some she said that she had got so far over that she had no desire to return, but rather to depart and be with Christ; that she had many ties to bind her to earth, but that heaven was far more desirable.

On the evening of the 19th she remarked to Mr. C. that some time before her mind had been much impressed by the words of the Saviour, "If it be possible, let this cup pass from me," &c., and by the statement, that an angel was sent to strengthen him. She had considered these passages in connection with the case of her afflicted daughter Amelia, and had derived much comfort from them; but now she felt them to apply to herself, and still they afforded comfort. Through grace she could say, "Thy will be done," and patiently endure the Lord's pleasure.

Next day she observed, that she did not wish to remain here, unless it were the Lord's will; she longed to go to her heavenly home, where she trusted that she would be welcomed, and be forever happy. It was not that she wished to get rid of trouble or suffering, for she was willing to bear all that the Lord was pleased to lay upon her, and to live all her appointed time till her change should come; but she would be with Christ, and that would be "far better." She could leave her husband and her children in the hands of God, for she felt assured that he would take care of them all.

Having requested that portions of Scripture might be repeated, to refresh her memory and direct her thoughts, Mr. C. mentioned the Apostle Paul's words, "For I am now ready to be offered,"
&c. "I have often thought of that passage," she said, "but I 241
feel that I have not 'fought the good fight' as I should have done, and I have not been so faithful to my household as I should have been; I trust you will do your duty to them, and make up my deficiency." The following text was then recited, "It doth not yet appear what we shall be," &c. "Yes," she observed, "eye

hath not seen, nor ear heard, what God hath prepared for them that love him; that portion has afforded me much comfort." Other suitable passages, such as "Thanks be unto God, which giveth us the victory," &c., were repeated: they sustained and consoled her, as heart and flesh failed.

She was very anxious to see Mr. C.'s surviving children by his first marriage, but only Mr. W. H. Chipman, with his wife and four children, were able to reach the house in time. She conversed with them all (it was the afternoon before her death) with great earnestness, evidently laboring under deep emotion, and gave them her parting blessing with peculiar solemnity.

She retained her consciousness, with slight and occasional exceptions, nearly to the last. Her hearing did not appear more than usually affected till late on Saturday evening, when it became extremely difficult for her to distinguish sounds. After ten o'clock her mind seemed somewhat wandering, although it was thought that she partially understood what was said to her. "My dear," Mr. C. said, "you are drawing near the closing scene, and will soon go over Jordan." As if roused and startled, she asked, with considerable energy, and in a hurried manner, "Do you mean Amelia?" "No, my dear, yourself." "*Ah! best!*" she replied. These were the last words she was heard to utter. They indicated at once her anxiety about her afflicted daughter, and her entire submission to the divine will respecting herself. After that, there were no earthly communings. But doubtless the soul, about to be released, had fellowship with God. The final struggle was hardly perceptible. At two o'clock on Lord's day morning, Oct. 23, 1853, she gently passed into life.

During the affliction she had enjoyed the "peace which passeth all understanding." She had borne her sufferings with exemplary patience, meekly surrendering herself to the Lord. The inward calm was expressed in her placid features. And when the lifeless form was prepared for the grave, there was still "a sweet and heavenly smile upon her countenance;" it was the smile of one who "slept in Jesus."

The funeral took place on Tuesday, Oct. 25. The Rev. T. S. Harding preached an excellent sermon on the occasion, from Colossians 3. 3, 4. The congregation was very large, and all were
242 deeply affected, for all felt that they had lost a friend.

Mrs. Chipman's character is so fully depicted in her Journal, in which she has unconsciously drawn her own likeness, that but few observations are now necessary.

The reader cannot but have observed that she was gifted with clearness of perception and sound judgment, and that she was intellectually as well as morally qualified for the position which Providence assigned her.

But the foundation of her varied excellencies was laid in earnest piety. Youthful ardour was disciplined betimes by grace. She early learned to view all things in the light of the Bible, and to govern herself by the revealed will of the Saviour. At all times the inquiry was, "Lord, what wilt thou have me to do?" and amid the toils, cares, and embarrassments of life, she sought peace in walking with God. Nor did she seek in vain. Notwithstanding the anxious questionings which humility prompted, and the recurrence of occasional seasons of darkness, she experienced largely the blessedness of faith, love, and hope, and exhibited the effects in habitual holiness and evangelical consistency. Conscious of innumerable defects and failings, she "groaned within herself, waiting for the adoption;" while others, when they saw the grace of God in her, were gladdened and encouraged. They knew that she was imperfect, like her fellow-believers, but they rejoiced in her as an intelligent, honest, straightforward christian.

Strongly attached to the principles and polity of the Baptist denomination, as derived from the New Testament, she manifested deep interest in the state of the Church to which she belonged. The members of that Church will not soon forget the manifold tokens of her love and solicitude. She was justly endeared to them all, and her removal, so sudden and unexpected, filled their hearts with sorrow. For she had sympathised with them in their griefs, and in many ways had sought to soothe and alleviate; and they saw that her happiness was inseparably connected with the prosperity of the cause. When sinners were converted she rejoiced, though with trembling, because she knew the devices of the enemy and the deceitfulness of the human heart. When any cases of backsliding occurred, or indifference and sloth appeared, her soul was grieved. It gladdened her exceedingly to witness liberality and zeal on behalf of denominational institutions. Our domestic and foreign missions, and our educational enterprises, were justly esteemed by her, and warmly recommended to the members of the Church. Other Societies, also, were much prized, among which Bible and Tract Societies held a high place, since in them are embodied the noblest purposes of christian benevolence.

In her domestic relations, Mrs. Chipman's deportment was truly exemplary. She was called to occupy a difficult post, (for two of her husband's children by his first marriage were older than herself,) but she discharged its duties with such prudence and discretion, and evinced such an amiable, conciliatory spirit, that preju-

dices vanished, and the step-mother became the object of sincere affection. Her own numerous family—eight of whom, the survivors of twelve, deplore the loss they have sustained by her unlooked-for death—experienced in full measure a christian mother's care and love. She laboured incessantly for their welfare; she cheerfully submitted to sundry inconveniences, that they might enjoy the advantages of education; and she agonized in prayer for their conversion to God, as may be seen in many pas-
243 sages of her Journal. But it is needless to multiply words on these points. None but her husband and her children could fully appreciate her character, and *they* "call her blessed."

It only remains to observe, that Mrs. Chipman was much beloved and respected by the Church. The members knew that their pastor's wife cherished anxious care on their behalf. They felt that they could confide in her. Kind, hospitable, and discreet, she was ever ready to render aid where it was required, and always desirous of promoting love and unity. A hasty and injudicious choice may cause a pastor to be linked for life to a *hindrance:* but Mrs. C. was a *help-meet.*

An extract from a letter written by Dr. Van Buren, formerly of Pleasant Valley, but now resident in Tennessee, U. S., will
244 appropriately close this brief sketch of Mrs. Chipman's character. The letter was addressed to a friend in Pleasant Valley, and was dated "Feb. 8, 1854":

"The Church and community have indeed sustained a loss of which they are not probably yet duly sensible; but our dear pastor and his lovely children have sustained a loss that can never be repaired. She was indeed and in truth a most estimable woman. As a christian, most exemplary; as a wife, affectionate and kind; as a mother, indefatigable in contributing to the comfort and happiness of her children, imparting christian instructions and all other necessary information in regard to domestic and social habits; as a friend, she was warm and sincere, never losing sight of her professions, attachments, or predilections; as a member of society, she was absolutely a pattern to all who felt inclined to act consistently. And what shall I say more—unless it be that we shall never look upon her like again? But she has only preceded us a few days, and is now resting in the bosom of that Redeemer whom she loved and served so faithfully on earth, ready to embrace all who have the same precious faith, and follow her through the resurrection, as they successively enter the same blessed abode."

Subjoined are a few extracts from Mrs. Chipman's letters to her friends. They are illustrations of her habitual spiritual-mindedness:

To Professor Chipman. May 3, 1846.—"I was sorry to 245
find your health again impaired. It is no more than I feared, when I hear of your constant application to perplexing business. I sincerely hope such means may be resorted to as will effect speedy and permanent relief. *I* am not willing to spare you just now (selfish motives, no doubt) set aside the Denomination. * * * * * I want to be more engaged for the welfare of souls around us and elsewhere. Often of late does time appear very short, and eternal realities of the utmost consequence. Oh for a light estimate of all earthly things, with right views of duty, and strength and wisdom to perform it!"

To Mrs. H. Lyons. Nov. 26, 1848.—"Your letter found 246
me conflicting with the powers of darkness in many forms. Sometimes I thought the dark weather had a great influence to help me look on the dark side, and I often feared I had forgotten to cast my burden on the Lord. These lines were some solace—

'Ye fearful saints, fresh courage take,
The clouds ye so much dread
Are big with mercy, and shall break
In blessings on your head.' 247

I have felt somewhat lightened of late, but it does not proceed wholly, I fear, from religious principles. My time and attention are so taken up with domestic duties that I have but little leisure for reading and retirement; and without these, no wonder I go lean from day to day. Though for the most part I do not allow my mind to be disturbed with trifles, or with things that cannot be helped, yet it is far from that life and peace which belong to a spiritual mind. How often are we 'perplexed, but not in despair!'"

To the same. Aug. 19, 1849.—"What beautiful lines the following are—

'Christian, walk prayerfully! oft wilt thou fall,
If thou forget on thy Saviour to call.
Safe shalt thou walk through each trial and care,
If thou art clad in the armour of prayer.'

I fear the two first too much apply to me. I have not felt that constant disposition to look up to God in all my straits which I know is necessary.

'Freely my spirit would converse
With Jesus all the day,'—

I want to be the language of my heart. When the Most High, who sits upon a throne high and lifted up, has condescended to permit such rebel worms to approach this throne of mercy, what an insult is offered to a God of spotless purity if we are backward to spread our wants before him."

To the same. January 14, 1850.—"Since I last wrote you we have entered upon another year. How seldom do persons giving and receiving the compliment usual on this occasion realize the full or proper meaning of their words! How unsatisfying is the pleasure that thousands anticipate! Instead of feeling deep heartfelt sorrow for sin, the many omissions and commissions of our lives, I feel for one that I enter upon it entirely too unconcerned, for an immortal being. I think I do feel some gratitude for the distinguishing favors of the past year, as well as all my life; but oh! what poor returns do I make for such amazing mercy bestowed upon one so unprofitable! * * * * How true are the words of the poet—

'We should expect some danger near,
When we possess delight.'

It is well for us that there is a rod in the covenant.

To the same. Feb. 4, 1851.—(Referring to the death of Fa-
248 ther Manning)—"I hope she (Mrs. M.) may continue to be supported under the heavy bereavement, and know of such testimonies of regard and veneration for her dear departed husband, from friends and foes, as may make amends for all the sorrow she has had on account of the enemy thrusting sore at Mr. Manning in various ways. I did esteem him highly for his work's sake; and one of his precious works used to be to watch over the children of families. Well do I remember much he said to me when I was a child, and how he cared for me when my mind was seriously exercised. It was he that welcomed me to the privileges of the Church, and led me down the banks of Jordan. Such a pastor is very near and dear." [The following passage from Mr. Manning's Diary may be appropriately introduced here:—"Sept. 16, 1825. Went to Deacon Homes Chipman ..... Some agreeable conversation with Sister Eliza, who is an amiable young christian, and possesses powers of mind of some considerable promise. Asked me some important questions respecting knowing the divine influences from natural affections, &c., and also in what communion with God consisted—the which I had an opportunity to explain. This was interesting. I am much pleased to have young converts modestly inquisitive; there seems to be an opportunity of doing them good."]

To the same. Jan. 15, 1853.—I know not why it was, but I felt impressed with the belief, or idea, when the beloved Isaac was taken from us, that it was the beginning of sorrows; and it seems as if there had been but one succession of sorrows since,—some visible and apparent to beholders, and others, not. I know I am dealt with far better than I deserve, and I need frequent chastisements to break my hold of the world, though it has few, if any, charms for me. * * * * I think I can say to-day,

> 'In all my fears, in all my straits,
> My soul on his salvation waits.'

I hope I have experienced some of the joys of this great salvation this autumn. The plan of redemption has appeared very precious at times."

To Mrs. S. T. Rand. April 7, 1840.—"Although you have 249
to mourn over the low state of religion with you, yet if the Church is in peace and union that is truly comforting; and I fully coincide with you in opinion, that there is much more hope of a person continuing in the good ways of the Lord; who embarks in the cause of Christ when there seems but little encouragement from the Church. Happy for us, that the power and love of God are the same at all times; and if we lived as near the fountain as we might, the enjoyment of religion (in private, at all events), would be precious."

To the same. 1844.—"I have passed through many changes since I saw you, enough to humble a heart not so proud as mine; but I fear mine is yet unhumbled. I have thought of you a great deal, and longed to tell you to seek much for the grace of the Spirit in training your children, for I can see sad deficiencies on this ground in myself. Rest assured, it is a small matter to nurse and take care of them in their infant days, compared with the anxiety a parent feels as they emerge into the society of the world. But here I often find myself leaning on my own strength, instead of saying,

> 'Accept the trust, accept the care,
> O Father, which I bring to thee;
> And let this holy act of prayer
> Exert its soothing power on me.'

May we live to the honor of our Lord and Master more than we have ever done, quiet and submissive to the allotments of Providence concerning us. A Minister's wife needs the whole armour of God, if any one."

To the same. May 17, 1848.—"Let us count it all joy when we fall into divers temptations, &c., if they only help us to make our way to God. I fear we too often exclaim, 'O land of rest, for thee I sigh.' O may you count it an honor to suffer for the furtherance of the Redeemer's cause, in the way in which your husband is engaged. * * * Have patience, and pray for more. Our work will soon be done; how careful we should be what impress we leave behind!"

To the same. Nov. 5, 1848.—"The wise man says, 'The Lord will not suffer the soul of the righteous to famish,' and I am sometimes encouraged to hope that it is somewhat verified in me, although I too often manifest that I am 'rich, and have need of
250 nothing.' Yet such are the straits a mother and a Minister's wife are placed in at times, I think they cannot be satisfied without imploring help from above.

'Weaker than a bruised reed,
Help I every moment need.'

But oh! how far short do I come in applying to the fountain for the supply of my numberless wants! 'Lord, teach us to pray aright,' should be our constant cry."

To the same. October 1, 1849.—"Grace dwells beside a bad neighbour in the best of us, and the sad temptations of our great adversary often find a ready reception within our troubled breast. * * * I am greatly cheered and revived in my pilgrimage since the Lord has dealt so graciously with me and mine, and added such a goodly number to the Church among us. It is true, dear sister, I ought more than any other human being to lie in the valley of humiliation, and forever adore the matchless grace of God. * * * Many times last winter, when cast down with the state of the Church and other things, this passage would come to my mind, 'Be patient, for the coming of the Lord draweth nigh.' I little thought it would be in the way of a revival. But I am one of those that rejoice with much trembling. You will, I hope, bear us on your mind at a throne of grace, that God may preserve the lambs as well as the sheep."

To the same. March 19, 1850.—"What a work the mother has to perform! Is it not to be feared those precious little immortals are too much neglected? I feel, for one, that while attending to the wants of their bodies, I have sadly neglected their minds. It is true, there will no more be laid upon us than we are able to bear, but are we 'instant, in season, out of season'—'sowing beside all waters'—not knowing whether this or that will prosper—laboring every moment as though the next might find them in an awful eternity? The more I reflect upon past life the more I have to plead for forgiveness, for my unfaithfulness in every thing of a spiritual or moral nature."

To the same. October 2, 1852.—"But our domestic matters are but small, to the irreparable loss we and the denomination have
251 met with. What breaches does death make! We feel the loss most sensibly here; every day makes me feel sad about it—save when I think of the reward they have all gone to receive. One of the strongest pillars of Acadia College has done his work and entered into glory. How Acadia will get on now, if the endow-

ment is not finished up, seems to human view to look dark;—but God will order all things well. * * * Could I see you for one hour, I could tell you many things I cannot write. I thought the language of the poet worthy of adoption—

'Let saints in sorrow lie resigned,
And trust a faithful God.'

But it has not been all sorrow with me, though my sins have deserved it. I sometimes get weary of toil and care, and wish for rest, so that the mind may have some food by reading, &c., and it may be that eternal rest is nearer at hand than I have any idea of. But it will soon come."

To the same. April 22, 1853.—[Referring to her recovery from severe illness]—"Through much mercy I have been spared to my family, and I increasingly feel the need of wisdom from on high to guide and direct me into all truth. You know the wisdom that cometh from above is represented as being 'pure, gentle, easy to be intreated, full of mercy and good fruits.' How much we need all those traits of character, or virtues, in every situation, but especially in ours, as mothers and Ministers' wives! 'Beloved self must be denied'—for as we would have our children to be, we ought to be ourselves. O the many deficiencies of my past life, and present, too, in regard to them and all others with whom I have to do!"

To the same. Sept. 22, 1853.—(Written a fortnight before the commencement of her last illness)—"Feeling in rather a melancholy mood, under the visitations of the Almighty through my past life, and the gloom of the autumn making its appearance, (though autumn has its beauties too, whether rightly considered or not,) with a sick, *drooping* daughter, as, I fear, I am often led to say with Job, 'Shew me wherefore thou contendest with me.' But I dare not complain, for 'why should a living man complain for the punishment of his sins?' We are often inclined to say of our light troubles, as the Saviour did, 'Father, if it be possible, let this cup pass from me'—but find it harder to feel and say, 'not my will, but thine, be done.' Oh that in all our straits and trials ministering spirits may be vouchsafed to us, strengthening us for the afflictions, toils, and duties of life! I know my mercies *far*, *very far*, outweigh judgments. What should we not be willing to endure, since the knowledge of salvation has been granted to us, while so many are left to perish? But alas, how little are we doing to make it known to others (or *I*)! How much have we to do around our own fireside! I can most sincerely sympathise with you in your bustle, and toil, and depression of spirits, at viewing so much left undone that ought to have been done, and like you feel the energies of life often failing, but—

'When we can hear our Saviour say,
Strength shall be equal to our day,
Then we rejoice in deep distress,
Leaning on all-sufficient grace.'

O let us, my dear sister, aim to bear our lot cheerfully and calmly,
knowing that the 'Angel over the right shoulder' makes a faithful
record of those, who, by patient continuance in well-doing seek for
glory, honour, immortality, and eternal life.' Have you seen that
252 little work, 'The Angel over the right shoulder'?"

"Who can find a virtuous woman? for her price is far above rubies.

"The heart of her husband doth safely trust in her, so that he shall have no need of spoil.

"She will do him good, and not evil, all the days of her life.

* * * * * * *

"She openeth her mouth with wisdom; and in her tongue is the law of kindness.

"She looketh well to the ways of her household, and eateth not the bread of idleness.

"Her children arise up, and call her blessed; her husband also, and he praiseth her.

"Many daughters have done virtuously, but thou excellest them all.

"Favour is deceitful, and beauty is vain: but a woman that feareth the Lord, she shall be praised.

"Give her of the fruit of her hands, and let her own works praise her in the gates." Proverbs xxxi. 10—12, 26, 31.

NOTES
TO THE TEXT

1. The First Baptist Church of Cornwallis was formerly an Open Communion Newlight Congregationalist-Baptist congregation until the minister, Edward Manning, adopted the Close Communion platform of the (Calvinistic) Baptist Association of Nova Scotia in 1807. He and a few followers separated from the Newlight majority to found the First Baptist Church. The initial members included William Chipman (Eliza Ann's future husband) and his first wife Mary, Eliza's father Holmes Chipman, along with William Cogswell, Walter Reid, Mrs. Edward Manning, Mrs. Handley Beckwith and Mrs. Dorcas Hall. A. W. H. Eaton, *The History of Kings County, Nova Scotia* (Salem, Mass., 1910), pp. 311-12; Edward M. Saunders, *History of the Baptists of the Maritime Provinces* (Halifax, N.S., 1902), pp. 126-27.
2. Edward Manning (1767-1851), son of Irish immigrant Peter Manning and his wife Nancy Carrol. He was a resident of Falmouth Township during the Great Awakening ignited by Henry Alline (1748-1784). Converted to Alline's version of Newlight Congregationalism, he was temporarily caught up by the antinomian New Dispensation movement of the 1790s before coming into the Calvinistic Newlight tradition just prior to his adopting the Baptist stand on immersion. As a minister, Manning remained a staunch supporter of the Baptists till his death; he was an active promoter of Horton Academy and Acadia College, in addition to several missionary and publication efforts. Manning also kept up a voluminous correspondence, and an extensive diary which differed from Eliza Ann's by inclusion of far more observations about his secular and church-related business. Barry M. Moody, "Edward Manning,"*Dictionary of Canadian Biography* Vol. 8, s.v.; John V. Duncanson,

Falmouth—A New England Township in Nova Scotia (Windsor, Ont., 1965), pp. 311, 318-19.

3. See Introduction.
4. Eliza Ann was sixteen years old at this time.
5. Luke 12:40 [All scriptural references taken from the King James Version]. This was probably her brother James Andrews Chipman (b. 1802): John Hale Chipman, *A Chipman Genealogy* (Norwell, Mass., 1970), p. 40.
6. Cf. traditional five stages of conversion as described by seventeenth century Puritan theologians in New England: Christian knowledge; conviction; grace; doubt and despair; conversion. J. M. Bumsted, *Henry Alline 1748-1784* (Toronto, 1971), p. 33. [Reprint: Bumsted, *Henry Alline 1748-1784,*Hantsport, N.S.: Lancelot Press, 1984.]
7. Eliza Ann often presents a compact vision of her spiritual peaks and valleys. Unlike references to mundane affairs, these are instances of the spiritual life in which Eliza Ann, even in using the set language of the genre, can reveal spontaneous outpourings.
8. Edward Manning; it would be a standard feature of the Baptist newspapers and journals of the Maritimes to print extracts from missionary-tour journals kept by ministers of the three provinces. Saunders, *Baptists of the Maritime Provinces,* pp. 160-61. Eliza Ann's future husband, William Chipman, kept his own diary of the soul from which segments were printed in Saunders. David G. Bell has uncovered diary transcriptions apparently taken from Chipman's diaries for the 1830s, now mistakenly attributed to Theodore Porter (son of Baptist minister Rev. Theodore H. Porter Sr. of Cornwallis Twp.): Provincial Archives of New Brunswick: MG300: MS59 (Theodore Porter Papers) #10.
9. This is a youth's descriptive exaggeration on the idea of consumption (tuberculosis). Henry Alline (1748-1784), the torchbearer of the Great Awakening in Nova Scotia (1776-1784), died a martyr to missionary work from consumption; Harris Harding (1761-1854) emulated the appearance of dying

in his early preaching career. Bumsted, *Henry Alline*, p. 31; George A. Rawlyk, "From Newlight to Baptist: Harris Harding and the Second Great Awakening in Nova Scotia," *Repent and Believe: The Baptist Experience in Maritime Canada,* ed. Barry M. Moody (Hantsport, N.S., 1980), p. 12.

10. William Elder (1784-?): excluded by the Bridgetown Baptist Church when converted to the Methodist belief in infant baptism 1833/34; author of *Infant Sprinkling weighed in the balance and found wanting* and *A Further Attempt to substantiate the legitimacy of Infant Baptism.* T. Watson Smith, *History of the Methodist Church within the Territories embraced in the Late Conference of Eastern British America, 2* Vol. (Halifax, N.S.: 1877-90), vol. 2: pp. 114-16.
The 'coloured man' was probably Richard Preston (1791/2-1861), a former Virginian slave who arrived in Nova Scotia during the War of 1812. Under the tutelage of Rev. John Burton, Preston became active in the Baptist ministry first as a Black delegate to the 1821 Nova Scotia Baptist Association and in 1823 when he was licensed to preach. An eventual split between Black Baptists and the Association led to Preston's 1831 ordination in England and creation of the African Baptist Association. Preston was particularly noted for his eloquent style of preaching. Frank S. Boyd, "Richard Preston," *D.C.B.* Vol. 8, s.v.
Elder's sermon was based on Romans 1:14; Preston's on 2 Cor. 5:1.

11. The lesson was literally engraved on local tombstones with the sentiment best summed up by these lines:

> Remember me as you pass by,
> As you are now, so once was I
> As I am now, soon you shall be
> So Prepare for Death to follow me.

(Tombstone in Old Wolfville Cemetery, Kings Co., N.S.). See also: Deborah Trask, *Life how short, Eternity how long: Gravestone Carving and Carvers in Nova Scotia (Halifax, N.S., 1978).*

12. Mason Cogswell (26 Aug. 1799-11 Sept. 1823), a son of William and Eunice (Beckwith) Cogswell. E. O. Jameson, *The Cogswell in America* (Boston, Mass., 1884), p. 385.

13. Although Eliza Ann states that late in 1823 she underwent conversion, she is unable to specify the time and circumstances (a most curious omission from a spiritual diary); this may account in part for her repeated doubts about her spiritual condition.

14. John 14:2

15. Eliza Ann blends scripture and her own writing. In a Bible-literate society it was not uncommon to break into recitations of extracts from the Bible in letters to express feelings both of joy and despair. For earlier examples, see: George A. Rawlyk, *New Light Letters and Songs* (Hantsport, N.S., 1983). Cf. Northrop Frye, *The Great Code: The Bible and Literature* (Toronto, 1983), pp. xi-xiii; Frye's study underscores the degree to which Western thinking is permeated with Biblical imagery.

16. Belial: "worthlessness; wickedness," Deut. 13:13, 2 Cor. 6:15. Here it is equated with the Temptor (i.e. Satan).

17. John 14:15; Matthew 10:38.

18. Grigg, "Jesus, and shall it ever be—": 2nd verse: Richard Fuller and J. B. Peter, ed., *The Psalmist: A Collection of Hymns for the Use of Baptist Churches . . .* (New York, 1879), p. 340. (Hereafter, *Psalmist*).

19. Rev. David Harris (c. 1785-15 April 1853); b. Cornwallis Twp., N.S.; baptized by Rev. T. S. Harding. His ministerial career included pastorates in Nova Scotia and New Brunswick. Saunders, *Baptists of the Maritime Provinces,* pp. 166, 485.

20. The language is misleading. Eliza Ann has made her relation of conversion—unfortunately not described—to the Church elders and been received as a candidate for baptism. See her entry of 20 June 1824.

21. Without further comment by Eliza Ann it is not possible to determine the exact nature of the treatise, whether detailed

theology or inspirational/devotional, though the latter is hinted at. Communion, always a solemn rite, was received only by covenanted church members.

22. Presumably reference to the annual meeting of the Baptist Association of Nova Scotia, held that year in Cornwallis Twp. I. E. Bill, *Fifty Years with the Baptist Ministers and Churches of the Maritime Provinces of Canada* (Saint John, N.B., 1880), p. 54. These were special occasions for sermons which attracted considerable public attention. Saunders quotes William Chipman's description of such a meeting at Aylesford in 1828: *Baptists of the Maritime Provinces,* p. 221.

23. Candidates for baptism were usually baptised one day, received the right hand of fellowship the next, and often were participants in a communion service held to highlight the significance of the event. Charles Deweese, "Church Covenants and Church Discipline among Baptists in the Maritime Provinces," in Moody, *Repent and Believe,* pp. 27-45.

24. If this if original, it is an example of how poetically expressive and moving Eliza Ann could be on occasion.

25. Cf. spiritual highs and lows of Henry Alline: G. A. Rawlyk, *Ravished by the Spirit: Religious Revivals, Baptists and Henry Alline* (Montreal, 1984), pp. 24-25.

26. Probably Rev. Theodore Seth Harding (1773-1855), pastor of First Horton Baptist Church at the village later known as Wolfville. Reared in the Newlight Congregationalist faith, he joined the Methodists before being won over to Baptist doctrines and accepted baptism at the hands of Rev. John Burton. Harding was ordained pastor of the Horton church in 1793 where he served till his death. There was a brief flirtation with Presbyterianism before Edward Manning brought Harding back to the orthodox Baptist fold. Saunders, *Baptists of the Maritime Provinces,* pp. 456-57, 464-85.

27. Robinson, "Come, thou Fount of every blessing": last verse: *Psalmist,* p. 368. Eliza Ann's entreaties often end with an invocation and prayer.

28. Job. 18:14: 'king of terrors' is death; here Eliza Ann expresses concern for finality and judgement beyond the opportunity for repentance, conversion and hope. Till the moment of death itself a Calvinistic Baptist may be waiting for evidence of predestined salvation, therefore God is perceived as allied with death as a judge of wrath. Contrast this to other passages by Eliza Ann where she exalts in the love of an omnipotent Lord. This dual perception and the tension it produces continues throughout the Chipman journal. These two poles of emotion are discussed in Philip Greven, *The Protestant Temperament: Patterns of Child-Rearing, Religious Experience and the Self in Early America* (New York, 1980), p. 22.

29. Deweese, "Church Covenants and Church Discipline," pp. 29-30.

30. The stress on the importance of immediate family as expressed here by Eliza Ann in some respects presages the Victorian cult of the family wherein the household was protection from a depersonalized work place, and from a world which did not universally share one's sense of morality or religious faith. Parochialism, of course, is another facet of close-knit family structure. For a comparable sense of isolation see Mrs. John Hicks's lament on her husband's death in *The Novascotian* 15 May 1843 (John Hicks was a deacon in the Bridgewater Baptist Church). Consult also Sandra S. Sizer, *Gospel Myths and Social Religion: The Rhetoric of Nineteenth-Century Revivalism* (Philadelphia, Pa., 1978), p. 118.

31. William Cogswell, Jr. (8 Sept. 1801-2 Oct. 1824) son of William and Eunice (Beckwith) Cogswell. His brother Mason died Sept. 1823. Jameson, *Cogswells,* p. 385.

32. Rebecca Cogswell (1 July 1805-15 July 1845) only daughter of William and Eunice Cogswell. Three of her brothers died young: Mason, William Jr. and Holmes (1810-1815). Her brother Hezekiah would marry (1819) as his first wife Nancy, daughter of Rev. Edward Manning; Rebecca herself married 19 February 1826 Caleb Rand Bill. Jameson, *Cogswells,* p. 385; Duncanson, *Falmouth*, p. 319.

33. Ps. 119:67.

34. Watts, "My soul, how lovely is the place": 1st verse: *Psalmist,* p. 56.

35. The Methodist was perhaps John B. Strong (1789-1870), an Englishman ordained in 1813. Arrived 1814 in Lower Canada; in Prince Edward Island 1816 and subsequently served on circuits in all three Maritime provinces. E. Arthur Betts, *Bishop Black and His Preachers* (Sackville, N. B., 1976), pp. 70, 158.

36. Wesley, "Thee we adore, eternal Name!" 2nd verse: John Wesley, *A Collection of Hymns, For the use of People called Methodists* (London, 1847), pp. 44-45. (Hereafter: Wesley, *Hymns*).

37. Ps. 84:2.

38. Acts 8:32.

39. Christmas was long observed in New England and Nova Scotia from the eighteenth to nineteenth centuries an occasion for sermons as contrast to any feasting or secular observances of the day. Not all Nova Scotians of Planter stock, however, excluded gatherings for good meals and company as witness Simeon Perkin of Liverpool, (a Methodist):

    (25 Dec. 1810) Christmas we have a Sermon by Mr. Bamford in the Chapel from Luke 2d, vii, very good Discourse. The Chapel decorated with Ever Greens . . .
    (25 Dec. 1811) CHRISTMAS Mr. Black preaches a suitable Sermon from Isaiah.
    We have a Christmas dinner Mr. Black and Family, Mr. Newton and Family, my son John and Family and my daughter Freeman & Family were our Guests we had a very pleasant afternoon and evening.

    Simeon Perkins, *The Diary of Simeon Perkins 1804-1812,* ed. Charles Bruce Fergusson (Toronto, 1978), pp. 269, 357.

40. This passage is one of the best descriptions by Eliza Ann showing her reverence and love for Rev. Edward Manning, that of a church member for her spiritual guide and father.

41. Steele, "Eternity is just at hand!": 2nd verse: *Psalmist,* pp. 690.

42. Watts, "Lord of the worlds above": 1st refrain: *ibid.*, p. 54.

43. Watts, "My drowsy powers, why sleep ye so?": 2nd verse: *ibid.*, p. 728.

44. Watts, "And must this body die?": 4th verse [Last line "power" instead of "praise"]: *ibid.*, p. 639.

45. There was a persistent prejudice against the reading of written sermons, a legacy left to the denomination by the eighteenth century charismatic preaching of Henry Alline and his followers. Although Edward Manning prepared notes beforehand he would not depart from 'inspired' precedent: Barry M. Moody, "The Maritime Baptists and Higher Education in the Early Nineteenth Century," in *Repent and Believe,* pp. 90-91.

46. Isa. 38:17.

47. C. Wesley, "O For a heart to praise my God!": *Psalmist,* p. 394.

48. This commentary on death is one example of Eliza Ann coming to terms with mortality as she grew from adolescence to adulthood.

49. Eliza Ann is not condemning the survivor's grief as such; instead she is observing that Christians should find consolation in the belief in the soul's immortality.

50. Cf. entry for 18 January 1825.

51. Heb. 11:38.

52. Watts, "Why should the children of a King": *Psalmist,* p. 250.

53. A reference to American Baptist Mission work in Burma by Adoniram Judson and his wife. There had been support for foreign missions in Nova Scotia by Baptists as early as 1814: Saunders, *Baptists of the Maritime Provinces,* pp. 207-10.

54. Phil. 4:18. The collection was apparently for Baptist missionary work, possibly for the Burma cause.

55. This is Rev. Thomas Handley Chipman (1756-1830), pastor of the Baptist Church at Nictaux. For his career and role in creating a Close-Communion Baptist Association see: Saunders, *Baptists of the Maritime Provinces,* pp. 86-89, 92;

Brian C. Cuthbertson, ed. *The Journal of John Payzant* Hantsport, N.S., 1981), pp. 9-10, 78-83.

56. This passage offers a clue to Eliza Ann's awakening to Christian knowledge on her initial path to conversion. Cf. Henry Alline's revelation on reading a passage of Scripture: James Beverley and Barry Moody, ed. *The Journal of Henry Alline* (Hantsport, N.S., 1982), pp. 60-61, and St. Augustine of Hippo's conversion: John J. O'Meara, ed., *An Augustine Reader* (Garden City, N.Y., 1973), p. 16.

57. Watts, "Tis by the faith of joys to come": *Psalmist*, p. 320.

58. Prayer meetings constituted one of the few approved outings for young women (or men) in evangelical Protestant society. Eliza Ann's attitude stands in contrast to a more liberal-minded approach to entertainment in another Baptist woman's diary, that of Margaret Michener of Hantsport, N.S., twenty years later:

    > [28 Sept. 1849]: . . . Ann came down with me, expecting the boys to come later to Mr. Frost's to sing . . . . After a short call we started for Mr. Frost's and met Esther coming for us. Charlotte and Amelia were at the door. Mr. Lockhart brought his bass viol. Mary Ann Robinson and Mary Faulkner came in, and shortly after David Huntly arrived. It was a lovely evening.

    "Diary of Margaret D. Michener", printed serially in *The Acadian* (Wolfville, N.S.,) 24 August 1924. John V. Duncanson, *Newport, Nova Scotia: A Rhode Island Township* (Belleville, Ontario, 1985), p. 316.

59. Rev. 15:2-3.

60. Foreign mission work excited much attention during the early nineteenth century and was seen in many ways as comparable to the writing of a new Book of Acts. Eliza Ann's observation shows her enthusiasm and at the same time a restraint in acknowledging to herself that she is unqualified for such work—both in theological training and, at this stage, in her social position as a woman in rural Nova Scotia. Not until the latter part of the nineteenth-century would single Canadian

Baptist women go overseas as teachers and nurses. Saunders, *Baptists of the Maritime Provinces,* p. 487; Jane Hunter, *The Gospel of Gentility: American Women Missionaries in Turn-of-the-Century China* (New Haven, Ct., 1984).

61. Watts, "Come, we that love the Lord": 4th verse: *Psalmist,* p. 450.

62. Public and denominational fasts were both observed by early nineteenth century Nova Scotia Baptists. The passage given is unclear as to whether Eliza Ann is adding personal fast days, or trying to avoid the sin of gluttony (a companion of sloth as one of the Seven Deadly Sins).

63. Eliza Ann was seeking to learn from the dying how to better live in her faith. While it is true that death was more present to nineteenth century Nova Scotians it did not form the basis for driving people to God. Coming to terms with one's own mortality is the essential thing being described here. Cf. Margaret Conrad, *Recording Angels: The Private Chronicles of Women from the Maritime Provinces of Canada 1750-1950* (Ottawa, 1982), p. 10.

64. There was a desire among evangelicals for the community of believers and the individual both to exist at a perpetual heightened sense of spiritual awareness.

65. Much anxiety was expressed at death beds by relatives anxious to be reassured that the dying individual had received a sign from God of election to salvation. In part this came from the belief in reunion after death of family members who were saved. Cf. death-bed scene of Methodist layman Robert Barry at Liverpool, N.S. September 1843 in letter of his son John A. Barry to Rev. T. Watson Smith, 27 February 1868: Public Archives of Nova Scotia [P.A.N.S.]: Mfm.: Churches: Nova Scotia: Methodist [Early Methodist Papers].

66. E. N. Harris, son of Rev. David Harris; ordained 1827. He preached in the Maritimes and United States, and eventually left the Baptists. Saunders, *Baptists of the Maritime Provinces,* p. 485.

67. Watts, "Welcome, sweet day of rest": *Psalmist,* p. 70. Given in *Psalmist*, as 3rd verse:

One day, amid the place,
  Where Christ, my Lord, has been,
Is sweeter than ten thousand days
  Of pleasure and of sin.

68. This was the first Mrs. William Chipman [see Introduction] whom Eliza Ann would replace in May 1827.

69. Rev. John Hull had started his preaching career as a Congregationalist [coming from an English background] before conversion to Baptist doctrine and acceptance into the ministry; his brother Hezekiah also became a Baptist preacher. Saunders, *Baptists of the Maritime Provinces,* p. 487; Bill, *Fifty Years,* p. 238; George Edward Levy, *The Baptists of the Maritime Provinces 1753-1946* (Saint John, N.B., 1946), p.94.

70. Eliza Ann is using the language of St. Paul to express a moving religious service and its effect on herself: II Cor. 12:1-5. Though she does use highly poetic phrasing, it remains within a pietistic as distinct from the mystical experience. Cf. F. C. Happold, *Mysticism: A Study and an Anthology* (Harmondsworth, England, 1970 rev. ed.), pp. 185-89.

71. One motive for Eliza Ann's journal: an act of spiritual devotion to praise God.

72. Rev. Thomas Ansley (1769-1831) came from a New Brunswick Loyalist household; he was converted by Rev. T. S. Harding. Res. 1810 Bridgetown, N.S. where he became the local Baptist congregation's long-time minister. He had been ordained at Sedgwick, Me. Saunders, *Baptists of the Maritime Provinces,* p. 471.

73. Cf. Watts, "My drowsy powers, why sleep ye so?": *Psalmist,* p 728.

74. Watts, "Come, Holy Spirit, heavenly Dove": *ibid.*, p. 286.

75. Dreams were as liable to be means of truth communicated from God as were sermons. The Bible of course furnishes many examples. In the Nova Scotian context see Harris Harding's dream of the fishes in J. Davis, *Life and Times of the late Rev. Harris Harding* (Charlottetown, P. E. I., 1866), p. 206.

76. There is a danger when emphasizing E. A. Chipman's rural life that she is depicted as narrowly confined to a specific geographical region. This reference, in addition to those of Association gatherings attended outside Cornwallis Township, and occasional trips after marriage with her husband, dispel the impression that she was unfamiliar with the world beyond Cornwallis.

77. Rev. George Richardson (1790-1878), a native of Ireland, came from an Episcopal background (Church of Ireland?); he was ordained at Hammond Plains, N.S., 1822. Eventually Richardson moved to Sydney in Cape Breton. Saunders, *Baptists of the Maritime Provinces,* p. 498.
It is strange that Eliza Ann has not mentioned Richardson earlier, especially as he seems to have competed with the 'beloved pastor' Edward Manning in her religious devotion or allegiance.

78. Social gatherings such as dances were frowned on by Baptists and Methodists alike as being without communal purpose (i.e. the utility of a barn-raising or quilting bee). Repeatedly accounts of conversions for the eighteenth and nineteenth centuries often included renunciations of dancing or card playing. See William Chipman's own conversion relation: Bill, *Fifty Years*, pp. 251-54.

79. Watts, "What sinners value I resign": *Psalmist,* p. 662.

80. An allusion to the widower William Chipman. See entry for 31 March 1827.

81. Eliza Ann's first cousin William Chipman has proposed marriage to her.

82. Part of Eliza Ann's psychological turmoil stemmed from her realization that she would at marriage be responsible for a large family which in itself was a daunting prospect for a young woman not yet twenty years old. She also is to be exposed to the dangers of child-birth which was bound to affect an individual of her often morbid introspective character. Finally, there was a conflict with the evangelical Protestant emphasis on becoming a 'bride of Christ' and possibly betraying that union by an unwise marriage. Conrad,

Recording Angels, p. 10; Greven, *Protestant Temperament,* pp. 124-40.

83. Steele, "Father, whate'er of earthly bliss": verses 1-3: *Psalmist,* p. 396, ["Prayer for Submission"].

84. E. A. Chipman's wedding day. In keeping with the structure of a spiritual diary, she has refrained from commenting on personal feelings toward William Chipman. All of life's activities must be seen through the prism of evangelical Baptist faith.

85. It would be the arrival of children of their own which curtails Eliza Ann's travels with William.

86. John Newton (1725-1807), a slave-owner turned evangelical clergyman, was the author of this hymn. Tony Jasper, ed. *The Illustrated Family Hymn Book* (New York, 1980), pp. 20-21.

87. From her marriage in May 1827 till her death Eliza Ann's family responsibilities would leave her with little time to write as detailed a journal as she kept from 1824 to mid 1827. Though she couches it in religious idiom Eliza Ann repeatedly laments her lack of time to have privacy for self-study and reflection. Much later thoughts on a related sense of the need for individual growth and writing by a far more secular-minded person may be found in Virginia Woolf's *A Room of One's Own* (1929).

88. "Guide me, O thou great Jehovah": *Psalmist,* p. 336, attributed to Oliver. The composer was William Williams (1717-1791), a Welsh convert to Calvinistic Methodism [Countess of Huntingdon Connexion]: Jasper, *Family Hymn Book,* pp. 56-57.

89. There is a suggestion in this that she suspects that her husband may enter the ministry, and she is not entirely willing to submit to a change from businessman-farmer's wife to that of a clergyman's spouse. In part this resentment may stem from her expectations in marriage of a settled, established social position with commensurate income (and security).

90. An allusion to advanced pregnancy.

91. William Allen Chipman, elected for Cornwallis Township.

92. Another reference to pregnancy.

93. Eliza Ann was not exaggerating the dangers of childbirth, particularly for a first child where the strength of the mother is untested. Conrad, *Recording Angels*, p. 10.

94. Birth of Leander Van Ess Chipman (1828-1830). Here is a new mother's anxiety, in a Calvinistic tradition, about the election (i.e. predestined fate) of her child. Moreover Eliza Ann feared that to love him too much would make her unwilling to accept God's decision if the child died young. The former worry is associated with attempts to save by domestic training, as noted by Peter Gregg Slater in *Children in the New England Mind in Death and in Life* (Hamden, Ct., 1977), p. 133:

> By the 1830s, the theme of the redemption of mankind through correct domestic education had become more explicit as the "Protestant Counter-Reformation" evolved from defensiveness to an extravagant optimism. If parents cultivated sound character and beliefs in their offspring, it would be "among the principal means of reforming the world and introducing the day of millenial glory."

95. Probably I. E. Bill and Ezekiel Marsters: see Saunders, *Baptists of the Maritime Provinces*, p. 214. Saunders states that after ordination (1829), Marsters served at Aylesford, and St. Martin's, N. B.; he left the ministry, "on account of irregularity of conduct". *Ibid.*, p. 490. I. E. Bill (1805-1891) was to be the author of *Fifty Years with the Baptist Ministers and Churches of the Maritime Provinces of Canada* (1880), an editor of the *Christian Visitor*, supporter of Acadia College, and minister at several churches in Nova Scotia and New Brunswick. *Ibid.*, p. 473.

96. I. E. Bill. He was to assist Eliza Ann's uncle Rev. Thomas H. Chipman at Nictaux. *Ibid.*, p. 214.

97. William Chipman was ordained 29 March 1829; that same spring I. E. Bill and Ezekiel Marsters were ordained: *ibid.*, p. 214.

98. The property for the Second Cornwallis Baptist Church was bought from Rev. William Chipman's father while the

burying ground was purchased from John Worth. The site of the Chipmans' new home had belonged also to William A. Chipman, Esq. Atlantic Baptist Archives [A.B.A.]: Berwick Baptist Church Records 1829-1858. Eliza Ann now had to face public scrutiny as a minister's wife, a worry only partly alleviated by moving to a house not associated with the first Mrs. Chipman.

99. Watts, "Let me but hear my Saviour say": *Psalmist:* p. 336.

100. Second Cornwallis Meeting house.

101. Zachariah Chipman (1779-1860), an uncle to William and Eliza Ann, had moved to Yarmouth from Annapolis County 1807. He was a Baptist deacon, captain in the militia, and an active member of his community in local government and development schemes. Chipman, a successful tanner and shoemaker, no doubt housed Rev. William Chipman and his wife while they attended the Yarmouth Association meeting. Chipman, *Chipman Genealogy*, pp. 40-41.

102. I. e., baptism.

103. Wesley, *Hymns* [1874 ed.]: "O Thou that hear'st when sinner's cry": 3rd verse: # 659.

104. Mary Eliza Chipman born 11 April 1830-died 6 May 1834.

105. The rapidly expanding Second Cornwallis church was experiencing growing pains in association with increased settlement in the region. Some members at a remove from the present meeting house wished a place of their own. Edward Manning recorded that a conference was held in November to settle matters. James D. Davison, *Eliza of Pleasant Valley* Wolfville, N.S., 1983), p. 73.

106. Cowper, "O For a closer walk with God!": *Psalmist,* p. 410.

107. The death of Leander reminds us of the high infant mortality rate in early nineteenth-century Nova Scotia. In this instance however, one wonders how the child was permitted to be in proximity to danger, the pot apparently having been removed from a hearth fire; reference to parasitic infection also calls into question the neglect of vermifuge treatment. Was Eliza Ann's acceptance of 'divine chastisement' eased by awareness

of neglect on her part hence deserved punishment? The matter remains open to speculation. Leander Chipman's funeral sermon was delivered by Rev. Edward Manning. Davison, *Eliza,* p. 85.

108. Christmas, as usual, was not observed by the local Baptists.

109. The loss of her son has obviously returned to affect Eliza Ann; it brought home to her the degree to which the death of someone near to the heart can try the Christian understanding of the individual.

110. Rebecca Chipman (b. 14 Aug. 1805), m. 17 February 1831, John Ross of Scotland, a merchant who settled in Wilmot, though earlier resided at Lawrencetown; Rev. Edward Manning performed the marriage. Chipman, *Chipman Genealogy,* p. 79; Jean Holder, ed., *Nova Scotia Vital Statistics from Newspapers, 1829-1834* (Halifax, 1982), p. 48.

111. The fate of infants and very young children in death had haunted both the Puritans of New England and their descendants in Nova Scotia. It had been a matter of such sensitivity that few ministers had written forthrightly on the subject, leaving parents to hope (but not in full assurance) that young ones were spared by God. By the 1830s there was a decided shift in thought that children were indeed granted God's grace and salvation, though this outlook was slower to spread among conservative, evangelical calvinistic sects. "The 1820s and 1830s were the last period in which the theological complexities of original sin as relating to infants, and the doctrinal arguments for and against their damnation could summon any interest from the general populace." Slater, *Children in the New England Minds,* p. 90.

112. Watts, "When I can read my title clear": *Psalmist:* p. 658.

113. Watts, "Let me but hear my Saviour say,": *ibid.,* p. 336.

114. The establishment of a female prayer society is the first important role Eliza Ann must accept as the incumbent minister's wife. It would serve as well as an outlet for earlier desires to more actively engage in missionary work.

115. Amelia Spurr Chipman (Born 7 December 1832); married 1857, Alfred G. Dodge (born 1822), son of John Dodge and his wife Mehitable Ruloffson; Alfred had married (1) Harriet Randall, and would marry (3) Charlotte Lamont. Chipman, *Chipman Genealogy,* p. 80; W. A. Calnek, *History of the County of Annapolis* (Belleville, Ontario, 1972; 1st. published 1897), p. 503.

116. Watts, "My God, permit my tongue": *Psalmist,* p. 391. "Within thy temple, Lord" and the succeeding lines belong to another hymn; "qulckening" as in original printed version of Memoir ["quickening"].

117. St. Vitus' dance, or chorea, is a nervous disorder in children resulting in jerking or twitching of muscles in the face and extremities; possibly related in this instance to worm infestation (Cf. Leander's last illness).

118. While it is evident that Eliza Ann makes liberal use of Scripture, it is difficult to determine how much may be taken from other devotional reading unless explicitly referred to as in this passage.

119. Watts, "My soul lies cleaving to the dust": *Psalmist:* p. 410.

120. Elizabeth (nee Gesner) Chipman (1793-1833) first wife of Eliza Ann's brother-in-law and first cousin Samuel Chipman, Esq. (1790-1891), and sister to Dr. Abraham Gesner (credited with the discovery of kerosene). Her husband Samuel sat in the Assembly for King's County (succeeding his father) and served in the Assembly and Council to 1870; along with other public duties, he was a long-standing member of the Masonic Order which may explain objections to Elizabeth's profession of Baptist belief as referred to in Eliza Ann's memoirs. Chipman, *Chipman Genealogy,* p. 81.

121. George E. Levy, *The Baptists of the Maritime Provinces 1753-1946* (Saint John, N.B., 1946), pp. 96-101, 132.

122. Isa. 44:22.

123. The earlier references to multiple baptisms by William Chipman belong to the revival period 1828-1833. 1834 witnessed renewed activity along the North Mountain, and at

Liverpool in Queen's County. Saunders, *Baptists of the Maritime Provinces,* pp. 220-21. This upsurge in Baptist activity coincided with the entry to the ministry of newly ordained men, William Chipman among them.

124. As with the death of her brother Leander, Mary Eliza's death reveals the belief that in this Calvinistic home even young children are judged by God without assurance of salvation. Eliza Ann is able to cope only by accepting the just judgement of God; she does, however, hold out hope as expressed in the entry for 9 May.

125. Rev. Edward Manning, who had preached at Leander's funeral too.

126. Cowper, "O For a closer walk with God!": 5th verse: *Psalmist:* p. 410.

127. Eliza Ann may be referring to the widely used hymnal commonly known as Winchell's Watts after the editor, James M. Winchell (pastor of the First Baptist Church in Boston, Mass.): *An Arrangement of the Psalms, Hymns, and Spiritual Songs of the Rev. Isaac Watts, D. D. To Which is added a Supplement of more than Three Hundred Hymns from the Best Authors, including All the Hymns of Dr. Watts, Adapted to Public Worship* (Boston, 1832).

128. Alfred Chipman (11 August 1834—24 April 1918); attended both Acadia College, and Andover-Newton Theological Institute in Newton, Mass.; entered the Baptist ministry; in 1912 he received an Honorary D.D. from Acadia. Alfred's wife Alice T. Shaw (1832-1921) graduated from Mt. Holyoke Seminary, and became the first principal of Acadia Seminary for Women. Chipman, *Chipman Genealogy,* p. 157; James D. Davison, *Alice of Grand Pre* (Wolfville, N.S., 1981); Levy, *Baptist,* p. 180.

129. Ps. 62:1: "Truly my soul waiteth upon God: from him cometh my salvation."

130. C. Wesley, "O For a heart to praise my God!": *Psalmist:* p. 395.

131. Mary, daughter of Joseph Troop, and first wife of Winkworth Allen Chipman (born 1804); she died 7 December at age 22

years, having had three children. Winkworth married twice more, and none of his issue survived beyond early adulthood. Eliza Ann and William's son John P. Chipman lived with his uncle while attending Acadia College following requests by the latter that he might foster one of Rev. William Chipman's twenty-one offspring. Jean Holder, ed. *Nova Scotia Vital Statistics from Newspapers, 1835-1839* (Halifax, N.S., 1984), p. 27; Chipman, *Chipman Genealogy*, pp. 82-83.

132. John S. C. Abbott, *The Mother at Home or; the principles of maternal duty familiarly illustrated* (London, 1835?); a publication of the Religious Tract Society. In 1832 the women of the Nictaux Baptist Church had formed two societies, one for funds to be sent to the Baptist Mission in Burma, and the second a Religious Tract Society: Bill, *Fifty Years*, p. 86. This may account for the speed in Eliza Ann gaining access to a recent British book. It also accords with the growing body of literature aimed at women for the promotion of Christian nuture: Slater, *Children in the New England Mind*, pp. 133-40.

133. Maria Chipman (born 3 July 1836), married 9 September 1858, Rev. J. E. Balcom (died 7 June 1872 age 46 years). Balcom studied at Acadia and held pastorates as a Baptist minister in Nova Scotia. Chipman, *Chipman*, p. 80; Saunders, *Baptists of the Maritime Provinces*, p. 472.

134. At the Halifax June 1836 Baptist Association meeting it was voted that William Chipman's expences be paid to attend a Baptist convention in Maine. Bill, *Fifty Years*, p. 46.

135. Richard McLearn was ordained at Rawdon, Hants County 8 March 1828, died 17 August 1860 at Halifax. Saunders notes that McLearn studied at Kings College in Windsor (a primarily Anglican institution) while holding a pastorate there: *Baptists of the Maritime Provinces*, p. 492.

136. Watts, "My soul lies cleaving to the dust": *Psalmist:* p.410.

137. Possibly Theodore Harding Porter Sr. (5 April 1805-12 April 1869), son of Stephen and Ruby Porter of Cornwallis Twp., who entered the Baptist ministry. Eaton, *Kings County*, p. 781; Saunders, *Baptists of the Maritime Provinces*, p. 496.

138. Protracted meetings were revival services lasting several days. They had been held as early as the second decade in Nova Scotia growing out of Baptist Conference meetings and partly from the idea of American Methodist revival services which presaged 'camp meetings'. Smith, *Methodist Church,* vol. 2: p. 89; William H. Williams, *The Garden of American Methodism: The Delmarva Peninsula 1769-1820* (Wilmington, Del.: Scholarly Resources, 1984), pp. 79-81. Cf. "great Communion" services held in Cape Breton among the evangelical Presbyterians: Laurie Stanley, *The Well-Watered Garden: The Presbyterian Church in Cape Breton, 1798-1860* (Sydney, N.S.: University College of Cape Breton Press, 1983), p. 140 ff.

139. Sabbath [or Sunday] Schools had started among Baptists as early as 1820 in the province and received continued attention during the ensuing decades; by 1832 churches were encouraged to give an account of these schools in their annual submissions to the Baptist Association. Levy, *Baptists,* pp. 139-40.

140. Cf. entry 26 June 1836 with reference to literature on the 'moral mother'.

141. Eliza Ann continually reflects on the difficulty of pursuing a life of Christian meditation while performing daily chores, including those of a busy mother. She has not reached the solution of making her work itself an act of prayer, nor of regarding each day's trials as a way of imitating Christ, perhaps revealing that Calvinistic Baptist belief of the early 1800s suffered from a too rigid exclusion of works as a means of devotion. There is not enough of Eliza Ann's view of life which would enable her to follow the scriptural injunction, "If any man will come after me, let him deny himself, and take up his cross daily, and follow me." Luke 9:23. For comparison with a twentieth-century example of work and prayer, see: Malcolm Muggeridge, *Something Beautiful for God: Mother Teresa of Calcutta* (London: William Collings and Sons, 1973).

142. John 1:29.

143. Chipman and I. E. Bill had visited the Island earlier in 1833

and published the results of that tour in the *Baptist Missionary Magazine* November 1834, p. 247 ff. Levy, *Baptists,* p. 132.

144. Silas Tertius Rand (1810-1889), son of Silas and Deborah (nee Tupper) Rand and first cousin to the future Prime Minister Charles Tupper. Rand was ordained 1834 as a Baptist minister (following the lead of his uncle Rev. Charles Tupper); he held pastorates at Parrsboro, Horton, Liverpool and Windsor, and Charlottetown, P. E. I., before settling permanently in Hantsport. He was known primarily as a missionary to the Micmac, an accomplished philologist, and an ethnologist, with an extensive list of publications to his credit. Rand broke with the Baptist denomination in 1872 to join the Plymouth Brethren but returned to the Baptists in 1885. His former home in Hantsport is commemorated in Rand Street. Judith Fingard, "Silas Tertius Rand," *D. C. B.* Vol. 11, s. v.; Levy, *Baptists,* pp. 166-70; M. V. Marshall, "Silas Tertius Rand and his Micmac Dictionary," *The Nova Scotia Historical Quarterly* 5, no. 4 (Dec. 1975): 391-410.

145. Alfred Chipman.

146. Bill, *Fifty Years,* pp. 97-98.

147. Isaac Logan Chipman (17 July 1817—7 June 1852), son of Rev. William Chipman by his first wife Mary Dickie. Studied at Horton Academy and Waterville College (Colby University), Maine; returned to teach at Acadia College as professor of Mathematics and Natural Philosophy; initiated the Baptist Historical Collection, and was an active fund-raiser for the College. Chipman with E. D. Very and four College students and a boatman drowned near Boot Island on returning from a geological expedition to Blomidon. Ronald S. Longley, *Acadia University, 1838-1938* (Wolfville, N.S., 1939) pp. 39-41, 68-70; Bill, *Fifty Years,* pp. 736-38.

148. Eliza Ann finally has the opportunity to realize a desire to be a witness to the Gospel, and at the same time to step outside the usual bounds of an early nineteenth-century housewife's sphere. In spite of protestations (and at thirty she was hardly a child) she was well suited to teach given her education and self-instruction in devotional literature.

149. Either Rev. William Forsyth (died 1840) of Established Church of Scotland training or his son-in-law the Reverend Mr. George Struthers. Eaton, *Kings County,* pp. 298-301.

150. Wesley, *Hymns* [1874 ed.]: "And let this feeble body fail": 7th verse: # 734.

151. Which son this was or the reason for his dibility is unknown.

152. Achan: "he that troubleth": Josh. 7:18-26. C. H. Wright, *The Bible Reader's Encyclopaedia and Concordance* (London: Collins' Clear Type Press, rev. ed. 1962), p. 12. This entry may refer to pastoral troubles, or more likely reflects Eliza Ann's conviction that there must be continual revivals to show that the church community is spiritually alive. Cf. Eliza Ann's own desire to be in a perpetual state of ecstatic awareness.

153. Mary Eliza Chipman born 11 March 1838 [not '22 March' as in the printed *Memoir*—a typographical error?]. She married 10 June 1861, Rev. D. O. Parker, son of Deacon Abel and Susan (nee Morse) Parker; David Obadiah's father was a deacon in Rev. William Chipman's Second Cornwallis Baptist Church. Eaton, *Kings County,* pp. 402, 770-71; Chipman, *Chipman,* p. 80; A. B. A.: Berwick Baptist Church Records 1829-1858.

154. Watts, "Come, Holy Spirit, heavenly Dove": *Psalmist:* p. 236.

155. Here is an allusion going back to the older Puritan belief in the truculant will of children which needs to be broken and the trouble this will can cause parents. Greven, *Protestant Temperament,* pp. 32-43.

156. The implication is that a renewed awareness of death might inspire some church attendents to pursue more fervently the steps of conversion. The absence of sympathy for the parents of sick children, however, cannot be passed over in silence. One is tempted to discern a relief that households other than Eliza Ann's own are experiencing difficulties.

157. The Beckwith family came from Connecticut to Kings County in the Planter migration of 1760-63; there were inter-marriages with the Chipmans. Eaton, *Kings County*, pp. 555-60.

158. William Chipman wishes to assure the reader that his wife

cheerfully took on the role of hostess during the protracted meeting. Earlier entries in the *Memoir* and the comment on Martha and Mary instead reveal discontent on Eliza Ann's part at missing too much of the revival services.

159. The protracted meeting apparently had its desired effect. See: G. A. Rawlyk's comments on planned revivals during the 1820s-1830s in Nova Scotia: *Ravished by the Spirit,* pp. 132-34.

160. Rev. Samuel Elder (1817-1852), son of Rev. William Elder (a Baptist minister who entered the Anglican priesthood after a flirtation with Methodism); graduate of Acadia College 1844; ordained Fredericton, N.B. 1845; known both for his pulpit deliveries and poetic abilities. Duncanson, *Falmouth,* pp. 248-49; Saunders, *Baptists of the Maritime Provinces,* p. 482; Eaton, *Kings County,* pp. 361, 367-68, 655-56. There had been Universalists in the county since the 1820s at least, one of whom was Dr. William Baxter (1760-1832), son of a New Brunswick Loyalist. The denomination believed in the final salvation of all souls (an extreme reaction to predestinarianism). A.B.A.: Diary of Edward Manning: 20 August 1820; D. G. Bell, ed. *The Newlight Baptist Journals of James Manning and James Innis* (Hantsport, N.S., 1984), pp. 32-33; Eaton, *Kings County,* pp. 463-64, 554-55.

161. The Association that year was at Wilmot, Annapolis County. Bill, *Fifty Years*, p. 99.

162. Newport in Hants County; Onslow in Colchester County.

163. Cf. entry 22 September 1838.

164. Toplady, "Rock of ages, cleft for me": *Psalmist:* p. 197. Eliza Ann's reflections on death increase whenever childbirth is near, a not unnatural concern for the era.

165. Andrew Fuller Chipman (16 April 1840-1 June 1906); married 28 January 1862 Mary Newcomb—seven children. Andrew became a successful merchant, and a deacon in the Berwick Baptist Church. Chipman, *Chipman,* p. 157.

166. Watts, "My God, permit me not to be": *Psalmist*: p. 377.

167. Though it is unspoken, Eliza Ann obviously finds it difficult to raise a family when her husband is away for several weeks at a time on missionary tours.

168. This unidentified excerpt is one more example of the literature to which Eliza Ann had exposed herself and which shaped her own writing style and diary contents.

169. Horton Academy (1828) and Acadia College (1838) were Baptist institutions of higher learning. Rev. William Chipman sat on the first Board of Governors for Acadia; his son Isaac joined the faculty in 1840 as professor of Mathematics and Natural Philosophy. Longley, *Acadia University*, pp. 36, 39-41. The *Memoir* entry raises two matters: the original difficulty the founders of Acadia had faced in convincing Baptists of the need for an institution to train Baptist youth, and the denominational struggles which by the 1820s and 1830s were starting to figure prominently in provincial politics. Moody, "Maritime Baptists and Higher Education"; J. Murray Beck, *Joseph Howe* 2 vol. (Montreal, 1982-83), vol. 1: pp. 249-53.

170. Bill, *Fifty Years,* pp. 100-101.

171. Edward Payson (1783-1827) was the author of several tracts and sermons; see his book, *Sermons for Christian Families, on the most important relative duties* (Boston, Mass. 1832).

172. William Chipman laboured under debt for several years before finally paying off his obligations. This business failure tarnished family reputation, and for Eliza Ann added a new sense of insecurity to her own household's economic situation. However, in December she was becoming reconciled to the situation: see entry for 20 December.

173. A son was born 2 December 1841 to William and Eliza Ann. Lack of reference in the *Memoir* may indicate a still-birth or death within a very short time of delivery. Chipman, *Chipman,* p. 80.

174. In her distress at the grave sickness of her husband Eliza Ann reveals how much she interprets every occurance as a sign of God's favour or displeasure; there is a decided bent toward self-centeredness in thinking that God is so concerned with her

that every illness or family reversal is the visible result of of God's malediction.

175. Watts, "What shall I render to my God": *Psalmist:* p. 57.

176. Obed Parker (1803-1890), a son of William and Lydia; he married (1) Hannah M. Morse, and (2) Mary Balcom. Obed was ordained 22 February 1844 and engaged in provincial missionary work. His brothers included Rev. James Parker (ordained 1842, and later a governor of Acadia College), and Deacon Abel Parker of Second Cornwallis Baptist Church. Calnek, *Annapolis,* p. 559; Saunders, *Baptists of the Maritime Provinces* , p. 495.

177. See Introduction.

178. The deafness may have been a complication connected with the birth of the son she lost in December 1841.

179. William Chipman as editor of the original publication of the *Memoir* was at pains to offer constructive criticism of Eliza Ann's failings at certain junctures; it is noteworthy that the passage and comment show how much Eliza Ann kept from her husband.

180. Amelia S. Chipman.

181. Lucilla Chipman. The Chipman genealogy gives 28 February as her birthdate. Chipman, *Chipman,* p. 80.

182. Col. 1:14.

183. Association for 1843 was held at Yarmouth; Rev. William Chipman's father was given special thanks for his services as treasurer of the Missionary Society. Bill, *Fifty Years,* pp. 102-103.

184. Cf. Fawcett, "I my Ebenezer raise": *Psalmist*: p. 745.

185. Watts, "My spirit looks to God alone": *ibid.:* p. 364.

186. Unity Ann Chipman born November 1844; married 26 February 1890 G. W. Eaton. Chipman, *Chipman,* p. 80.

187. Rev. Richard E. Burpee (died February 1853, Florida), a native of New Brunswick and the first Baptist foreign missionary from what became Canada (if one excludes preaching tours to the United States by earlier ministers). He

and his wife Laleah (a daughter of Dr. Lewis Johnstone of Wolfville, and a niece to the Hon. J. W. Johnstone, premier of Nova Scotia), sailed for Burma in 1845 where they established a mission to the Karens. His story is related more fully in Saunders, *Baptists of the Maritime Provinces,* pp. 294-97, 474; Levy, *Baptists*, pp. 138-39, 156; Bill, *Fifty Years,* pp. 277-80.

188. Elizabeth, wife of William Handley Chipman and a daughter of Joseph Troop of Granville, N.S., died 22 September 1844 in her 42nd year; she was survived by her husband and four children. The second sister-in-law of Eliza Ann was probably Olivia Lucilla (nee DeWolfe), the second wife of Winkworth Allen Chipman of Kentville.

189. Eliza Ann is trying to impose on her son Alfred a sense of continuous spiritual questing, and perpetuates her obsession with the evangelical desire to exist at a constant level of ecstatic awareness.

190. 'Parliament' is in reference to the provincial House of Assembly at Halifax.

191. Newton, "Saviour, visit thy plantation": *Psalmist:* p. 738.

192. William Allen Chipman died 28 December 1845: Chipman, *Chipman,* p. 39. Elizabeth (nee Andrews) Chipman died 2 February 1846: ibid., p. 40.

193. 'Sprinkling' is a reference to infant baptism as practised by Congregationalists and Anglicans.

194. Cf. Amos 4:11.

195. John Angell James, *The Anxious Inquirer after Salvation* (New York, 18--); a publication of the American Tract Society.

196. Maria Chipman.

197. Watts, "Behold the glories of the Lamb": *Psalmist:* p. 231.

198. The Methodists were Arminians (free-will) in doctrine hence it is strange that Eliza Ann offers no comment.

199. 1846 Association was held at Bridgetown in neighbouring Annapolis County. Rev. Joseph Dimock (1768-1846), son of Daniel and Betsy (nee Bailey) Dimock of Newport Township, N.S.; the first Baptist minister born in what is now Canada.

Joseph Dimock knew Henry Alline, and was an ardent New Light with a Baptist background. Following an extensive itinerent career he settled as the pastor of a Baptist congregation at Chester. Dimock is considered one of the founders of Acadia College and is numbered among the "Baptist Patriarchs" of the Maritimes. George E. Levy, ed. *The Diary of Joseph Dimock* (Hantsport, N.S., 1979); Saunders, *Baptists of the Maritime Provinces,* pp. 73, 330-34; see also historical essay in George A. Rawlyk, ed., *The New Light Letters and Spiritual Songs 1778-1793* (Hantsport, N.S., 1983), pp. 37-66.

200. I Cor. 15:57.

201. Watts, "Welcome, sweet day of rest"; *Psalmist*, p. 70; this is a Wesleyan hymn which was included apparently in Winchel's *Watts,* and in turn by the editors of *Psalmist.*

202. A daughter of Rebecca (nee Chipman) and her husband John Ross of Wilmot; she was an only child.

203. Held this year in Yarmouth.

204. This is in reference to a private school (outside the direct surveillance and supervision of either William or Fliza Ann). Educational opportunities for Baptist women were limited till after mid-century with the founding of Grand Pre Seminary at Wolfville. There were various private schools operated by a staff of one or two, as noted in Saunders, *(Baptists of the Maritime Provinces*, pp. 272-93); however, there has been to date no adequate research into this area in comparison to attention given to formally established institutions. A son of Eliza Ann's, Rev. Alfred Chipman, would marry Alice T. Shaw who as a graduate of Mt. Holyoke Seminary carried those principles to Nova Scotia: see Davison, *Alice of Grand Pre.*

205. A vague allusion to loss of church attendants; it may be in reference to political dissension in the province over a provincial or state college versus denominational colleges. The Baptists led by J. W. Johnstone favoured the latter yet not all were convinced that they should desert support for Joseph Howe the provincial college proponent. One 1843 supporter

of Howe's stand had been the member for Annapolis, which no doubt occasioned much local gossip in Pleasant Valley for a few years. Saunders, *Baptists of the Maritime Provinces*, pp. 269-79; Chipman, *Chipman*, p. 41; Barry M. Moody, "William Henry Chipman," *D. C. B.* Vol. 9, s. v.; Beck, *Joseph Howe*, Vol. 1, pp. 264-65; W. E. Boggs and Burpee R. Bishop , "The Genealogy of the Bishop Family of Horton, N.S." (MSS, 1918), p. 19.

206. Alfred Chipman had begun studies at Horton Academy in Wolfville. A. C. Chute, *Records of the Graduates of Acadia University 1843-1926* (Wolfville, N.S., 1926), p. 12.

207. This is the first clear glimpse of William and Eliza Ann Chipman's family's past-times and evidence of the pervasiveness of literacy in the household. Eliza Ann's journal too often masks the fact that the Chipman home cultivated study of the Bible, devotional literature, and (in light of William's sons' careers) access to secular material as well.

208. Revivals in connection with Acadia College and the Baptist Church at Wolfville were seen as evidence of divine blessing on the denomination's educational enterprise, and incidently also served to allay Baptist suspicions of too much study being injurious to a spiritually alive ministry. A. C. Chute, *The Religious Life of Acadia* (Wolfville, N.S., 1933), pp. 26-27. The 1848 revival was considered to have been most noteworthy; for Alfred Chipman's own observations see *ibid.*, pp. 41-42.

209. Her son John Pryor Chipman was born on the 29 March 1848.

210. John Pryor Chipman (1848-1917), graduate of Acadia College and Harvard Law School; practised law in Nova Scotia at Kentville where he twice served as mayor; associate of members of the Federal cabinet. He married 21 November 1853 Susan May Brown of Halifax; there were nine children. Chipman, *Chipman*, p. 158.

211. Liverpool in Queen's County was the site of the 1848 Association.

212. See extracts of this correspondence in 'Chapter III' of the *Memoir*.

213. The extreme language supposedly reflects Eliza Ann's continual worry for the spiritual health of her family, and the time that related household duties keep her from private devotions. There is a hint of bitterness, though, which belies laudatory assessments about Mrs. Chipman.

214. Perhaps an indirect comment on the 1848 revolutionary uprisings across Europe.

215. C. Wesley, "Come, let us anew": *Psalmist*: p. 602.

216. William Chipman had brought in a private tutor for his children, a Miss Cylina [Selina] Millett; later the children attended school at Miss Millett's nearby residence in Lower Aylesford. The 'Daybook' of William Chipman contains entries referring to payments for school supplies, books, teacher's salary, board, etc. The subjects taught were not solely literature and manners; texts covered astronomy, history and French conversation. Davison, *Eliza of Pleasant Valley*, pp. 142-44; ABA: Rev. William Chipman: Daybook, 1837-1857.

217. The *Christian Messenger.*

218. Association was held at Nictaux, Annapolis County.

219. The Nova Scotia Association was to be divided into three bands or districts with home mission service confined to each area. Saunders, *Baptists of the Maritime Provinces,* p. 342.

220. Robert Allen Chipman (1819-1850).

221. Possibly the sister of Rev. Samuel Elder, Amelia (born 1815—died 28 December 1851). Duncanson, *Falmouth*, p. 248.

222. Abigail Bigelow (born 20 March 1785) married 17 March 1803 Alfred Skinner (born 20 June 1778)—twelve children. William Skinner, Alfred's brother, was a deacon of Second Cornwallis Baptist Church. Eaton, *Kings County,* pp. 568, 821.

223. A clear statement that as long as she suffers from a hearing loss Eliza Ann will consider that she has been or continues to be guilty of a sin punishable by God. This attitude appears to go deeper than any pre-birth mental distress.

224. Holmes Samuel Chipman (born 22 December 1850), youngest child of William and Eliza Ann Chipman; educator, publisher, merchant. After a teaching career in Nova Scotia, Holmes entered the firm of Bancroft Publishing and Printing in San Francisco, California. As a friend of a future premier of Japan he introduced the use of merchanized printing in that country. Later in his career Holmes engaged in the mercantile field in Australia, and was an active promoter of funding for troops in the Boer War to aid the British. Holmes Chipman married 1 August 1882 Julia Ann Ventrillion Tortat (daughter of an 1848 French Revolution refugee); they had one son. Holmes S. Chipman's life was by far the most removed from and different in pursuit from the world of his parents. Chipman, *Chipman,* pp. 158-59.

225. Isa. 41:10.

226. There were two female boarding schools at Wolfville, one operated by Mrs. Margaret Best and her daughters (c. 1835-1855), and the other (which the Chipmans attended) kept by the Troop family (1850-1855); Mary and Charlotte Troop taught with their father William Troop (who had started the family teaching profession). The Troops were Baptists and among the first of the denomination to promote women's education prior to the establishment of Grand Pre Seminary. Saunders, *Baptists of the Maritime Provinces,* pp. 337, 380; Davison, *Eliza of Pleasant Valley,* p. 114; James D. Davison, ed., *Mud Creek: The Story of the Town of Wolfville, Nova Scotia* (Wolfville, 1985), pp. 117-18.

227. Wesley, *Hymns* [1874 ed.]: "Thee We adore Eternal Name": 7th verse: p. 45.

228. A rare instance where Eliza Ann allowed herself to be a concerned mother instead of an anxious pastor.

229. Elizabeth (Stuart) Phelps, *The Sunny Side; or The Country Minister's Wife.* (Philadelphia, Penn., 1851).

230. These comments on ministerial support go counter to tradition among Congregationalist and Baptist ministers of late eighteenth and nineteenth century Nova Scotia who usually had to engage in a trade to supplement their income.

Eliza Ann certainly is bitter in her observations but the Chipmans were not alone in finding it difficult to obtain regular support from their congregation.

231. Wesley, *Hymns*: "Thee we adore Eternal Name": 2nd verse: p. 45.

232. See *Memoir* entry for 8 July 1837 and references to Isaac Chipman's career. The funeral sermon at the Wolfville Baptist Church is still remembered by Acadia University, town, and Gaspereau Valley residents for the segregating line, 'The loss of six precious souls and the man from Gaspereau.'

233. A psalm of reproof from God and a call to worship Him in righteousness. Ps. 50:23: "Whoso offereth praise glorifieth me: and to him that ordereth his conversation aright will I shew the salvation of God."

234. Amelia S. Chipman.

235. Another example of Eliza Ann allowing a veil of concern to be partly lifted back but she soon returns to stock phasing and an inward look at herself.

236. Unidentified.

237. Eliza Ann does not observe that in the Gospel account of Martha and Mary there was no injunction from Jesus that Martha should cease to serve. We are left, in Eliza Ann's case, with a picture of a discontented housewife who longed to devote herself to some form of contemplative life; yet, her *Memoir* entries do not lead one to believe that she would have been fully satisfied even with that opportunity.

238. Probably Hannah (nee Hand) Calkin, (daughter of Marchant and Hannah Hand) who married 20 December 1809 Edmund Calkin (born 16 November 1781), a grandson of Cornwallis Twp. grantee Ezekiel Calkin. Eaton, *Kings County*, p. 595.

239. Alfred Chipman.

240. Dr. Adoniram Judson, Baptist missionary to Burma. Saunders, *Baptists of the Maritime Provinces,* pp.208-209, 225-29.

241. 2 Tim. 4:6.

242. The obituary appeared in *The Christian Messenger* 3 November 1853.

243. This statement contradicts numerous entries in the *Memoir* by Eliza Ann in which she complained about finances and spoke of motherhood as a crucifixion.

244. The Van Buerens were Loyalists who settled in Annapolis County 1783, and were of New York Dutch-American ancestry. Calnek, *Annapolis County*, p. 251. John J. Van Beuren was a member of Second Cornwallis Baptist Church. A. B. A.: Berwick Baptist Church Records, 1824-1858.

245. Isaac L. Chipman, Eliza Ann's step-son.

246. Perhaps the former Harriet Sophia Reid (born 16 September 1815) daughter of Walter Reid and his second wife Ann Starr; Harriet married Henry Lyons (born 22 May 1810) of Cornwallis Twp. Eaton, *Kings County*, pp. 738, 800.

247. Wesley, *Hymns* [1874 ed.]: "God moves in a mysterious way": 2nd verse: p. 520.

248. Rev. Edward Manning.

249. Mrs. Silas T. Rand (nee Jane Elizabeth McNutt).

250. Prov. 10:3.

251. Death of Isaac L. Chipman.

252. Elizabeth (Stuart) Phelps, *The Angel over the Right Shoulder, or The Beginning of a New Year*. (Andover, Mass., 1852).

APPENDIX I

George Armstrong to Mrs. William Chipman, 26 Jan. 1839, from Queen's College, Horton. [Acadia College, Wolfville]:[1]

Good Mother!

I sit down to address a few lines to you, as being one in whom I place the fullest confidence, as regards the exercise of christian sympathy towards a poor, weak, and trembling member of Jesus Christ. I feel under peculiar obligations to you for the kind attention you extended towards me, while under your immediate notice, and for that christian feeling you manifested for my future welfare in bringing to my view many things as regards the care of health, which I had almost neglected, as well as for your endeavours to encourage me in the work of the Lord. I know that I ought to thank God for the assistance I have received from you, and I have, and do thank him. But what have [ ] that you have not received? Nothing "By the Grace of God," says St. Paul, "I am what I am." If you are a christian (as I believe you are) and moreover a christian Mother, bless God for it, and ascribe all to free grace, through the glorious Lord Jesus Christ.

Since I left Pleasant Valley I have had a deep and sore conflict in my poor soul, I have been tossed hither and thither; I could not rest either by day or night, could neither eat nor drink, until I became perfectly miserable and unfit for everything good [ ]. To finish all I got shut up in the whale's belly and a horrible place it is, sure enough.[2] I remained Monday night [at] you[r] Pa, had a ve[r]y good night's repose.[3] The angles [angels] of God guarded my bed from ferocious demons, and my soul dwelt beneath the winds of the Almighty.

I remained till the Monday following in Cornwallis, my soul felt awfully burdened in viewing the desolations of Zion, and I was led in my soul to pray for a reformation.[4] And I hope, yea, I believe in my soul that it will come. However, if it dont come, all I can say is that poor George Armstrong was mistaken, and that is no wonder for he is often so. You have a reformation in P. V. [Pleasant Valley] and I rejoice in it, O, what cause have you to bless God for such distinguishing and extraordinary displays of divine grace, as he hath exhibited and made known among the people in your vicinity. There is a famine in the region, but there is no cry for bread. Sinners are going to hell and they don't know, or at least, don't believe it, and worse than all, professed christians are helping them on to the flames of the bottomless pit. Good God! what a fearful picture!—Will not sinners go to Hell fast enough without the professed people of God lying in their way to give them a premature fall into the awful gulf of woe! I sometimes look round me, and ask myself, where are the christians, or those in whom the Spirit of Christ dwells? I hear half or more than half of the professed christians in Horton know nothing about the love of Jesus Christ in their souls.[5] I proceed no further. Unless God sends us a reformation from Heaven, we shall all go to Hell, body and soul, root and branch. O pray for Horton—for backsliding Horton. I awfully fear that the Devil will overthrow my soul by his ungodly ingenuity, for he is watching me continually endeavouring to entrap me in his [ ]. Jesus I know is able to keep and to make me more than conquorer over Satan and all his posse of devils. Pray for me, O pray for me. O I feel in my soul that I want to love Jesus Christ and feel my heart swallowed up in his everlasting love. Draw me, oh draw me, Blessed Saviour, and captivate my affections with [ ] glories. I fear that my studies will freeze my heart. I feel that I need more piety to God, faith in his divine work and perfections, love for his holy and lovely name. I sometimes think of leaving the College, giving up all ideas of preaching and gospel and going about my business, and yet if preaching is not my business, I know not what is. Oh! the Devil gives me a sore time, he shoots many venomed arrow at me, from his deadly quiver.

I feel for the young at Pleasant V.[alley] lest the wolf should come and take them in his paws. Oh that the "good Shepherd" would guard them from every beast of prey!

I desire to be remembered to Sister Sarah Pearce in the gospel. Tell her not to be faithless, but believing. Look to her living head, Jesus, the blessed intercessor. Also to Father Chipman, with all the thanks I can give him, for his kindness towards me in the bowels of Jesus Christ. I shall ever remember him. Tell him to be strong and of a good courage, feeding the church of God, purchased with his own blood. He has a great work, I try to pray for him. The brethren, Stubbert & Ross send christian salutations, desiring their regards to be presented to you.[6]

If you shall think it worth your while, on the reception of this poor letter, to send me one in return, I shall feel especially gratified for the favour. By the Bye you have promised me a letter.

Dear Mrs. Chipman, will you pray for me? O do, do for heaven's sake! The prayers "of the rightous availeth much."

I sign myself with unfeigned respect your unworthy son in the gospel of Christ.

George Armstrong

I tried to converse with your sister Harriet about her soul, she says that she is not a christian, but that she has had serious impressions and hopes that she will be a christian. I endeavoured to talk with her as solemnly as I could, I know not what effect it will have. Pray for her.

1. Rev. Dr. George Armstrong (1815-1886) was a native of Dumbaum,Tipperary Co., Ireland and emigrated as a child with his parents to Cape Breton. A member of the second graduating class of Acadia College (B. A. 1844). Ordained at Port Medway, Queen's County, 31 Dec. 1848; served at Port Medway, Chester, Bridgetown, Kentville and Port Hawkesbury. From 1870 to 1880 he was the editor and publisher of the *Christian Visitor*; also served as an Inspector of Schools for Annapolis County. Became a governor and senator of Acadia. Received his M. A. 1851, and D. D. in 1881. George Armstrong married twice: (1) Mary Ann Johnson of Wolfville, (2) Elizabeth Dykeman of St. John, N. B. A. C. Chute, *Records of the Graduates of Acadia University 1843-1926* (Wolfville, N.S., 1926), p. 8; Edward M. Saunders, *History of the Baptists of the Maritime Provinces* (Halifax, N.S., 1902), p. 471, and portrait opposite p. 34.
2. An allusion to Jonah in the belly of the whale (or seamonster): Jonah 1:17.
3. Holmes Chipman in Cornwallis Township.
4. 'Reformation' was an alternate term for revival.
5. 'Professed Christians' refers both to other denominations, and to Baptists whom Armstrong believes have lost evangelical fervour. Wolfville, the site of Acadia College, was in Horton Township.
6. William F. Stubbert (B. A. 1844, D. D. 1870) of North Sydney, Cape Breton, graduated with Armstrong from Acadia. Most of his preaching career spent in the United States. Died 6 April 1891. Malcolm Ross, also of Cape Breton, studied at Horton Academy 1838-42 and preached actively in the Annapolis Valley. Ordained 1843 at North River, P. E. I., in which province he devoted his remaining career; died 1844 at Charlottetown. His brother the Rev. Hugh Ross also studied at Wolfville ca. 1844. Chute, *Graduates of Acadia*, p. 8; Saunders, *Baptists of the Maritime Provinces*, p. 499.

APPENDIX II

Eliza Ann Chipman made it a habit in her journal entries to note the text of sermons she heard delivered, or which were preached by her husband. In addition there are scarcely any pages devoid of direct scriptural quotations, and none without Biblical allusions. Only the more significant citations have been identified for the main text of the *Memoir.*

It may be thought that there was a disproportionate emphasis on the Old Testament in Calvinistic Baptist sermons (a belief in part based on the erronious assumption that New England Puritans had been obsessed with Old Testament legalisms). However, a sample identification of Biblical passages in the *Memoir* 20 July 1823-24 Dec. 1825 of fifty-nine citations yields twenty-eight Old Testament and thirty-one New Testament entries. Here one may see in practice the mirroring of the two parts of the Bible as discussed in Northrop Frye's *The Great Code* (Toronto, 1983). The whole of the Bible came under study and reflection although certain books were favoured, especially Psalms and Isaiah, and the Gospels. The following listing is provided to indicate the texts to which Eliza Ann and those in the congregation with her were exposed from Sunday to Sunday (and on special occasions). [P=Citation by Eliza Ann Chipman not referring to sermon.]

1823: July 20 (Luke 12:40 [P]); Aug. 10 (Rom. 1:14; 2 Cor. 5:1); Aug. 25 (Ruth 1:16; Cant. 5:1).

1824: March 26 (John 14:2 [P]); April 13 (Luke 16:13); April 19 (John 14:15; Matthew 10:38 [P]); April 25

(Ex. 14:13 or 2 Chr. 26:17; Cant. 1:4?); June 25 (I Cor. 15:10); July 18 (Ps. 90:14; Deut. 33:29; Deut. 33:12; Rom. 8:14; Eph. 5:27); July 26 (Isa. 33:14; Isa. 33:16); Aug. 2 (Acts 13:16); Aug. 6 (Matt. 25:10); Aug. 9 (Isa.42:16) Oct. 2 (Ps. 119:67 [P]); Oct. 11 (Phil. 2:12); Dec. 11 (Ps. 84:2 [P]); Dec. 13 (Acts 8:32 [P]; Rev. 3:4).

1825: Jan. 5 (John 10:27-28); Jan. 28 (Rev. 14:4); Feb. 8 (Ps. 116:7); Feb. 16 (Rom. 8:6); April 9 (Isa. 38:17 [P]); April 13 (Ps. 103:1 [P]); April 17 (Ps. 31:23); April 24 (Ps. 139:23-24); May 22 (Job. 13:1-2; John 4:14); May 29 (Luke 2:52; Luke 2:35); June 6 (2 Pet. 1:4); June 12 (Isa. 11:10); June 19 (Phil. 4:18); Aug. 1 (Prov. 13:20; Prov. 14:25); Aug. 14 (Isa. 49:22?; Acts 8:32); Aug. 28 (Deut. 32:3); Sept. 5 (Rom. 8:28; I Pet. 2:25); Sept. 11 (Isa. 26:2); Oct. 12. (Luke 24:46); Oct. 30 (Jer. 32:40); Nov. 6 (Mic. 6:8; Mark 10:15); Nov. 16 (Isa. 28:9); Nov. 19 (Ps. 119:105; 2 Cor. 5:17); Dec. 7 (Rev. 15:2-3 [P]); Dec. 24 (Rev. 3:5).

APPENDIX III

Handley Chipman, Esq. (1717-1799) m. (1) 1740, Jean Allen, daughter of Col. Jonathan and Margaret (Homes) Allen; m. (2) 1775, Nancy Post, daughter of Stephen and Elizabeth (Clarke) Post:

1. Elizabeth, b. 1741
2. John, b. 1742, d. infancy
3. Margaret, b. 1743
4. John, b. 1744
5. Catharine, b. 1746
6. dau., d. infancy
7. Handley, d. 1748
8. Rebecca, b. 1750
9. Thomas Handley, b. 1756
10. William Allen, b. 1757
11. Anthony, b. 1776
12. Nancy, b. 1776
13. Holmes, b. 1778, d. 1844
14. Zachariah, b. 1779
15. Major, b. 1780
16. Stephen, b. 1784
17. Jacob, b. 1797 [A grandson raised by Handley Chipman]

Holmes Chipman (1778-1844) m. 1798, Elizabeth Andrews, daughter of John Iśrael Andrews of Windsor, N. S. (1777-1846); eleven children, including Eliza Ann Chipman (b. 3 July 1807).

Rev. William Chipman (1781-1861) son of William

Allen and Ann (Osborne) Chipman, M. H. A.; William m. (1) 1803, Mary McGowan Dickey (d. 1826); m. (2) 24 May 1827, Eliza Ann Chipman (1827-1853.) Nine children by first marriage, twelve by the second:

1. Dr. Joseph Chipman, b. 28 Dec. 1803
2. Rebecca, b. 14 Aug. 1805, m. merchant John Ross; res. Wilmot, N.S.
3. William Henry Chipman, b. 3 Nov. 1808
4. David Chipman, b. 13 Sept. 1809
5. James Edward Chipman, b. 14 May 1811, d. 1843
6. John Chaloner Chipman, b. 16 Aug. 1813, d. 1842
7. Isaac Logan Chipman, b. 17 July 1817, d. 1852
8. Robert Allen Chipman, b. 16 Sept. 1819, d. 1850
9. Leander VanEss Chipman, b. 23 Feb. 1822, d. infancy.

By Eliza Ann

10. Leander VanEss Chipman, b. 9 March 1828, d. 1830
11. Mary Eliza, b. 11 April 1830, d. in infancy
12. Amelia Spurr, b. 7 Dec. 1832
13. Rev. Alfred Chipman, b. 11 Aug. 1834, d. 1918
14. Maria, b. 3 July 1836
15. Mary Eliza, b. 11 March 1838
16. Andrew Fuller Chipman, b. 16 April 1840, d. 1 June 1906
17. son, b. 2 Dec. 1841, d. infancy
18. Lucilla, b. 28 Feb. 1843, d. infancy
19. Unity Ann, b. Nov./Dec. 1844
20. John Pryor Chipman, b. 31 March 1848, d. 5 Dec. 1917.
21. Holmes Samuel Chipman, b. 22 Dec. 1850

INDEX